IMMIGRATION IN THE 21ST CENTURY: POLITICAL, SOCIAL AND ECONOMIC ISSUES

VISAS

CATEGORIES, WORK VISAS AND THE VISA WAIVER PROGRAM

Immigration in the 21st Century: Political, Social and Economic Issues

Additional books and e-books in this series can be found on Nova's website under the Series tab.

IMMIGRATION IN THE 21ST CENTURY:
POLITICAL, SOCIAL AND ECONOMIC ISSUES

VISAS

CATEGORIES, WORK VISAS AND THE VISA WAIVER PROGRAM

BRIAN A. SHELTON
EDITOR

New York

Library of Congress Cataloging-in-Publication Data

ISBN: 978-1-53619-966-6

Published by Nova Science Publishers, Inc. † New York

CONTENTS

PREFACE

U.S. immigration policy is governed largely by the Immigration and Nationality Act (INA). The United States has long distinguished temporary immigration from permanent immigration. Temporary immigration occurs through the admission of visitors for specific purposes and limited periods of time. Permanent immigration occurs through family- and employer-sponsored categories, the diversity immigrant visa lottery, and refugee and asylee admissions. This book looks at key issues concerning visas.

Chapter 1 - Congress has expressed interest in the visa categories by which foreign nationals may enter or be present in the United States. U.S. immigration policy is governed largely by the Immigration and Nationality Act (INA), which was first codified in 1952 and has been amended significantly several times since. The United States has long distinguished temporary immigration from permanent immigration. Temporary immigration occurs through the admission of visitors for specific purposes and limited periods of time, and encompasses two dozen categories (which are commonly referred to by the letter and numeral that denote their subparagraph in the INA). Permanent immigration occurs through family- and employer-sponsored categories, the diversity immigrant visa lottery, and refugee and asylee admissions. This brief chapter provides the following information:

- a list of nonimmigrant (i.e., temporary) visa categories and lawful permanent resident (LPR) categories,
- a description of each category,
- the allowed duration of stay in the United States for each nonimmigrant visa category,
- the annual numeric limit (or "cap") for each nonimmigrant and LPR category, and
- the number of visas that were issued/individuals obtaining LPR status for each category in the most recent year for which data are available.

Chapter 2 - The purpose of the diversity immigrant visa program (DV program, sometimes called "the green card lottery" or "the visa lottery") is, as the name suggests, to foster legal immigration from countries other than the major sending countries of current immigrants to the United States. Current law weights the allocation of immigrant visas primarily toward individuals with close family in the United States and, to a lesser extent, toward those who meet particular employment needs. The diversity immigrant category was added to the Immigration and Nationality Act (INA) by the Immigration Act of 1990 (P.L. 101-649) to stimulate "new seed" immigration (i.e., to foster new, more varied migration from other parts of the world). The DV program currently makes 50,000 visas available annually to natives of countries from which immigrant admissions were less than 50,000 over the preceding five years combined. The formula for allocating these visas is specified in statute: visas are divided among six global geographic regions, and each region and country is identified as either high-admission or low-admission based on how many immigrant visas were given to foreign nationals from each region and country over the previous five-year period. Higher proportions of diversity visas are allocated to low-admission regions and countries. The INA limits each country to 7% (3,500, currently) of the total and provides that Northern Ireland be treated as a separate foreign state. Because demand for diversity visas greatly exceeds supply, a lottery system is used to select individuals who may apply for them. Those selected by lottery ("lottery winners"), like all other foreign nationals wishing to come to the United States, must undergo reviews performed by Department of State consular officers abroad and Department of Homeland Security immigration officers upon entry to the United States. These reviews are intended to ensure that the foreign nationals are not ineligible for visas or admission to the United States under the grounds for inadmissibility spelled out in the INA. To be eligible for a diversity visa, the INA requires that a foreign national have at least a high school education or the equivalent, or two years' experience in an occupation that requires at least two years of training or experience. The foreign national or the foreign national's spouse must be a native of one of the countries listed as a foreign state qualified for the diversity visa program. The distribution of diversity visas by global region of origin has shifted over time, with higher shares coming from Africa and Asia in recent years compared to earlier years when Europe accounted for a higher proportion. Of all those admitted through the program from FY1995 (the first year it was in full effect) through FY2017 (the most recent year for which data are available), individuals from Africa accounted for 40% of diversity immigrants, while Europeans accounted for 31% and Asians for 25%. Some argue that the DV program should be eliminated and its visas re-allocated for employment-based visas or backlog reduction in various visa categories. Critics of the DV program warn that it is vulnerable to fraud and misuse and is potentially an avenue for terrorists to enter the United States, citing the difficulties of performing background checks in many of the countries whose citizens are eligible for a diversity visa. Critics also argue that admitting immigrants on the basis of their nationality is discriminatory and that the reasons for establishing the DV program are no longer germane. Supporters of the program argue that it provides "new seed" immigrants for a system weighted disproportionately to family-based immigrants from a handful of countries. Supporters contend that fraud and abuse have declined following measures put in place by the State Department, and that the system relies on background checks for criminal and national security matters that are performed on all prospective immigrants seeking to come to the United States, including those applying for diversity visas. Supporters also contend that the DV program promotes equity of opportunity and serves important foreign policy goals.

Chapter 3 - Certain foreign workers, sometimes referred to as guest workers, may be admitted to the United States to perform temporary labor under two temporary worker visas: the H-2A visa for agricultural workers and the H-2B visa for nonagricultural workers. The H-2Avisa is not subject to any numerical limitations, while the H-2B visa is subject to a statutory annual cap of 66,000. H-2A and H-2B workers fill jobs that do not require much formal education. H-2A workers perform seasonal or temporary agricultural labor. They also engage in range herding and livestock production. H-2B workers perform temporary jobs in a variety of fields including landscaping, meat and seafood processing, and construction. The H-2A and H-2B programs are administered by the Department of Homeland Security (DHS) and the Department of Labor (DOL). These agencies and the Department of State (DOS) have made adjustments, and in the case of DHS issued H-2A and H-2B temporary final rules, related to guest worker visas in response to the coronavirus pandemic. Statutory and regulatory provisions establish processes for bringing in workers under the H-2A and H-2B programs that are intended to protect similarly employed U.S. workers. As an initial step in the process, a prospective H-2Aor H-2B employer must apply for DOL labor certification to ensure that U.S. workers are not available for the jobs in question and that the hiring of foreign workers will not adversely affect the wages and working conditions of U.S. workers. After receiving labor certification, the employer can submit an application, known as a petition, to DHS to bring in foreign workers. If the petition is approved, a foreign worker who is abroad can then go to a U.S. embassy or consulate to apply for an H-2A or H-2B nonimmigrant visa from DOS. If the visa application is approved, the worker is issued a visa that he or she can use to apply for admission to the United States at a port of entry. The final steps are different if the foreign worker is already in the United States; in such a case, there is no visa application. Over the years, a variety of legislative measures have been put forward concerning foreign temporary agricultural and nonagricultural workers. These have included bills to establish new temporary worker visas for agricultural and nonagricultural workers as well as proposals to change the existing H-2A and H-2B programs. In recent Congresses, the latter proposals have been more common. H-2A-related measures have sought to revise H-2Aprogram requirements on temporary need, wages, U.S. worker recruitment, and housing, among other items. Recent bills on the H-2B visa have focused largely on the annual cap. The H-2A and H-2B programs—and guest worker programs broadly—strive both to be responsive to legitimate employer needs for temporary labor and to provide adequate protections for U.S. and foreign temporary workers. There is much debate, however, about how to strike the appropriate balance between these goals. Key policy considerations for Congress include the labor market test to determine whether U.S. workers are available for the positions; required wages; and enforcement. The issue of unauthorized workers also arises in connection with guest worker programs.

Chapter 4 - The Trump administration is expected to unveil an executive action in the near future that would significantly restrict temporary ("nonimmigrant") work visa categories, potentially including:

- H-1B visas for skilled "specialty occupation" workers
- H-2B visas for nonagricultural seasonal workers
- H-4 visas for the spouses or children of H-1B and H-2B visa holders (among others)
- J-1 visas for exchange visitors
- J-2 visas for the spouses or children of J-1 visa holders
- L-1 visas for employees of multinational companies
- L-2 visas for the spouses or children of L-1 visa holders
- F visas for those international students staying in the United States after graduation to gain on-the-job training with a U.S. employer through the Optional Practical Training (OPT) program

While there are multiple public data sets available from the Department of Homeland Security (DHS) and the Department of State (DOS) relevant to these visa categories, they are unfortunately not sufficient to answer these basic questions with great precision:

- How many individuals enter the country each year, for the first time, using each of these visa categories?
- How many individuals are already in the United States at any given moment, having previously entered using each of these visa categories?

Our goal below is to synthesize the relevant data and clearly present what it can—and cannot—reveal about the number of individuals potentially impacted by work visa restrictions.

Chapter 5 - The Immigration and Nationality Act (INA) of 1952, as amended, enumerates categories of foreign nationals, known as nonimmigrants, who are admitted to the United States for a temporary period of time and a specific purpose. One of these nonimmigrant visa categories— known as the H-2B visa—is for temporary nonagricultural workers. The H-2B visa allows for the temporary admission of foreign workers to the United States to perform nonagricultural labor or services of a temporary nature if unemployed U.S. workers are not available. Common H-2B occupations include landscaping worker, housekeeper, and amusement park worker. The H-2B program is administered by the U.S. Department of Homeland Security's (DHS's) U.S. Citizenship and Immigration Services (USCIS) and the U.S. Department of Labor's (DOL's) Employment and Training Administration. DOL's Wage and Hour Division also has certain concurrent enforcement responsibilities. The H-2B program operates mainly under regulations issued by DHS in 2008 on H-2B requirements, by DHS and DOL jointly in 2015 on H-2B wages, and by DHS and DOL jointly in 2015 and 2019 on H-2B employment. Bringing workers into the United States under the H-2B program is a multiagency process involving DOL, DHS, and the Department of State (DOS). A prospective H-2B employer must apply to DOL for labor certification. Approval of a labor certification application reflects a finding by DOL that there are not sufficient U.S. workers who are qualified and available to perform the work and that the employment of foreign workers will not adversely affect the wages and working conditions of U.S. workers who are similarly employed. If granted labor certification, an employer can file a petition with DHS to bring in the approved number of H-2B workers. If the petition is approved, a foreign worker overseas who the employer wants to employ can go to a U.S. embassy or consulate to apply for an H-2B nonimmigrant visa from DOS. If the visa application is approved, the worker is issued a visa that he or she can use to apply for admission to the United States at a port of entry. H-2B workers can be accompanied by eligible spouses and children.

Chapter 6 - Under the Immigration and Nationality Act (INA), there are five categories of employment-based visas in the permanent immigration system. The EB-5 immigrant investor visa, the fifth employment preference immigrant visa category, was created in 1990 to benefit the U.S. economy through job creation and foreign capital investment. It provides lawful permanent residence (LPR status) to foreign nationals who invest $1,800,000 or more, or $900,000 or more in a rural area or an area with high unemployment (referred to as targeted employment areas [TEAs]), in a new commercial enterprise (NCE) in the United States and create or preserve at least 10 jobs. Approximately 10,000 visas annually, 7.1% of all employment-based visas, are allotted to immigrant investors and their family members. The majority (80% in FY2019) of EB- 5 visas are issued to investors from Asia, with 46% issued to Chinese-origin investors in FY2019. The EB-5 visa grants foreign national investors conditional residence status. After approximately two years, the foreign national must apply to remove the conditionality (i.e., adjust to full-LPR status). If the foreign national has met the visa requirements (i.e., invested the required money and created the required jobs), he/she will receive full LPR status. If the foreign national has not met the requirements or does not apply to have the conditional LPR status removed, his or her conditional status is terminated, and, generally, the foreign national is required to leave the United States, or will be placed in removal proceedings. In 1992, Congress established the Regional Center (Pilot) Program, which created an additional pathway in the EB-5 visa category. Regional centers are "any economic unit, public or private, which [are] involved with the promotion of economic growth, including increased export sales, improved regional productivity, job creation, and increased domestic capital investment." The program allows investors to pool their investment in a regional center to fund a project in a specific geographic area. The Regional Center Program now accounts for nearly all EB-5 visas (96% in FY2019). Unlike the standard EB-5 visa category, which does not expire, funding for the Regional Center Program requires reauthorization. In recent years, funding has been appropriated through a series of continuing resolutions. A 2019 Department of Homeland Security (DHS) regulation implemented major changes to the EB-5 program, including increases to the minimum investment amounts, changes to the TEA designation process, and allowing petitioners to retain the priority dates of approved EB-5 petitions for subsequent EB-5 petitions. These changes addressed some longstanding concerns about the EB-5 program. Nevertheless, the EB-5 visa continues to be the subject of ongoing policy debates. Proponents contend that providing visas to foreign investors benefits the U.S. economy through economic growth and job creation. Opponents argue that the visa allows wealthy individuals to buy their way into the United States and have highlighted instances of fraud and threats to national security associated with the EB-5 program. Some have moved to eliminate it entirely. Compared with other immigrant visas, the EB-5 visa presents additional risks of fraud. Such risks are associated with difficulty verifying that investors' funds are obtained lawfully and with the visa's potential for large monetary gains, which could motivate individuals to take advantage of investors and make the visa susceptible to the appearance of favoritism. U.S. Citizenship and Immigration Services (USCIS) has reported improvements in fraud detection but also states it is restricted by statutory limitations. EB-5 stakeholders have voiced concerns over the delays in processing EB-5 applications and possible effects on investors and time sensitive projects as well as uncertainty generated by the short-term reauthorizations of the Regional Center Program, the most common pathway for EB-5 visas.

Chapter 7 - The ability to repatriate foreign nationals (aliens) who violate U.S. immigration law is central to the immigration enforcement system. The Immigration and Nationality Act (INA) provides broad authority to the Department of Homeland Security (DHS) and the

Department of Justice (DOJ) to remove certain foreign nationals from the United States. Any foreign national found to be inadmissible or deportable under the grounds specified in the INA may be ordered removed. Those ordered removed may include unauthorized aliens (i.e., foreign nationals who enter without inspection, enter with fraudulent documents, or enter legally but overstay their temporary visas). Lawfully present foreign nationals who commit crimes or certain other acts may also be subject to removal. To effectuate a removal, the alien's country of citizenship must confirm the alien's nationality, issue travel documents, and accept his or her physical return by commercial flight or, where necessary, charter flight. A 2001 Supreme Court ruling, Zadvydas v. Davis, generally limits the government's authority to indefinitely detain aliens who have been ordered removed. As a result, detained aliens subject to removal orders but for whom there is "no significant likelihood of removal in the reasonably foreseeable future," must be released into the United States after six months, with limited exceptions.

Chapter 8 - The Visa Waiver Program(VWP), originally established in 1986 as a trial program and made permanent in 2000 (P.L. 106-396), allows nationals from 39 countries, many of which are in Europe, to enter the United States as temporary visitors (nonimmigrants) for business or pleasure without first obtaining a visa. Generally, temporary visitors for business or pleasure from non- VWP countries must obtain a visa from Department of State (DOS) officers at a consular post abroad before traveling to the United States. Some observers argue that the VWP strengthens national security because it sets standards for travel documents, requires information sharing between the member countries and the United States on criminal and security concerns, and mandates reporting of lost and stolen travel documents. VWP travelers have to present e-passports (i.e., passports with a data chip containing biometric information), which tend to be more difficult to alter than other types of passports. Nevertheless, some observers of the program have raised concerns about the possibility that terrorists will enter the United States under the VWP because those entering under the VWP undergo a biographic, rather than a biometric (i.e., fingerprint and digital photograph), security screening and do not need to interview in person with a U.S. consular official before embarking for the United States. There is also interest in the VWP as a mechanism to promote tourism and commerce. In FY2018, there were more than 22.8 million admissions to the United States under this program, constituting nearly a third of all visitor admissions. The inclusion of countries in the VWP indicates a shared approach to national security and eases consular workloads abroad. To qualify for the VWP, a country must offer reciprocal travel privileges to U.S. citizens; have had a nonimmigrant visa refusal rate of less than 3% for the previous year; issue their nationals machine-readable passports that incorporate biometric identifiers; issue tamper-resistant, machine-readable visa documents that incorporate biometric identifiers which are verifiable at the country's port of entry; report the loss and theft of passports; share specified information regarding nationals of the country who represent a threat to U.S. security; and not compromise the law enforcement or security interests of the United States by its inclusion in the program. Countries can be terminated from the VWP if they fail to meet any of these conditions or otherwise threaten the United States' security or immigration interests. All foreign nationals (i.e., aliens) entering under the VWP must present passports that contain electronic data chips (e-passports). Under Department of Homeland Security (DHS) regulations, travelers who seek to enter the United States through the VWP are subject to the biometric requirements of the United States Visitor and Immigrant Status Indicator Technology (US-VISIT) program. In addition, aliens seeking to travel to the United States under the VWP must get an approval from the Electronic System for Travel Authorization (ESTA), a web-based system that checks the alien's information against relevant law enforcement and security databases, before they can board a plane to the United States. Under statute, the Secretary of Homeland Security has the authority to waive the nonimmigrant visa refusal rate requirement, provided certain conditions are met. However, the waiver authority was suspended on July 1, 2009, because DHS had not fully implemented an air-exit system that incorporates biometric identifiers. The waiver will not be available until such a system is implemented, and it is unknown when and if a biometric exit system will be fully implemented. Activity in the 116th

Congress related to the VWP seeks to expand the number of countries by changing the criteria or by designating specific countries. Other bills would rename the VWP to "Secure Travel Partnership" to reflect one of the program's main goals of securing travel to the United States. Legislation in the 116th Congress would also address the ESTA fee paid by VWP applicants. In December 2019, Congress authorized the continued use of the ESTA fee to partially fund Brand USA, a national tourism promotion program, through September 30, 2027. Congress also raised the ESTA fee from $14 to $21 (Division I, Title 8 of P.L. 116-94). The effective date of the new ESTA fee has not yet been announced.

Chapter 9 - The Visa Waiver Program (VWP), which allows citizens of certain countries to visit the United States for up to three months without a visa, has two explicit missions: to enhance national security and to boost the U.S. travel and tourism sectors. On November 8, 2019, the United States designated Poland into the VWP, bringing the number of participating countries to 39. A concern for Congress is whether the VWP exposes the United States to security threats, despite implementation of strict security requirements over recent years. At the same time, because of longstanding congressional interest in promoting the U.S. travel and tourism sectors, many lawmakers support adding more countries to the VWP. A key goal of the VWP is to improve standards for aviation security, travel documents, and law enforcement in countries around the world. To qualify for the VWP, countries must issue electronic passports, report information on all lost and stolen passports to the United States through the International Criminal Police Organization (INTERPOL), and share information on travelers who may pose a terrorist or criminal threat. Every VWP traveler must obtain preclearance to board a flight to the United States through the Electronic System for Travel Authorization (ESTA). Supporters of the VWP see admission into the program as an incentive for foreign countries to increase their security infrastructure and information sharing with the United States. A competing view is that despite security improvements following the 2015 terrorist attacks in Europe, such as screening of passengers entering under the VWP based on past travel to a country known as a terrorist sanctuary, the program remains a national security vulnerability. Another objective of the VWP is to facilitate and encourage foreign business and leisure travel from high-volume and low- risk countries to the United States. In FY2018, 22.8 million nonimmigrant visitors—constituting nearly one-third of all visitor admissions to the United States—arrived through the VWP. Figures from U.S. Travel, the industry group representing travel and tourism organizations, show that nationals from VWP countries generated an estimated $190 billion in economic activity and supported close to 1 million jobs in the United States in 2017. In addition, the U.S. government's National Travel and Tourism Office (NTTO) reports that a record 80 million international travelers visited the United States in 2018, with the number falling slightly in 2019. The number of foreign visitor arrivals in 2019 indicated that the United States would likely fall short of the goal set by the federal government's travel and tourism strategy of attracting 100 million visitors annually by the end of 2021. The COVID-19 pandemic has sharply reduced foreign tourism in 2020 as countries have discouraged international travel and required arriving passengers to quarantine themselves for extended periods, probably putting the 2021 goal out of reach. Nonetheless, advocates for the U.S. travel and tourism industries argue that adding more countries to the VWP would further promote tourism, trade, and commerce by increasing the number of overseas visitors traveling to the United States. Activity in the 116th Congress related to the VWP seeks to expand the number of countries by changing the qualification criteria or designating specific countries. Other bills would rename the VWP to "Secure Travel Partnership" to reflect one of its main goals of securing U.S. borders. Legislation in the 116th Congress also addresses the ESTA fee paid by VWP applicants. In December 2019, Congress authorized the continued use of the ESTA fee to partially fund Brand USA, a national tourism promotion program, through September 30, 2027. Congress also raised the ESTA fee from $14 to $21 (Division I, Title 8 of P.L. 116-94). The effective date of the new ESTA fee has not yet been announced.

Chapter 10 - On June 22, 2020 President Trump issued a proclamation (amended on June 29) suspending the entry of foreign nationals (aliens) in certain nonimmigrant (temporary) visa categories that allow foreign nationals to work in the United States. Citing the high unemployment rate resulting from public health measures to reduce the spread of COVID-19, Proclamation 10052 suspends the entry of foreign nationals—and their accompanying family members—on H-1B, H-2B, J, and L visas, with some exceptions. On December 31, 2020, President Trump issued a new proclamation extending the June proclamation through March 31, 2021. Proclamation 10052 follows Proclamation 10014 from April 22 (which it extends through December 31, 2020) suspending the entry of permanent immigrants (see CRS Insight IN11362). In Proclamation 10014, President Trump directed the Secretaries of Labor and Homeland Security to review nonimmigrant programs and recommend measures to prioritize the hiring of U.S. workers. According to the June 22 proclamation, the Secretaries found that admitting temporary workers in the aforementioned categories "poses a risk of displacing and disadvantaging United States workers during the current recovery." The President cited two immigration-related legal authorities. Under Section 212(f) (8 U.S.C. §1182(f)) of the Immigration and Nationality Act (INA), the President may suspend immigration when it would be detrimental to the interests of the United States. Under INA §215(a) (8 U.S.C. §1185(a)) the President may prescribe limitations and exceptions on who may enter or depart the United States.

In: Visas
Editor: Brian A. Shelton

ISBN: 978-1-53619-966-6

Chapter 1

NONIMMIGRANT AND IMMIGRANT VISA CATEGORIES: DATA BRIEF (UPDATED)*

Jill H. Wilson

INTRODUCTION

Congress has expressed interest in the visa categories by which foreign nationals may enter or be present in the United States. U.S. immigration policy is governed largely by the Immigration and Nationality Act (INA), which was first codified in 1952 and has been amended significantly several times since.[1] The United States has long distinguished temporary immigration from permanent immigration.

* This is an edited, reformatted and augmented version of Congressional Research Service Publication No. R45938, updated January 26, 2021.

[1] The INA is Title 8 of the U.S. Code. For an overview of U.S. immigration policy, see CRS Report R45020, *A Primer on U.S. Immigration Policy*.

Temporary immigration occurs through the admission of visitors for specific purposes and limited periods of time, and encompasses two dozen categories (which are commonly referred to by the letter and numeral that denote their subparagraph in the INA).[2] Permanent immigration occurs through family- and employer-sponsored categories, the diversity immigrant visa lottery, and refugee and asylee admissions.

This brief chapter provides the following information:

- a list of nonimmigrant (i.e., temporary)[3] visa categories and lawful permanent resident (LPR)[4] categories,
- a description of each category,
- the allowed duration of stay in the United States for each nonimmigrant visa category,
- the annual numeric limit (or "cap") for each nonimmigrant and LPR category, and
- the number of visas that were issued/individuals obtaining LPR status for each category in the most recent year for which data are available.[5]

This information is provided in two tables: Table 1 contains information for nonimmigrant visa categories, and Table 2 contains information for LPR categories.

---

[2] These categories are found in INA §101(a)(15), 8 U.S.C. §1101(a)(15).

[3] *Nonimmigrants* are foreign nationals lawfully admitted to the United Stat es for a specific purpose and period of time, including tourists, diplomats, students, temporary workers, and exchange visitors, among others. For more information, see CRS Report R45040, *Immigration: Nonimmigrant (Temporary) Admissions to the United States*.

[4] Lawful permanent residents (LPRs) are foreign nationals lawfully admitted to the United States to live permanently. For more information, see CRS Report R42866, *Permanent Legal Immigration to the United States: Policy Overview*.

[5] In this chapter, data on nonimmigrant visa issuances come from the Department of State, which has published data for FY2020. Data on persons obtaining LPR status come from t he Department of Homeland Security, which has not yet published FY2020 data; thus, LPR data in this chapter are for FY2019.

Table 1. Nonimmigrant Visas, FY2020

Visa Category	Description	Initial Duration of Stay[a]	Annual Numeric Limit	FY2020 Visa Issuances
A-1	Ambassador, public minister, career diplomat, or consul, and immediate family	Duration of assignment	None	7,106
A-2	Other foreign government official or employee, and immediate family	Duration of assignment	None	48,358
A-3	Attendant or personal employee of A-1/A-2, and immediate family	Up to three years	None	415
B-1	Visitor for business	Six months to one year	None	17,919
B-2	Visitor for pleasure	Six months to one year	None	5,276
B-1/B-2	Visitor for business and pleasure	Six months to one year	None	2,164,021
B-1/B-2/ BCC	Border crossing cards for Mexicans	Up to 30 days (or longer if coupled with B-1 or B-2)	None	625,726
B-1/B-2/ BCV	Mexican Lincoln Border Crossing Visa	Up to 30 days (or longer if coupled with B-1 or B-2)	None	36,810
C-1	Alien in transit	Up to 29 days	None	5,228
C-1/D	Alien in transit/crew member	Up to 29 days	None	161,076
C-2	Alien in transit to United Nations Headquarters	Up to 29 days	None	1

Table 1. (Continued)

Visa Category	Description	Initial Duration of Stay[a]	Annual Numeric Limit	FY2020 Visa Issuances
C-3	Foreign government official and immediate family, attendant, or personal employee in transit	Up to 29 days	None	2,355
CW-1	Commonwealth of the Northern Marianas (CNMI) transitional worker	Up to one year	For FY2020: 12,000 plus 3,000 for construction/extraction occupations	975
CW-2	Spouse or child of CW-1	Up to one year	None	140
D	Crew member	Up to 29 days	None	6,597
E-1	Treaty trader, spouse and child, and employee	Up to two years	None	3,278
E-2	Treaty investor, spouse and child, and employee	Up to two years	None	23,493
E-2C	CNMI treaty investor, spouse, and child	Up to two years	None	27
E-3	Australian specialty occupation professional	Up to two years	10,500	3,144
E-3D	Spouse or child of E-3	Up to two years	None	2,267
E-3R	Returning E-3	Up to two years	None	1,775
F-1	Foreign student (academic or language training program)	Duration of study (limited to 12 months for secondary school students)	None	111,387
F-2	Spouse or child of F-1	Duration of study	None	9,818

Visa Category	Description	Initial Duration of Stay[a]	Annual Numeric Limit	FY2020 Visa Issuances
F-3	Border commuter academic or language student	Duration of study	None	0
G-1	Principal resident representative of recognized foreign member government to international organization, staff, and immediate family	Duration of assignment	None	3,754
G-2	Other representative of recognized foreign member government to international organization, staff, and immediate family	Duration of assignment	None	5,026
G-3	Representative of nonrecognized or nonmember foreign member government to international organization, staff, and immediate family	Duration of assignment	None	162
G-4	International organization officer or employee, and immediate family	Duration of assignment	None	13,749
G-5	Attendant or personal employee of G-1 through G-4, and immediate family	Up to three years	None	149
H-1B	Temporary worker—professional specialty occupation	Specialty occupation: up to three years; Department of Defense	Specialty occupation or fashion model: 65,000, plus 20,000 for those with U.S.	124,983

Table 1. (Continued)

Visa Category	Description	Initial Duration of Stay[a]	Annual Numeric Limit	FY2020 Visa Issuances
		(DOD) research & development: up to five years	advanced degrees; renewals and certain research/educational employers are not counted against cap; DOD research & development: 100 at any time	
H-1 B-1	Free trade agreement professional from Chile or Singapore	Up to one year	1,400 for Chile; 5,400 for Singapore	Chile: 546 Singapore: 537
H-2A	Temporary worker—agricultural workers	Up to one year	None	213,394
H-2B	Temporary worker—nonagricultural workers	Up to one year (up to three years in the case of a one-time event)	66,000	61,865
H-3	Temporary worker—trainee	Alien trainee: up to two years Special education exchange visitor program: up to 18 months	Alien trainee: none Special education exchange visitor program: 50	475

Visa Category	Description	Initial Duration of Stay[a]	Annual Numeric Limit	FY2020 Visa Issuances
H-4	Spouse or child of H-1B, H-1B-1, H-2A, H-2B, or H-3	Same as H-1, H-2, or H-3 spouse/parent	None	66,323
I	Representative of foreign information media, spouse and child	Duration of employment	None	4,888
J-1	Cultural exchange visitor	Duration of program	None	108,510
J-2	Spouse or child of J-1	Duration of program	None	15,232
K-1	Fiancé(e) of U.S. citizen	Valid for four months; must marry within 90 days of entry to adjust to LPR status	None	16,849
K-2	Child of K-1	Same as parent	None	2,460
K-3	Spouse of U.S. citizen awaiting lawful permanent resident visa	Up to two years	None	2
K-4	Child of K-3	Up to two years or until 21st birthday	None	4
L-1	Intracompany transferee (executive, managerial, and specialized knowledge personnel continuing employment with international firm or corporation)	Up to three years; up to one year when beneficiary is coming to open or be employed in a new office	None	35,942

Table 1. (Continued)

Visa Category	Description	Initial Duration of Stay[a]	Annual Numeric Limit	FY2020 Visa Issuances
L-2	Spouse or child of L-1	Same as spouse/parent	None	35,710
M-1	Vocational student	Duration of study	None	3,928
M-2	Spouse or child of M-1	Same as spouse/parent	None	119
M-3	Border commuter vocational or nonacademic student	Duration of study	None	0
NATO-1	Principal permanent representative of member nations to North Atlantic Treaty Organization (NATO), high ranking NATO officials, and immediate family members	Tour of duty	None	6
NATO-2	Other representatives of member states to NATO (including any of its subsidiary bodies) and immediate family members; dependents of member of a force entering in accordance with provisions of NATO agreements, members of such force	Tour of duty	None	5,199
NATO-3	Official clerical staff accompanying a representative of a member state to NATO, and immediate family	Tour of duty	None	0

Visa Category	Description	Initial Duration of Stay[a]	Annual Numeric Limit	FY2020 Visa Issuances
NATO-4	Officials of NATO (other than those classifiable as NATO-1), and immediate family	Tour of duty	None	110
NATO-5	Experts employed in missions on behalf of NATO (other than NATO-4 officials), and their dependents	Tour of duty	None	14
NATO-6	Civilian employees of a force entering in accordance with the provisions of NATO agreements or attached to NATO headquarters, and immediate family	Tour of duty	None	437
NATO-7	Attendant or personal employee of NATO-1 through NATO-6, and immediate family	Up to three years	None	1
N-8	Parent of certain special immigrants (pertaining to international organizations)	Up to three years, as long as special immigrant remains a child	None	8
N-9	Child of N-8 or of certain special immigrants (pertaining to international organizations)	Up to three years, or until no longer a child, whichever is shorter	None	2

Table 1. (Continued)

Visa Category	Description	Initial Duration of Stay[a]	Annual Numeric Limit	FY2020 Visa Issuances
O-1	Person with extraordinary ability in the sciences, arts, education, business, or athletics	Up to three years	None	8,838
O-2	Person accompanying and assisting in the artistic or athletic performance by O-1	Up to three years	None	3,919
O-3	Spouse or child of O-1 or O-2	Up to three years	None	2,658
P-1	Internationally recognized athlete or member of an internationally recognized entertainment group and essential support	Up to five years for individual, up to one year for group or team	None	11,710
P-2	Artist or entertainer in a reciprocal exchange program and essential support	Up to one year	None	48
P-3	Artist or entertainer in a culturally unique program and essential support	Up to one year	None	3,585
P-4	Spouse or child of P-1, P-2, or P-3	Same as spouse/parent	None	968
Q-1	International cultural exchange program participant	Up to 15 months	None	755
R-1	Religious worker	Up to 30 months	None	1,732
R-2	Spouse or child of R-1	Up to 30 months	None	667

Visa Category	Description	Initial Duration of Stay[a]	Annual Numeric Limit	FY2020 Visa Issuances
S-5	Witness or informant in criminal matter	Up to three years	200	0
S-6	Witness or informant in terrorism matter	Up to three years	50	0
S-7	Spouse or child of S-5 and S-6	Up to three years	None	0
T-1	Victim of human trafficking	Up to four years; may adjust to LPR status if conditions are met	5,000	0
T-2	Spouse of T-1	Same as T-1	None	33
T-3	Child of T-1	Same as T-1	None	131
T-4	Parent of T-1	Same as T-1	None	18
T-5	Unmarried sibling under age 18 of T-1	Same as T-1	None	14
T-6	Adult or minor child of T-2, T-3, T- 4, or T-5	Same as T-1	None	24
TN	NAFTA professional	Up to three years	None	13,771
TD	Spouse or child of TN	Up to three years	None	6,055
U-1	Victim or informant of criminal activity	Up to four years; may adjust to LPR status if conditions are met.	10,000	79
U-2	Spouse of U-1	Same as U-1	None	71
U-3	Child of U-1	Same as U-1	None	544
U-4	Parent of U-1 under age 21	Same as U-1	None	6
U-5	Unmarried sibling under age 18 of U-1 under age 21	Same as U-1	None	8

Table 1. (Continued)

Visa Category	Description	Initial Duration of Stay[a]	Annual Numeric Limit	FY2020 Visa Issuances
V-1	Spouse of LPR who has had immigrant visa petition pending for three years or longer; transitional visa that leads to LPR status when visa becomes available	Up to two years	None	0
V-2	Child of LPR who has had immigrant visa petition pending for three years or longer	Up to two years, or until 21st birthday	None	0
V-3	Child of V-1 or V-2	Up to two years, or until 21st birthday	None	0
Total				4,013,210

Source: Visa Category, Description, Duration of Stay, and Annual Numeric Limit: §101(a)(15), §212, and §214 of the Immigration and Nationality Act; and §214 of 8 C.F.R. FY2020 Visa Issuances: U.S. Department of State, Report of the Visa Office 2020, Table XV (B).

[a] Some visas are renewable. For more information, see Appendix in CRS Report R45040, Immigration: Nonimmigrant (Temporary) Admissions to the United States.

Table 2. LPR Categories, FY2019

LPR Category	Description	Annual Numeric Limit	FY2019 LPR Recipients[a]
Employment-Based Preference Immigrants			
EB-1	Priority workers	40,040	39,471
EB-2	Professionals with advanced degrees or aliens of exceptional ability	40,040	39,506
EB-3	Skilled workers, professionals, and needed unskilled workers	40,040[b] (including up to 10,000 for unskilled “other	41,787

LPR Category	**Description**	**Annual Numeric Limit**	**FY2019 LPR Recipients**[a]
		workers")	
EB-4	Special immigrants (including religious workers, employees of U.S. government abroad, and juvenile court dependents)	9,940 (including up to 5,000 religious workers)	9,609
EB-5	Investors/employment creation	9,940	9,085
Family-Based Immigrants			
IR-1	Spouses of U.S. citizens	No annual limit	304,334
IR-2	Children of U.S. citizens (includes orphans and adoptees)	No annual limit	61,303
IR-3	Parents of U.S. citizens	No annual limit	140,128
F-1	Unmarried sons/daughters of U.S. citizens and their children	23,400	24,497
F-2	Spouses, children, and unmarried sons/daughters of LPRs	114,200	93,398
F-3	Married sons/daughters of U.S. citizens and their spouses and children	23,400	25,213
F-4	Brothers/sisters of U.S. citizens (age 21 or older) and their spouses and children	65,000	61,031
Diversity	Individuals from countries that send relatively few immigrants to the United States	55,000[c]	43,463
Refugees	Aliens admitted to the United States as refugees based on persecution claims who have been physically present in the United States for at least one year	No annual limit	80,908

Table 2. (Continued)

LPR Category	Description	Annual Numeric Limit	FY2019 LPR Recipients[a]
Asylees	Aliens granted asylum based on persecution claims who have been physically present in the United States for at least one year	No annual limit	26,003
Other	Includes parolees, children born abroad to alien residents, certain Iraqis and Afghans employed by the U.S. government, cancellation of removal, victims of human trafficking, and victims of crime	Various limits[a]	32,029
Total			*1,031,765*

Source: LPR Category, Description, and Annual Numeric Limit: CRS summary of INA §§203(a), 203(b), and 204 (8 U.S.C. §§1153(a) 1153(b), and 1154). FY2019 Recipients: U.S. Department of Homeland Security, Yearbook of Immigration Statistics FY2019, Table 6. [a] Categories in which the number of LPR recipients exceeds the statutory annual numeric limit are largely due to timing differences between when LPR status is officially granted, and when immigrants actually arrive in the United States and are counted by DHS as green card recipients. These differences also result from the "roll-downs" of unused visa numbers from higher-priority categories. For more information, see Table 1 in CRS Report R42866, *Permanent Legal Immigration to the United States: Policy Overview*. [b] The Immigration and Nationality Act provides 40,040 EB-3 immigrant visas each year. From FY2002 through FY2019, that annual ceiling was reduced by up to 5,000 each year to accommodate adjustments made under the Nicaraguan Adjustment and Central American Relief Act (NACARA, Title II of P.L. 105-100, as amended by P.L. 105-139, Section 1(e)). For FY2020, this reduction was limited to approximately 350, and for FY2021, this reduction will be limited to approximately 150. [c] The Immigration and Nationality Act provides for 55,000 diversity immigrant visas each year. From FY1999 through FY2020, that annual ceiling was reduced by up to 5,000 each year to accommodate adjustments made under the Nicaraguan Adjustment and Central American Relief Act (NACARA, Title II of P.L. 105-100 as amended by P.L. 105-139, Section 1(e)). For FY2020, this reduction was limited to approximately 350, and for FY2021, this reduction will be limited to approximately 150. [d] For more information on these categories, see CRS Report R42866, *Permanent Legal Immigration to the United States: Policy Overview*.

In: Visas
Editor: Brian A. Shelton

ISBN: 978-1-53619-966-6

Chapter 2

THE DIVERSITY IMMIGRANT VISA PROGRAM*

Jill H. Wilson

SUMMARY

The purpose of the diversity immigrant visa program (DV program, sometimes called "the green card lottery" or "the visa lottery") is, as the name suggests, to foster legal immigration from countries other than the major sending countries of current immigrants to the United States. Current law weights the allocation of immigrant visas primarily toward individuals with close family in the United States and, to a lesser extent, toward those who meet particular employment needs. The diversity immigrant category was added to the Immigration and Nationality Act (INA) by the Immigration Act of 1990 (P.L. 101-649) to stimulate "new seed" immigration (i.e., to foster new, more varied migration from other parts of the world).

The DV program currently makes 50,000 visas available annually to natives of countries from which immigrant admissions were less than 50,000 over the preceding five years combined. The formula for

* This is an edited, reformatted and augmented version of Congressional Research Service Publication No. R45973, dated October 15, 2019.

allocating these visas is specified in statute: visas are divided among six global geographic regions, and each region and country is identified as either high-admission or low-admission based on how many immigrant visas were given to foreign nationals from each region and country over the previous five-year period. Higher proportions of diversity visas are allocated to low-admission regions and countries. The INA limits each country to 7% (3,500, currently) of the total and provides that Northern Ireland be treated as a separate foreign state.

Because demand for diversity visas greatly exceeds supply, a lottery system is used to select individuals who may apply for them. Those selected by lottery ("lottery winners"), like all other foreign nationals wishing to come to the United States, must undergo reviews performed by Department of State consular officers abroad and Department of Homeland Security immigration officers upon entry to the United States. These reviews are intended to ensure that the foreign nationals are not ineligible for visas or admission to the United States under the grounds for inadmissibility spelled out in the INA. To be eligible for a diversity visa, the INA requires that a foreign national have at least a high school education or the equivalent, or two years' experience in an occupation that requires at least two years of training or experience. The foreign national or the foreign national's spouse must be a native of one of the countries listed as a foreign state qualified for the diversity visa program.

The distribution of diversity visas by global region of origin has shifted over time, with higher shares coming from Africa and Asia in recent years compared to earlier years when Europe accounted for a higher proportion. Of all those admitted through the program from FY1995 (the first year it was in full effect) through FY2017 (the most recent year for which data are available), individuals from Africa accounted for 40% of diversity immigrants, while Europeans accounted for 31% and Asians for 25%.

Some argue that the DV program should be eliminated and its visas re-allocated for employment-based visas or backlog reduction in various visa categories. Critics of the DV program warn that it is vulnerable to fraud and misuse and is potentially an avenue for terrorists to enter the United States, citing the difficulties of performing background checks in many of the countries whose citizens are eligible for a diversity visa. Critics also argue that admitting immigrants on the basis of their nationality is discriminatory and that the reasons for establishing the DV program are no longer germane. Supporters of the program argue that it provides "new seed" immigrants for a system weighted disproportionately to family-based immigrants from a handful of countries. Supporters contend that fraud and abuse have declined following measures put in place by the State Department, and that the system relies on background checks for criminal and national security matters that are performed on all prospective immigrants seeking to come to the United States, including those applying for diversity visas. Supporters also contend that the DV program promotes equity of opportunity and serves important foreign policy goals.

BACKGROUND

Family reunification and the admission of immigrants with needed skills are two of the major principles underlying U.S. immigration policy. As a result, current law weights the allocation of immigrant visas heavily toward individuals with close family in the United States and, to a lesser extent, toward individuals who meet particular employment needs. The diversity immigrant category was added to the Immigration and Nationality Act (INA) by the Immigration Act of 1990 (P.L. 101-649) to stimulate "new seed" immigration (i.e., to foster new, more varied migration from other parts of the world).[1] Diversity visas are allocated to natives of countries from which the combination of immediate relatives, family preference, and employment preference immigrant admissions were lower than a total of 50,000 over the preceding five years combined.

Legislative Origins

The Immigration Amendments of 1965 replaced the national origins quota system, which prioritized European source countries, with equally distributed per-country ceilings.[2] In the 1980s, some Members of Congress began expressing concern that U.S. legal immigration admissions were skewed in favor of immigrants from Asia and Latin America because of the 1965 amendments.[3] The first legislative response to this concern

---

[1] §203(c) of INA.

[2] P.L. 89-23679 Stat. 911 (1965).

[3] Legal permanent residents from Ireland, for example, fell from 6,307 in FY1964 to 1,836 in FY1986; see CRS Report 91-141, *A Brief History of U.S. Immigration Policy*, Joyce C. Vialet, January 25, 1991 (archived report, available upon request to congressional clients). For more on the legislative history of the diversity immigrant visa program, see Anna O.

occurred in Section 314 of the Immigration Reform and Control Act of 1986 (IRCA), which allowed an extra 5,000 immigrant visas per year for FY1987 and FY1988 to be distributed to natives of 36 countries that had been adversely affected by the 1965 changes to the INA. Over 1 million people applied for what was then called the NP-5 program, and visas were made available according to the chronological order in which qualified applications were mailed to the State Department (DOS). Natives of Ireland received the largest proportion (31%) of the NP-5 visas, followed by natives of Canada (21%) and Great Britain (11%).[4] In 1988, Congress extended the NP-5 program for two more years and made 15,000 additional immigrant visas available each year in FY1989 and FY1990.[5]

What is now known as the diversity immigrant category was added to the INA[6] by P.L. 101-649 and went fully into effect in FY1995. Section 132 of P.L. 101-649 provided 40,000 visas per year for a transitional program during FY1992-FY1994 for certain natives of foreign states that were adversely affected by the 1965 changes to the INA. At least 40% of these visas were earmarked for natives of Ireland. The current diversity visa category had an annual allocation of 55,000 visas when it went into effect in FY1995.

While the diversity visa category has not been directly amended since its enactment, P.L. 105- 100, the Nicaraguan Adjustment and Central American Relief Act of 1997 (NACARA), temporarily decreased the 55,000 annual ceiling to 50,000. Beginning in FY2000, the 55,000 ceiling has been reduced by 5,000 annually to offset immigrant visas made available to certain unsuccessful asylum seekers from El Salvador, Guatemala, and formerly communist countries in Europe who are being granted immigrant status under special rules established by NACARA. The 5,000 offset is temporary, but it is not clear how many years it will be in effect to handle these adjustments of status.

Law, "The Diversity Visa Lottery: A Cycle of Unintended Consequences in United States Immigration Policy," *Journal of American Ethnic History*, vol. 21, no. 4 (Summer 2002).

[4] "Irish Biggest Winners in NP-5 Nonpreference Visa Program," *Interpreter Releases,* vol. 64, no. 291 (March 9, 1987).

[5] "State Dept. Advises on New NP-5 Program," *Interpreter Releases*, vol. 65, no. 45 (November 22, 1988).

[6] §203(c) of INA.

Eligibility Criteria and Application Process

To be eligible for a diversity visa, the INA requires that a foreign national must have at least a high school education or the equivalent, or two years of experience in an occupation that requires at least two years of training or experience. The applicant or the applicant's spouse must be a native of one of the countries listed as a foreign state qualified for the DV program.[7] Minor children of the qualifying diversity immigrant, as well as the spouse, may accompany as lawful permanent residents (LPRs)[8] and are counted toward the 50,000 annual limit.

Because the demand for diversity visas is much higher than the supply, a lottery is used to randomly select who may apply for one of the 50,000 diversity visas available annually. (See *Figure 1* for an illustration of the process). There is no fee to enter the diversity lottery.[9]

Registration for the FY2020 diversity lottery began on October 3, 2018, and closed on November 6, 2018.[10] Beginning on May 7, 2019, and continuing through September 30, 2020, those who registered can use an online system to find out if they had been selected.[11] The FY2018 lottery

---

[7] 8 USC §1153(c) (INA §203(c)). An individual who is not a native of a qualifying country may also qualify for the diversity visa program based on his or her spouse's country of birth or his or her parent's country of birth if neither of the parents were born in or are permanent residents of the applicant's country of birth at the time of the applicant's birth (see "Instructions for the 2020 Diversity Immigration Visa Program," https://travel.state.gov/content/dam/visas/Diversity-Visa/DV-Instructions-Translations/DV-2020-Instructions-Translations/DV-2020-Instructions-English.pdf).

[8] LPRs are foreign nationals who are admitted to the United States on a permanent basis.

[9] On June 5, 2019, the State Department began requiring petitioners to have a valid, unexpired passport in order to enter the lottery; see U.S. Department of State, "Visas: Diversity Immigrants," 84 *Federal Register* 25989, June 5, 2019. Some predict that this new rule will exclude lower-income petitioners or those in more remote areas for whom obtaining a passport may be more difficult. A lawsuit was filed in September claiming that the Trump Administration did not follow the public notice and comment procedures in changing this policy (*E.B. et al. v. U.S. Department of State et al.*, case number 1:19-cv-02856, in the U.S. District Court for the District of Columbia).

[10] U.S. Department of State Bureau of Consular Affairs, "Registration for the Diversity Immigrant (DV-2020) Visa Program," 83 *Federal Register* 48499-48507, September 25, 2018. Registration for the FY2021 diversity visa lottery began on October 2, 2019, and is to close on November 5, 2019.

[11] The DOS instructs registrants to log onto "Entrant Status Check" at dvlottery.state.gov to see if they have been selected. Selected entrants are encouraged to complete the online DS-260 application immediately to schedule an interview appointment at the U.S. embassy or

had 14.7 million entries, representing over 23 million people (including family members). From the millions of entries, approximately 100,000 selectees are randomly chosen.[12] Being chosen as a selectee ("lottery winner") does not guarantee receipt of a diversity visa; rather, it identifies those who are eligible to apply for one. To receive a visa, selectees must successfully complete the application process (including security and medical screenings and in-person interviews) by the end of the fiscal year for which they registered for the lottery or they lose their eligibility.[13]

DV applicants, like all other foreign nationals applying to come to the United States, must pay applicable fees[14] and undergo reviews and biometric background checks performed by DOS consular officers abroad and Department of Homeland Security (DHS) immigration officers upon entry to the United States. Individuals selected for a diversity visa who are residing in the United States as nonimmigrants[15] must undergo reviews by U.S. Citizenship and Immigration Services (USCIS) prior to adjusting to LPR status.[16] These reviews, which include an in-person interview, are intended to ensure that the applicants are not inadmissible under the grounds spelled out in Section 212(a) of the INA. Grounds for inadmissibility include health, criminal history, security and terrorist concerns, public charge, illegal entry, and previous removal.[17]

---

consulate. For more information, see https://travel.state.gov/content/ travel/en/us-visas/immigrate/diversity-visa-program-entry.html.

[12] The State Department chooses approximately 100,000 selectees in order to yield 50,000 visas because historically about half of selectees do not successfully complete the visa application process by the deadline.

[13] Such individuals may register for the lottery again in subsequent years.

[14] Individuals outside the United States must pay $330 to DOS to apply for their visa and $220 to USCIS to receive their LPR status. DV applicants who are already present in the United States on a nonimmigrant visa and do not wish to leave and re-enter the United States using their diversity visa must pay $1,140 (plus an $85 biometrics fee) to USCIS to adjust their status from nonimmigrant to LPR and $330 to DOS for their visa.

[15] Nonimmigrants are foreign nationals who are lawfully admitted to the United States for a designated period of time and a specific purpose. These include students, temporary workers, exchange visitors, and tourists. For more information, see CRS Report R45040, *Immigration: Nonimmigrant (Temporary) Admissions to the United States*.

[16] Each year, a small percentage (2.8%, on average, over the last 10 fiscal years) of DV immigrants adjust status from within the United States.

[17] For more information on inadmissibility, see CRS Report R43892, *Alien Removals and Returns: Overview and Trends*.

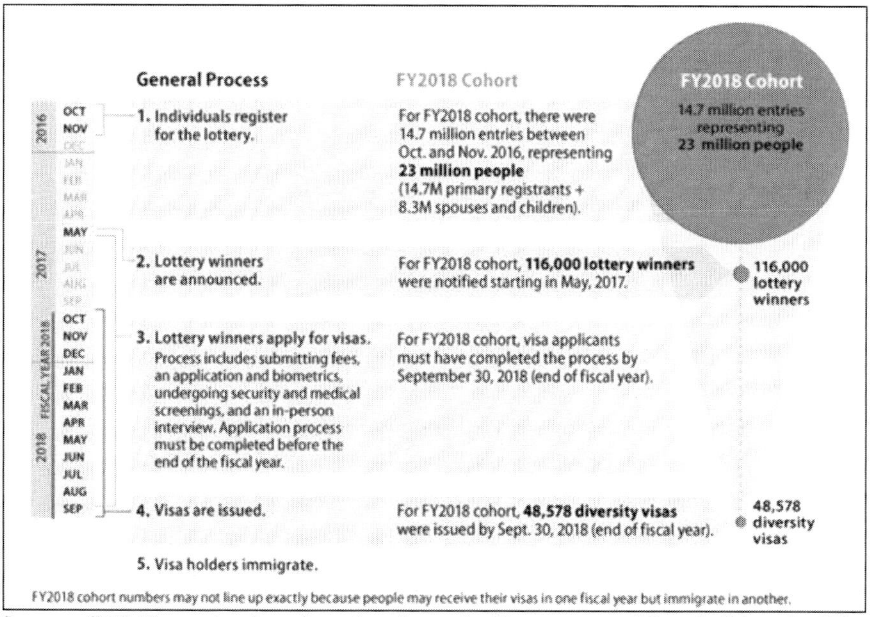

Source: CRS illustration based on data from the Department of State's Diversity Visa Selected Entrants, 2018, https://travel.state.gov/content/travel/en/us-visas/immigrate/diversity-visa-program-entry/dv-2018-selected entrants.html and from Table III of Report of the Visa Office, 2018, https://travel.state.gov/content/dam/visas/Statistics/AnnualReports/FY2018AnnualReport/FY18AnnualReport%20-%20TableIII.pdf.

Figure 1. Diversity Immigrant Visa Program. (General Process and FY2018 Cohort Information)

TRENDS IN SOURCE REGIONS AND COUNTRIES

The diversity immigrant visa program currently makes 50,000 visas available annually to natives of countries from which immigrant admissions were lower than a total of 50,000 over the preceding five years.[18] USCIS implements a formula for allocating visas according to statutory specifications:[19] visas are divided among six global geographic

[18] Only immediate relatives, family-based immigrants, and employment-based immigrants count toward the 50,000 total for the preceding five years.

[19] INA §203(c)(1).

regions, and each region and country is identified as either high admission or low admission based on how many immigrant visas each received over the previous five-year period. Higher proportions of diversity visas are allocated to low-admission regions and low-admission countries. Each country is limited to 7%, or 3,500,[20] of the total, and the INA provides that Northern Ireland be treated as a separate foreign state.[21]

The distribution of diversity visas by global region of origin has shifted over time (see Figure 2). From FY1995 through FY2001, foreign nationals from Europe garnered a plurality of diversity visas, ranging from 38% to 47% of the total. In the early 2000s, the share of DV recipients from Africa was on par with those from Europe. Europe's share dropped by nine percentage points from FY2005 to FY2006 as the shares from African and Asian countries continued to increase.

Since FY2008, Europe has accounted for smaller shares than Africa or Asia. Latin America (which includes South America, Mexico, Central America, and the Caribbean), Oceania, and North America accounted for less than 8% each year. In total, from FY1995 through FY2017 immigrants from Africa accounted for 40% of diversity immigrants, while Europeans accounted for 31% and Asians for 25%. These trends are consistent with the statutory formula Congress outlined to allocate diversity visas.[22]

Figure 3 presents the countries from which at least 1,000 DV immigrants were admitted in the first five years that the program was in full effect (FY1995-FY1999) and the most recent five years for which data are available (FY2013-FY2017). Early in the program, most of the top countries were in Europe (particularly Eastern Europe) and Africa. In more recent years, there has been a shift toward Africa and Asia. Certain countries—such as Ethiopia, Ukraine, and Egypt— rank high across many years of the program, while others—such as Ireland, Poland, and Venezuela—are limited to particular periods of time. From FY1995-FY2017, natives of six countries received at least 40,000 diversity visas in

---

[20] Given the temporary reduction in visas from 55,000 to 50,000, the 7% limit currently yields a maximum of 3,500 rather than 3,850 visas per country.

[21] INA §203(c)(1)(F).

[22] INA §203(c)(1).

total: Ethiopia (67,832), Nigeria (58,563), Egypt (56,862), Ukraine (52,654), Albania (47,136), and Bangladesh (40,847).

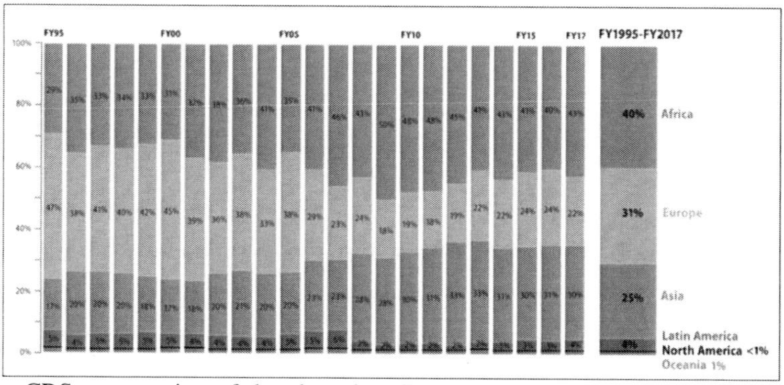

Source: CRS presentation of data based on Table 10 of the Yearbook of Immigration Statistics, DHS Office of Immigration Statistics, multiple fiscal years.

Note: CRS definitions of regions are based on diversity visa regions from U.S.C. §1153(c)(1)(F) and thus differ from definitions of regions used in the DHS Yearbook of Immigration Statistics.

Figure 2.World Region of Birth for Diversity Immigrants. FY1995-FY2017.

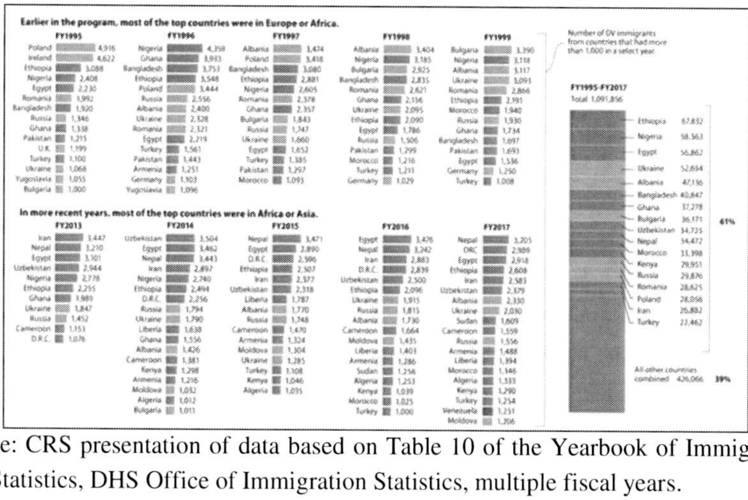

Source: CRS presentation of data based on Table 10 of the Yearbook of Immigration Statistics, DHS Office of Immigration Statistics, multiple fiscal years.

Notes: The colors of the bars correlate to the regions depicted in Figure 2 (Purple = Africa; Gold = Europe; Green = Asia).

Figure 3.Top Countries of Birth for Diversity Immigrants. FY1995-FY1999 and FY2013-FY2017.

CHARACTERISTICS OF DIVERSITY IMMIGRANTS

Regions of Birth

As one would expect, diversity immigrants come from different parts of the world that differ from the leading immigrant-sending regions. Department of Homeland Security data (*Figure 4*) reveal that Africa accounted for 43% of diversity immigrants admitted in FY2017, but 11% of all LPRs admitted that fiscal year. Europeans made up 7% of all LPRs admitted in FY2017, but 22% of diversity immigrants. In contrast, Latin America (Mexico, Central America, the Caribbean, and South America) was the sending region for 43% of all LPRs admitted in FY2017, but provided 4% of the diversity immigrants during that fiscal year. North America (excluding Mexico) and Oceania account for a small percentage of LPRs admitted by any means.

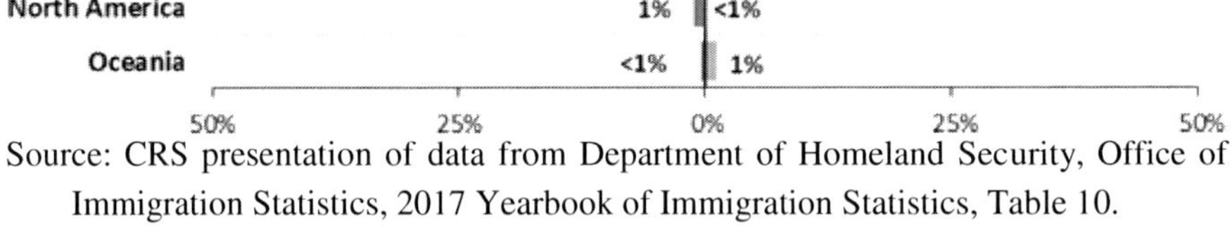

Source: CRS presentation of data from Department of Homeland Security, Office of Immigration Statistics, 2017 Yearbook of Immigration Statistics, Table 10.

Notes: In FY2017, 1.1 million LPRs were admitted, of which 51,592 were diversity LPRs. Some LPRs are admitted in a different fiscal year than the fiscal year in which the visa is issued, which explains why there can be more than 50,000 diversity LPRs admitted in a given year. Latin America includes Mexico, Central America, the Caribbean, and South America. North America includes Canada and The Bahamas.

Figure 4.World Region of Birth for LPRs in FY2017. Diversity LPRs Compared with Total LPRs.

The distribution of LPR admissions and DV admissions from Asia illustrates the impact of the two-step visa allocation formula, which considers both regional and national admissions levels. Asia includes many top-sending countries—such as China, India, and the Philippines—for family- and employment-based LPRs, making it a high-admission region. Yet it also includes low-admission countries—such as Nepal, Iran, and Uzbekistan—that rank high for their number of diversity visas. As a result, as Figure 4 illustrates, in FY2017 foreign nationals from Asia represented a somewhat more equivalent share of the 1.1 million LPRs (38%) in relation to their share (30%) of diversity LPRs in contrast to the other world regions.

Age and Sex

Diversity immigrants are, on average, younger than other LPRs. Department of Homeland Security data (see *Figure* 5) reveal that DV immigrants are more likely to be working-age adults and their children, and less likely to be over the age of 40 than LPRs overall. Also, the foreign- born population of the United States is more likely to be in the prime working-age group (i.e., ages 25 to 64) than the native-born population, and diversity immigrants have a younger age distribution than the foreign-born population as a whole.[23] In addition, 56% of diversity immigrants in FY2017 were male compared to 46% of all LPRs.

Marital Status

Diversity immigrants were less likely to be married than LPRs generally (47% versus 58%) in FY2017, perhaps a function of their relative youth. Over half (52%) of diversity immigrants were single, in contrast to

---

[23] For further analysis of the foreign-born populations, see CRS Report R41592, *The U.S. Foreign-Born Population: Trends and Selected Characteristics*.

36% of LPRs overall. Few of either group were likely to be widowed, divorced, or separated.

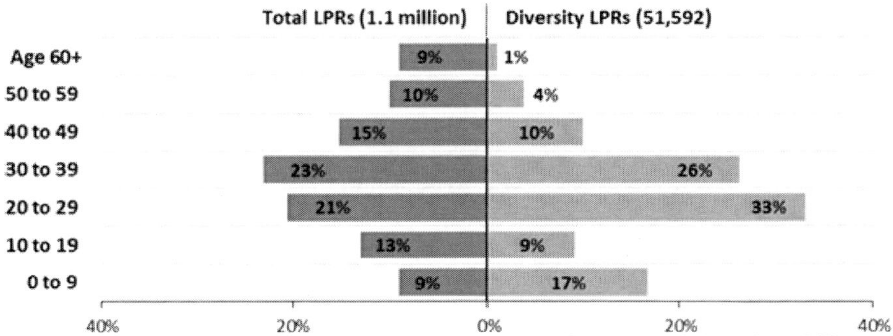

Source: CRS presentation of data from Department of Homeland Security, Office of Immigration Statistics,

2017 Yearbook of Immigration Statistics, Table 9.

Notes: In FY2017, 1.1 million LPRs were admitted, of which 51,592 were diversity LPRs. Some LPRs are admitted in a different fiscal year than the fiscal year in which the visa is issued, which explains why there can be more than 50,000 diversity LPRs admitted in a given year.

Figure 5. Age Distribution of LPRs in FY2017. Diversity LPRs Compared with Total LPRs.

Educational Attainment and Labor Market Characteristics

Recent critics of the diversity immigrant visa have argued against the program on the grounds that individuals do not need high levels of education or work experience to qualify for the DV program and that the U.S. admissions system should prioritize "high-skilled" immigrants.[24] Neither DHS nor DOS publish data on the educational attainment of DV immigrants, but other sources provide some information. According to

[24] Senator Tom Cotton and Senator David Perdue, "Reforming American Immigration for a Strong Economy Act (RAISE Act)," press release, August 2, 2017, https://www.cotton.senate.gov/files/documents/170801_New_RAISE_Act_One_Pager_FINAL.pdf; George J. Borjas, "Why Trump's New Immigration Bill Makes Sense," *Politico Magazine*, August 4, 2017; and RJ Hauman, *S. 1720: The RAISE Act*, Federation for American Immigration Reform, November 15, 2017.

now-dated data from the New Immigrant Survey,[25] a widely cited, nationally representative, longitudinal study of individuals who obtained LPR status in 2003, those who entered as principals[26] via the diversity visa category had, on average, 14.5 years of schooling when they entered the United States, which was higher than those who were admitted on family-based visas as spouses or siblings of U.S. citizens (13.0 and 11.5 years, respectively), but lower than those who were admitted as principal employment-based immigrants (15.6 years).[27] Similarly, DV immigrants were more likely to be fluent in English than most family-based immigrants (except for immigrant spouses of native-born U.S. citizens), but less likely than employment-based immigrants to be fluent in English.[28] Using the same data source, the Migration Policy Institute found that 50% of DV immigrants who entered in 2003 had a college degree (32% with a bachelor's and 18% with a graduate degree).[29] It is likely that the educational attainment of recent DV immigrants is higher than it was for those represented in the New Immigrant Survey, given that more recently arrived immigrants have higher levels of education overall than their predecessors.[30]

---

[25] Although data stopped being collected in 2009, the New Immigrant Survey remains the best available source of comparative information on the characteristics of LPRs by admission category. For more information on the New Immigrant Survey, see https://nis.princeton.edu/.

[26] Principals are foreign nationals who apply for a visa and from whom another foreign national (such as a spouse or child) may derive lawful status under immigration law.

[27] Guillermina Jasso and Mark R. Rosenzweig, "Labor Market Outcomes of Family Migrants in the United States: New Evidence from the New Immigrant Survey," unpublished; presented at the DHS-OECD Conference on Adapting to Changes in Family Migration: The Experience of OECD Countries, Washington, DC, November 2013.

[28] Guillermina Jasso, "Migration and stratification," *Social Science Research*, vol. 40 (2011), pp. 1292-1336.

[29] Julia Gellatt, "The Diversity Visa Program Holds Lessons for Future Legal Immigration Reform," Migration Policy Institute, February 2018.

[30] Jynnah Radford and Jens Manueal Krogstad, "Recently Arrived U.S. Immigrants, Growing in Number, Differ from Long-term Residents," Pew Research Center, June 3, 2019. In addition, using Census Bureau data, the Migration Policy Institute found that among recent arrivals (2012-2016) from 19 countries for which at least 25% of new green-card holders were admitted via diversity visas (from FY2012-FY2016), 50% had a bachelor's degree or higher, compared to 32% of the overall U.S. population in 2016. Julia Gellatt, "The Diversity Visa Program Holds Lessons for Future Legal Immigration Reform," Migration Policy Institute, February 2018.

Government data on other labor market characteristics of DV immigrants are also limited.[31] According to the New Immigrant Survey, DV immigrants who entered in 2003 had higher initial[32] unemployment rates than employment-based immigrants and those who immigrated as spouses of U.S. citizens, but lower unemployment rates than those who immigrated as siblings of U.S. citizens. Four to six years after U.S. entry, however, DV immigrants' unemployment rates had dropped significantly and were similar to those of all other groups except employment-based principals (who had the lowest rates at both initial entry and four to six years later). DV immigrants' hourly earnings were similarly situated between that of employment-based immigrant category (which had the highest earnings) and that of the sibling category (which had the lowest). Among male immigrants earning wages, those who entered on diversity visas had the highest percentage growth in real hourly wages between initial entry and re-sampling four to six years later.[33]

IMPACT OF THE DV PROGRAM ON IMMIGRANT DIVERSITY

Given its name and the discourse about "new seed" immigrants that preceded the creation of the diversity visa, the question arises whether the DV program has led to an increase in the diversity of immigrant flows to the United States. Leading up to and since its enactment, some observers have noted that, regardless of its name, the DV program was intended to

---

[31] Although DHS publishes annual data on occupations of DV immigrants (see Table 9 of the *Yearbook of Immigration Statistics*), the data cannot accurately portray the DV immigrant population because there are many missing values, the information is self-reported and difficult to categorize, the information reflects past work history not necessarily occupation in the United States, and the data are published in categories that are too broad to assess educational and occupational attainment.

[32] "Initial" refers to Round 1 of the New Immigrant Survey, in which interviews were conducted approximately four months, on average, after admission to LPR.

[33] Guillermina Jasso and Mark R. Rosenzweig, "Labor Market Outcomes of Family Migrants in the United States: New Evidence from the New Immigrant Survey," unpublished; presented at the DHS-OECD Conference on Adapting to Changes in Family Migration: The Experience of OECD Countries, Washington, DC, November 2013.

benefit Irish and Italian constituents who had been negatively affected by the Immigration Act of 1965 that resulted in an increase in immigration from Asia and Latin America.[34] During the transition period after the program was created (FY1992-FY1994), at least 40% of diversity visas were earmarked for Irish immigrants, and 92% of diversity visas in FY1994 went to Europeans. Since its full implementation in FY1995, however, immigrants from a wider range of countries and regions have entered via the program (see "Regions of Birth" above).

The DV program's small size relative to total annual immigrant admissions (DV admissions make up about 5% of annual LPR admissions) limits its impact on the make-up of the immigrant population. Former Representative Bruce Morrison, who helped create the program, stated in a 2005 hearing that it was not Congress's intent to diversify the immigrant flow as a whole ("It could not have possibly done so at the 50,000 number"),[35] but rather to add a new pathway for those who would not be able to enter under the family- or employment-based systems. By that standard, the program arguably fulfills its objectives, having admitted more than 1 million immigrants from under-represented countries since FY1995 (see Figure 3).

Another way to assess the program's impact is to analyze the diversity of annual LPR flows before and after the DV program was established. Using a measure of diversity called the entropy index, CRS found that in FY1990, before the DV program was in effect, the diversity of LPR

[34] See, for example, Anna O. Law, "The Diversity Visa Lottery: A Cycle of Unintended Consequences in United States Immigration Policy," *Journal of American Ethnic History*, vol. 21, no. 4 (Summer 2002), pp. 3-29; Walter P. Jacob, "Diversity Visas: Muddled Thinking and Pork Barrel Politics," *Georgetown Immigration Law Journal*, vol. 6, no. 297 (1992), pp. 297-343; Frank H. Retman, "Diversity and Transition Programs Under the Immigration Act of 1990," in *Understanding the Immigration Act of 1990*, American Immigration Lawyers Association Washington, DC, 1991, pp. 117-125; and Charles Gordon, Stanley Mailman, and Stephen Yale-Loehr, *Immigration Law and Procedure* §§ 40.01 to 40.04, revised annually.

[35] Testimony of Bruce A. Morrison, House Committee on the Judiciary, Subcommittee on Immigration, Border Security, and Claims, *Diversity Visa Program*, 109th Cong., 1st sess., June 15, 2005, H.Hrg. 109-49 (Washington: GPO, 2005), p. 5.

admissions was 0.52.[36] In every year from FY1995 (when the DV program went into full effect) through FY2017 (the most recent data available), the diversity of annual LPR admissions was higher than in 1990, ranging from 0.67 to 0.72. In each of those years, the diversity of LPR admissions not including the DV admissions was lower than it was with DV admissions included (see the Appendix), indicating that the admission of DV immigrants does increase the diversity of annual LPR admissions.

A full analysis of the impacts of the DV program on admission numbers would also take into account individuals whom DV immigrants subsequently sponsor through the family-based admissions system. Because administrative data on immigrant admissions do not specify these linkages, this type of direct analysis is not currently possible. However, admissions data suggest that, at least for Africans, the DV has led to an increase in immigration via the family-based system (particularly immediate relatives).[37] From 1992 to 2007, admissions of Africans based on family sponsorship grew faster than other categories of admissions for Africans, including diversity, which remained fairly stable over the time period.[38] The DV seems to have diversified the African flow itself by boosting emigration from non-English speaking African countries (whereas English-speaking African countries have longer histories of U.S. immigration and are therefore more likely to be the source of sponsoring immigrant family members).[39]

SELECTED LEGISLATIVE ACTION

Legislation related to the Diversity Immigrant Visa has focused largely on eliminating the program. Bills to eliminate the diversity visa category

---

[36] The entropy index (also called the Shannon index) is at its maximum when all groups are present in equal proportions, in which case the index is equal to one. See *Appendix* for details.

[37] Kevin J. A. Thomas, "What Explains the Increasing Trend in African Emigration to the U.S.?," *International Migration Review*, vol. 45, no. 1 (Spring 2011).

[38] Ibid.

[39] Ibid.

have been introduced in nearly every Congress since the program was created and have passed one chamber on more than one occasion. Most recently, S. 744 in the 113th Congress, a comprehensive immigration reform bill that the Senate passed in 2013 by a vote of 68 to 32, would have eliminated the program.[40] Other bills introduced in the past would have raised the annual limit of diversity visas or temporarily re- allocated diversity visas for other purposes. In the 116th Congress, several bills to eliminate the DV program have been introduced, including H.R. 479, H.R. 2278, S. 1103, and S. 1632. In contrast, H.R. 3799 would raise the annual diversity visa allocation to 80,000.

SELECTED POLICY QUESTIONS

As Congress weighs whether to eliminate or revise the diversity visa category, it may want to consider various policy questions pertinent to this discussion.[41]

Is It Fair to Have the Diversity Visa Category When There Are Family Members and Prospective Employees Who Have Been Waiting for Years for Visas to Become Available?

Given the 3.7 million approved family-based and employment-based petitions waiting for a visa to become available at the close of FY2018,[42]

---

[40] One of the bill's merit-based point systems included points (5 out of 100) for country of origin diversity. For more information on S. 744, see archived CRS Report R43097, *Comprehensive Immigration Reform in the 113th Congress: Major Provisions in Senate-Passed S. 744*.

[41] Despite recent debate about the DV program, no hearings have been held on this topic since 2011. Thus, many of the citations in this section come from hearings held in 2004, 2005, and 2011.

[42] U.S. Department of State, Annual Report of Immigrant Visa Applicants in the Family-sponsored and Employment- based preferences Registered at the National Visa Center as of November 1, 2018. These data do not include nationals already present in the United States with approved employment-based immigrant petitions who have not yet adjusted status. USCIS reported that figure to be 395,025 as of April 20, 2018. For more information on the

some argue that the 50,000 diversity visas should be used for backlog reduction in these visa categories.[43] Others might observe that the family-based, employment-based, and diversity visa categories are statutorily designed as independent pathways to LPR status and that the problems of the family-based and employment-based backlogs should be addressed separately.[44] Some also argue that the DV program *increases* fairness in the immigration system by making visas available to individuals who would not otherwise have a chance of obtaining one[45] and by discouraging illegal immigration through expanding access to the legal immigration system.[46]

---

visa queue, see CRS Report R45447, *Permanent Employment-Based Immigration and the Per-country Ceiling*.

[43] Testimony of Representative Bob Goodlatte, House Committee on the Judiciary, Subcommittee on Immigration Policy and Enforcement, *SAFE for America Act*, 112th Cong., 1st sess., April 5, 2011, H. Hrg. 112-27 (Washington: GPO, 2011); and testimony of Jan Ting, Professor of Law, Temple University, House Committee on the Judiciary, Subcommittee on Immigration, Border Security, and Claims, *Diversity Visa Program and Its Susceptibility to Fraud and Abuse*, 108th Cong., 2nd sess., April 29, 2004, H.Hrg. 108-82 (Washington: GPO, 2004).

[44] For more information on family-based and employment-based immigration, see CRS Report R42866, *Permanent Legal Immigration to the United States: Policy Overview*. For information on visa wait times in the employment-based system and efforts to reduce them, see CRS Report R45447, *Permanent Employment-Based Immigration and the Per- country Ceiling*.

[45] Testimony of Representative Zoe Lofgren, House Committee on the Judiciary, Subcommittee on Immigration Policy and Enforcement, *SAFE for America Act*, 112th Cong., 1st sess., April 5, 2011, H. Hrg. 112-27 (Washington: GPO, 2011); testimony of Representative John Conyers, House Committee on the Judiciary, Subcommittee on Immigration Policy and Enforcement, *SAFE for America Act*, 112th Cong., 1st sess., April 5, 2011, H. Hrg. 112-27 (Washington: GPO, 2011);and testimony of Ambassador Johnny Young, Executive Director, U.S. Conference of Catholic Bishops, House Committee on the Judiciary, Subcommittee on Immigration Policy and Enforcement, *SAFE for America Act*, 112th Cong., 1st sess., April 5, 2011, H. Hrg. 112-27 (Washington: GPO, 2011).

[46] Testimony of Ambassador Johnny Young, Executive Director, U.S. Conference of Catholic Bishops, House Committee on the Judiciary, Subcommittee on Immigration Policy and Enforcement, *SAFE for America Act*, 112th Cong., 1st sess., April 5, 2011, H. Hrg. 112-27 (Washington: GPO, 2011); and testimony of Senator Charles Schumer, House Committee on the Judiciary, Subcommittee on Immigration Policy and Enforcement, *SAFE for America Act*, 112th Cong., 1st sess., April 5, 2011, H. Hrg. 112-27 (Washington: GPO, 2011).

Should the United States Base Admissions Decisions on Nationality?

Some argue that the diversity visa program reverts to discriminatory national origin quotas, which Congress eliminated through the 1965 amendments to the Immigration and Nationality Act.[47] However, there are other examples of admissions policies that effectively discriminate based on nationality (e.g., H-2A,[48] H-2B,[49] E,[50] and TN[51] nonimmigrant visas, the Visa Waiver Program,[52] and the per country caps[53] on family- and employment-based LPR admissions, all of which limit admissions by nationality). Some also argue that admissions decisions should be based on higher levels of education, job experience, and language skills, or family ties to U.S. residents, rather than country of origin and being selected at random via a lottery.[54]

In contrast, others argue that the program bolsters equity of opportunity—a quintessential American value—by providing a pathway

---

[47] Stephen H. Legomsky, "Immigration, Equality and Diversity," *Columbia Journal of Transnational Law*, vol. 31, no. 2 (1993); testimony of Mark Krikorian, Executive Director, Center for Immigration Studies, House Committee on the Judiciary, Subcommittee on Immigration, Border Security, and Claims, *Diversity Visa Program*, 109th Cong., 1st sess., June 15, 2005, H. Hrg. 109-49;testimony of Rosemary Jenks, Director of Government Relations, NumbersUSA, House Committee on the Judiciary, Subcommittee on Immigration, Border Security, and Claims, *Diversity Visa Program*, 109th Cong., 1st sess., June 15, 2005, H. Hrg. 109-49; testimony of Jan Ting, Professor of Law, Temple University, House Committee on the Judiciary, Subcommittee on Immigration, Border Security, and Claims, *Diversity Visa Program and Its Susceptibility to Fraud and Abuse*, 108th Cong., 2nd sess., April 29, 2004, H.Hrg. 108-82 (Washington: GPO, 2004); and Walter P. Jacob, "Diversity Visas: Muddled Thinking and Pork Barrel Politics," *Georgetown Immigration Law Journal*, vol. 6, (1992), pp. 297-343.

[48] For more information, see CRS Report R44849, H-2A and H-2B Temporary Worker Visas: Policy and Related Issues.

[49] Ibid.

[50] For more information, see CRS Report R45040, Immigration: Nonimmigrant (Temporary) Admissions to the United States.

[51] Ibid.

[52] For more information, see CRS Report RL32221, *Visa Waiver Program.*

[53] For more information, see CRS Report R45447, Permanent Employment-Based Immigration and the Per-country Ceiling.

[54] Testimony of Representative Bob Goodlatte, House Committee on the Judiciary, Subcommittee on Immigration Policy and Enforcement, *SAFE for America Act*, 112th Cong., 1st sess., April 5, 2011, H. Hrg. 112-27 (Washington: GPO, 2011).

for individuals—particularly those from Africa, Eastern Europe, and the former Soviet Union—who do not have family or employer connections in the United States.[55] Some also argue that the more than one million immigrants who have moved to the United States as a result of the program have enriched the United States culturally and economically, and strengthened the nation's global connections.[56] Some also argue that efforts to end it are racially motivated[57] or point out that for most of U.S. history, Africans in particular had little opportunity to come to the United States other than as slaves.[58]

---

[55] estimony of Bruce A. Morrison, House Committee on the Judiciary, Subcommittee on Immigration, Border Security, and Claims, *Diversity Visa Program*, 109th Cong., 1st sess., June 15, 2005, H.Hrg. 109-49 (Washington: GPO, 2005). Testimony of Representative John Conyers, House Committee on the Judiciary, Subcommittee on Immigration Policy and Enforcement, *SAFE for America Act*, 112th Cong., 1st sess., April 5, 2011, H. Hrg. 112-27 (Washington: GPO, 2011). In addition, the House Judiciary Committee Report on H.R. 4300, which led to the enactment of the DV program, stated "The Committee is convinced that in order to correct ongoing inequities in current law, changes must be made to further enhance and promote diversity within the present system." U.S. Congress, House Committee on the Judiciary, *Family Unity and Employment Opportunity Immigration Act of 1990*, 101st Cong., 2nd sess., September 19, 1990, H. Rept. 101-723 (Washington: GPO, 1990), p. 48.

[56] Patrick Kennedy, "The Labor Economics Case for the Diversity Visa Lottery," *Stanford Law Review*, vol. 71 (October 2018), https://www.stanfordlawreview.org/online/the-labor-economics-case-for-the-diversity-visa-lottery/; Jeremy L. Neufeld, *The Diversity Visa: Part of a Merit-Based Immigration System*, Niskanen Center, Washington, DC, October 2018, https://niskanencenter.org/wp-content/uploads/2018/10/Diversity-Visa-and-Skills.pdf; Arun Peter Lobo, *U.S. Diversity Visas are Attracting Africa's Best and Brightest*, Population Reference Bureau, July 2001, https://www.prb.org/usdiversityvisasareattracting africasbestandbrightest/; Laura D. Francis, "Diversity Visas are a Trump Target, and That Could Hurt Employers," *Bloomberg Law*, November 14, 2018, https://news.bloomberglaw.com/daily-labor-report/diversity-visas-are-a-trump-target-and-that-could-hurt-employers- corrected; Testimony of Representative Zoe Lofgren, House Committee on the Judiciary, Subcommittee on Immigration Policy and Enforcement, *SAFE for America Act*, 112th Cong., 1st sess., April 5, 2011, H. Hrg. 112-27 (Washington: GPO, 2011); Testimony of Ambassador Johnny Young, Executive Director, U.S. Conference of Catholic Bishops, House Committee on the Judiciary, Subcommittee on Immigration Policy and Enforcement, *SAFE for America Act*, 112th Cong., 1st sess., April 5, 2011, H. Hrg. 112-27 (Washington: GPO, 2011).

[57] Rafael Bernal, "Five things to know about the diversity visa lottery," *The Hill*, November 1, 2017. Testimony of Representative John Conyers, House Committee on the Judiciary, Subcommittee on Immigration Policy and Enforcement, *SAFE for America Act*, 112th Cong., 1st sess., April 5, 2011, H. Hrg. 112-27 (Washington: GPO, 2011).

[58] Andowah A. Newton, "Injecting Diversity into U.S. Immigration Policy: The Diversity Visa Program and the Missing Discourse on Its Impact on African Immigration to the United

Is a Lottery the Best Way to Choose Applicants for Diversity Visas?

Some equate the use of a lottery system in the DV program to awarding "green cards" at random and argue that luck should not come into play in U.S. admissions decisions.[59] Others argue that, given the millions of interested applicants every year, a lottery is a fair method of reducing the applicant pool because it gives all entrants who meet the program's qualifications an equal chance to apply for a diversity visa. They also cite the use of a lottery in other over-subscribed visa categories such as the H-1B and H-2B temporary worker classifications to illustrate that U.S. immigration policy considers it a reasonable tool.[60]

Is the Diversity Visa Lottery More Vulnerable to Fraud and Misuse Than Other Immigration Pathways?

Some observers concerned about immigration fraud surrounding the DV program reference a 2003 State Department Office of Inspector General report and a 2007 GAO report which found fraud vulnerabilities in the DV program.[61] They may also cite the 2017 and 2018 complaints filed by the Department of Justice (DOJ) in two cases seeking the denaturalization of individuals who had gained admission (in 1997 and

---

States," *Cornell International Law Journal*, vol. 38, no. 3 (2005); Testimony of Bruce A. Morrison, House Committee on the Judiciary, Subcommittee on Immigration, Border Security, and Claims, *Diversity Visa Program*, 109th Cong., 1st sess., June 15, 2005, H.Hrg. 109-49 (Washington: GPO, 2005).

[59] Testimony of Representative Bob Goodlatte, House Committee on the Judiciary, Subcommittee on Immigration Policy and Enforcement, *SAFE for America Act*, 112th Cong., 1st sess., April 5, 2011, H. Hrg. 112-27 (Washington: GPO, 2011).

[60] For information on the H-1B visa program, see CRS Report R43735, *Temporary Professional, Managerial, and Skilled Foreign Workers: Policy and Trends*. For information on the H-2B visa program, see CRS Report R44849, *H- 2A and H-2B Temporary Worker Visas: Policy and Related Issues*.

[61] U.S. Department of State, Office of Inspector General, *Memorandum Inspection Report: Diversity Visa Program*, ISP-CA-03-52, September 2003; U.S. Government Accountability Office, *Fraud Risks Complicate State's Ability to Manage Diversity Visa Program*, GAO-07-1174, September 2007, https://www.gao.gov/products/GAO-07-1174.

2001) to the United States through the DV program. In the first case, DOJ filed a complaint to denaturalize four Somali-born diversity visa recipients who falsely claimed to be a family.[62] In the second case, DOJ filed a complaint to denaturalize a diversity visa recipient who obtained naturalization without having disclosed two prior orders of removal.[63]

Those defending the fraud protections of the DV program counter that DOS has since revised the diversity lottery procedures to address fraud vulnerabilities,[64] including a requirement to submit a recent photograph, the addition of biographic and facial recognition checks to reduce duplicate entries, a policy requiring the disqualification of entrants who fail to list their spouse and children on their entries, and technical improvements to limit manipulation of entries by automated bots.[65] They also argue that the risk of fraud is not unique to the DV program and refer to the numerous fraud investigations and arrests of immigrants who entered the United States via other visa categories[66] and the significant resources that DOS

---

[62] U.S. Department of Justice, "Denaturalization Sought Against Four Somalia-Born Individuals Who Falsely Claimed to be a Family and Were Admitted to the United States on Diversity Immigrant Visas," press release, November 6, 2017 https://www.justice.gov/opa/pr/denaturalization-sought-against-four-somalia-born-individuals-who-falsely-claimed-be-family.

[63] U.S. Department of Justice, "Department of Justice Files Complaint to Denaturalize Diversity Visa Recipient Who Obtained Naturalized Citizenship After Failing to Disclose Two Prior Orders of Removal," press release, February 15, 2018 https://www.justice.gov/opa/pr/department-justice-files-complaint-denaturalize-diversity-visa-recipient-who- obtained.

[64] U.S. Department of State, "Fraud Warning, Diversity Visa, Program Scammers Sending Fraudulent Emails and Letters," https://travel.state.gov/content/travel/en/us-visas/visa-information-resources/fraud.html.

[65] U.S. Department of State letter to the Chairman of the Committee on the Judiciary, Charles E. Grassley, December 15, 2017, https://www.judiciary.senate.gov/imo/media/doc/2017-12-19%20State%20Dept.%20to%20CEG%20-%20Diversity%20Visa%20Program.pdf.

[66] The Department of State's response to the 2007 GAO report on the diversity visa program stated, "It is a sad reality that *all* visa categories encounter sham marriages, suspect identities, fraudulent documents, use of agents, and unlikely stories." U.S. Department of State, *Comments on GAO Draft Report, 'Border Security: Fraud Risks Complicate State's Ability to Manage Diversity Visa Program,'* September 10, 2007, p. 1. USCIS maintains a website for the public to report immigration fraud, with specific sections for fraud related to marriage, asylum, and the H-1B, H-2B, and EB-5 programs: https://www.uscis.gov/report-fraud. For recent examples, see U.S. Immigration and Customs Enforcement, "Nearly 100 people indicted, 50 currently in custody in massive Houston-based marriage fraud conspiracy," press release, May 13, 2019; U.S. Government Accountability Office, *Student and Exchange Visitor Program: DHS Can Take Additional Steps to Manage Fraud Risks Related to School Recertification and Program Oversight*, GAO-19-297, March 18, 2019, https://www.gao.gov/products/GAO-19-297; U.S. Government Accountability Office,

commits to fraud prevention for all immigrant and nonimmigrant visa applications through its Fraud Prevention Units at posts overseas.[67] In addition, on June 5, 2019, DOS published an interim final rule to require diversity visa entrants to provide certain information from a valid, unexpired passport on the electronic entry form.[68] This rule is intended to make it more difficult for third parties to submit unauthorized entries, because third parties are less likely to have individuals' passport numbers.[69]

Are There National Security Reasons to Eliminate the Diversity Visa?

Some assert that the difficulties of performing background checks in many of the countries whose natives currently qualify for the DV program, as well as broader concerns about terrorism, justify the elimination of the category.[70] Some cite the 2004 warning of the DOS Deputy Inspector General that the diversity visa lottery "contains significant vulnerabilities to national security" from state sponsors of terrorism.[71] They argue that DV

Immigrant Investor Program: Progress Made to Detect and Prevent Fraud, but Additional Actions Could Further Agency Efforts, GAO-16-828, September 13, 2016; U.S. Department of Justice, "International Employee Recruiter Sentenced to Two Years in Prison for Visa Fraud," July 2, 2014; and U.S. Government Accountability Office, *H-2B Visa Program: Closed Civil Criminal Cases Illustrate Instances of H-2B Workers Being Targets of Fraud and Abuse*, GAO-10-1053, September 30, 2010.

[67] U.S. Department of State letter to the Chairman of the Committee on the Judiciary, Charles E. Grassley, December 15, 2017, https://www.judiciary.senate.gov/imo/media/doc/2017-12-19%20State%20Dept.%20to%20CEG%20-%20Diversity%20Visa%20Program.pdf.

[68] U.S. Department of State, Visas, Diversity Immigrants: Interim Final Rule, 84 *Federal Register* 25989, (June 5, 2019), https://www.federalregister.gov/documents/2019/06/05/2019-11762/visas-diversity-immigrants.

[69] Ibid. at 25990, "Why is the Department promulgating this rule?" Some argue that this new rule's effect will be to limit lottery entries from low-income individuals and those who live in remote areas or who otherwise have difficulty obtaining a passport.

[70] Testimony of Janice L. Kephart, Center for Immigration Studies, House Committee on the Judiciary, Subcommittee on Immigration Policy and Enforcement, *SAFE for America Act*, 112th Cong., 1st sess., April 5, 2011, H. Hrg. 112-27 (Washington: GPO, 2011).

[71] U.S. Congress, House Committee on the Judiciary, Subcommittee on Immigration, Border Security, and Claims, *The Diversity Visa Program, and Its Susceptibility to Fraud and Abuse*, 108th Cong., 2nd sess., April 29, 2004.

immigrants, by definition, are not required to have employer or family ties in the United States and thus may be more likely to have nefarious intent.[72] They cite the case of a New Jersey resident responsible for killing eight people with his rental truck in lower Manhattan in 2017, who had immigrated to the United States from Uzbekistan on a diversity visa.[73] In response to that event, the Trump Administration called on Congress to immediately terminate the diversity visa lottery program.[74]

Others respond that immigrants coming to the United States in other immigrant visa categories are not restricted if they come from these same countries, and further argue that background checks for national security risks are performed on all prospective immigrants seeking to come to the United States. They also point to the 2005 DOS Inspector General's testimony that DOS's Bureau of Consular Affairs strengthened the DV program by complying with most of the recommendations in the OIG's 2003 report.[75] They similarly note the testimony of one of the creators of the DV Program who contended that "it is absurd to think that a lottery would be the vehicle of choice for terrorists" and that attention should instead be focused on greater security risks.[76] They also point out that since the creation of the Visa Security Program in 2003, DHS has aided consular officers in extensively vetting individuals applying for visas.[77] They also

---

[72] Testimony of Janice L. Kephart, Center for Immigration Studies, House Committee on the Judiciary, Subcommittee on Immigration Policy and Enforcement, *SAFE for America Act*, 112th Cong., 1st sess., April 5, 2011, H. Hrg. 112-27 (Washington: GPO, 2011).

[73] Benjamin Mueller, William K. Rashburn, Al Baker, "Terror Attack Kills 8 and Injures 11 in Manhattan," The New York Times, https://www.nytimes.com/2017/10/31/nyregion/police-shooting-lower-manhattan.html; U.S. Congress, Senate Judiciary Committee, "Grassley Seeks Details on NYC Attacker," press release, November 1, 2017, https://www.grassley.senate.gov/news/news-releases/grassley-seeks-details-nyc-attacker.

[74] The White House, "National Security Threats—Chain Migration and the Visa Lottery System," February 1, 2018, https://www.whitehouse.gov/articles/national-security-threats-chain-migration-visa-lottery-system/.

[75] Testimony of DOS Inspector General Howard J. Krongard, House Committee on the Judiciary, Subcommittee on Immigration, Border Security, and Claims, *Diversity Visa Program*, 109th Cong., 1st sess., June 15, 2005, H. Hrg. 109- 49 (Washington: GPO, 2005).

[76] Testimony of Bruce A. Morrison, House Committee on the Judiciary, Subcommittee on Immigration, Border Security, and Claims, *Diversity Visa Program*, 109th Cong., 1st sess., June 15, 2005, H.Hrg. 109-49 (Washington: GPO, 2005).

[77] Through the Visa Security Program, special agents from ICE's Homeland Security Investigations are assigned to diplomatic posts worldwide to conduct law enforcement visa

reference a 2007 GAO report stating: "We found no documented evidence that DV immigrants from these, or other, countries posed a terrorist or other threat. However, experts familiar with immigration fraud believe that some individuals, including terrorists and criminals, could use fraudulent means to enter or remain in the United States."[78]

Are There Foreign Policy Reasons to Continue the Diversity Visa Program?

Citing the millions of diversity visa lottery entries every year from around the world, some argue that the DV program is an efficient means of boosting American goodwill and "soft power" abroad, and that a diversity of immigrant origins helps the United States better respond to the challenges of globalization.[79] Some also cite the value of remittances sent by diversity immigrants to their countries of origin as international development assistance without U.S. government expense.[80] Others argue

---

security activities. For more information, see U.S. Immigration and Customs Enforcement, *Visa Security Program*, https://www.ice.gov/visa-security-program#

[78] U.S. Government Accountability Office, Border Security: Fraud Risks Complicate State's Ability to Manage Diversity Visa Program, GAO-07-1174, September 21, 2007, Highlights.

[79] Carly Goodman and Charles Piot, "Diversity visa lottery doesn't make us less safe, but ending it might," *The Hill*, November 29, 2017; Klara Bilgin, "It is called hope! Why we should keep the U.S. diversity immigrant visa program," *International Policy Digest*, November 6, 2017; Onoso Imoagene, "Affecting Lives: How Winning the U.S. Diversity Visa Lottery Impacts DV Migrants Pre- and Post-Migration," *International Migration*, vol. 55, no. 6 (2017), pp. 170- 183; Testimony of Representative John Conyers, House Committee on the Judiciary, Subcommittee on Immigration Policy and Enforcement, *SAFE for America Act*, 112th Cong., 1st sess., April 5, 2011, H. Hrg. 112-27 (Washington: GPO, 2011); Testimony of Ambassador Johnny Young, Executive Director, U.S. Conference of Catholic Bishops, House Committee on the Judiciary, Subcommittee on Immigration Policy and Enforcement, *SAFE for America Act*, 112th Cong., 1st sess., April 5, 2011, H. Hrg. 112-27 (Washington: GPO, 2011). "Dissenting Views," U.S. Congress, House Committee on the Judiciary, *SAFE for America Act*, Report to accompany H.R. 704, 112th Cong., 1st sess., November 10, 2011, H.Rept. 112-275 (Washington: GPO, 2011); Testimony of Bruce A. Morrison, House Committee on the Judiciary, Subcommittee on Immigration, Border Security, and Claims, *Diversity Visa Program*, 109th Cong., 1st sess., June 15, 2005, H.Hrg. 109-49 (Washington: GPO, 2005).

[80] B. Ikubolajeh Logan and Kevin J.A. Thomas, "The U.S. Diversity Visa Programme and the Transfer of Skills from Africa," *International Migration*, vol. 50, no. 2 (2012); John Gibson and David McKenzie, "The Economic Consequences of 'Brain Drain' of the Best and

that the DV program encourages "brain drain" from developing countries, a concern which acknowledges that many DV immigrants—particularly from Africa— possess education and skills beyond the minimum requirements for program eligibility.[81]

Are the Reasons That Led to Establishment of the Diversity Visa (E.G., to Stimulate "New Seed" Immigration) Still Germane?

Supporters of the DV program argue that it honors the United States' history as a destination for enterprising immigrants—the "self-selected strivers"[82]—who arrive without family ties but with a desire to work hard for a better life.[83] Some point to the present-day preponderance of immigrants from a handful of countries and argue that the diversity visa fosters new and more varied migration to counterbalance an admissions system weighted disproportionately to family-based immigration, which tends to perpetuate the dominance of certain countries. They also point to wide support for legislation that would remove or raise the 7% per-country limits on family- and employment-based immigrant admissions,[84] which would likely result in further concentration of immigrant flows from the

Brightest: Microeconomic Evidence from Five Countries," *The Economic Journal*, vol. 122, no. 560 (May 2015).

[81] Onoso Imoagene, "Affecting Lives: How Winning the U.S. Diversity Visa Lottery Impacts DV Migrants Pre- and Post-Migration," *International Migration*, vol. 55, no. 6 (2017), pp. 170-183; B. Ikubolajeh Logan and Kevin J.A. Thomas, "The U.S. Diversity Visa Programme and the Transfer of Skills from Africa," *International Migration*, vol. 50, no. 2 (2012); Arun Peter Lobo, "Unintended Consequences: Liberalized U.S. Immigration Law and the African Brain Drain," in *The New African Diaspora in North America: Trends, Community Building, and Adaptation*, ed. Kwado Konadu-Agyemang, Baffour K. Takyi, and John Arthur (New York: Lexington Books, 2006), pp. 189-208.

[82] Testimony of Bruce A. Morrison, House Committee on the Judiciary, Subcommittee on Immigration, Border Security, and Claims, *Diversity Visa Program*, 109th Cong., 1st sess., June 15, 2005, H.Hrg. 109-49 (Washington: GPO, 2005).

[83] Testimony of John P. Collins, National Chairman of the American Irish National Immigration Committee, House Committee on the Judiciary, Subcommittee No. 1, *The Effect of the Act of October 3, 1965, on Immigration from Ireland and Northern Europe*, 91st Cong., 1st sess., December 10, 1969, H. Hrg. 91-28 (Washington: GPO, 1970).

[84] On July 10, 2019, H.R. 1044, the Fairness for High-Skilled Immigrants Act, passed the House by a vote of 365-65. It would remove the 7% per country limit for employment-based immigrant visas and raise the per-country limit to 15% for family-based immigrant visas.

top sending countries.[85] Even with the per-country limits and DV program in place, the total foreign-born population has become more concentrated in the top ten source countries compared to 1990[86] (see "Impact of the DV Program on Immigrant Diversity").

Others argue that, after almost 30 years, the diversity visa category has run its course.[87] They might cite the countries—such as Pakistan, Brazil, Nigeria, and Bangladesh—that formerly qualified for the DV program and no longer do due to their increase in admissions, or the growth in immigration from Africa, Eastern Europe, and parts of Asia as an indication that the need for "new seed" immigration has been met.[88] Others counter that these trends indicate that the program is meeting its goals and should be continued. They further argue that in many countries around the world, the diversity visa remains the only accessible avenue for immigrating to the United States.[89]

---

[85] For more information on the 7% per-country caps, see CRS Report R42866, *Permanent Legal Immigration to the United States: Policy Overview*.

[86] In 1990, 52.2% of foreign-born individuals were born in the top ten countries of origin for the U.S. foreign-born population; in 2017, that number was 57.4%. At the same time, a higher proportion of the foreign born are concentrated in the bottom ten source countries (0.42% in 2017 compared to 0.21% in 1990). These statistics have been used to argue both for and against keeping the DV program in place. Those who support the DV program argue that without it, the foreign-born population would be dominated to an even greater extent by the high-admission countries. Those against it argue that the increased concentration at the top shows that the DV program does not actually diversify the foreign-born population and therefore should be eliminated, but this argument does not take into account what would have happened if the DV program had not been in place. See "Impact of the DV Program on Immigrant Diversity" above.

[87] Institute of the Electrical and Electronic Engineers, *Promoting Diversity through the STEM Visa: A White Paper on High-Skill Immigration Reform*, 2012, https://ieeeusa.org/wp-content/uploads/2017/07/IEEEUSAWP- DiversityVisa2012.pdf; and Laura D. Francis, "Diversity Visas are a Trump Target, and That Could Hurt Employers," *Bloomberg Law*, November 14, 2018, https://news.bloomberglaw.com/daily-labor-report/diversity-visas-are-a-trump- target-and-that-could-hurt-employers-corrected.

[88] Ibid.

[89] Testimony of Representative John Conyers, House Committee on the Judiciary, Subcommittee on Immigration Policy and Enforcement, *SAFE for America Act*, 112th Cong., 1st sess., April 5, 2011, H. Hrg. 112-27 (Washington: GPO, 2011); and testimony of Bruce A. Morrison, House Committee on the Judiciary, Subcommittee on Immigration, Border Security, and Claims, *Diversity Visa Program*, 109th Cong., 1st sess., June 15, 2005, H.Hrg. 109-49 (Washington: GPO, 2005).

APPENDIX. ENTROPY INDEX METHODOLOGY AND RESULTS

The entropy index (also called the Shannon index)[90] is a measure of the diversity of a population. Diversity can be defined as the "relative heterogeneity of a population."[91] It is at its maximum when all subpopulations are present in equal proportions (for the purposes of this chapter, when each country of birth receives an equal number of LPR admissions). The formula for the entropy index is

$$\mathrm{H} = -\sum_{k=1}^{K} P_k \, log P_k$$

where H is the entropy index, k is the country-of-origin group, and P is the proportion of the total from each country-of-origin group. The index can be standardized by dividing by its maximum, log K. Doing so results in a range of 0 (for the case where all of the population is in one subpopulation) to 1.0 (for the case where all subpopulations are present in equal proportions).

For this chapter, the standardized entropy index was calculated by year for country of birth of total LPR admissions, LPR admissions minus DV admissions, and DV admissions. This was calculated after creating a standardized list of countries across all years so that K was held constant. As shown in *Figure A-1*, between FY1995 and FY2017, the entropy index varied, but in all years the index was higher when DV LPRs were included.

---

90 The entropy index used in this chapter is explained in greater detail in Michael J. White, "Segregation and Diversity Measures in Population Distribution," *Population Index*, vol. 52, no. 2 (Summer 1986).

91 91 Ibid, p. 199.

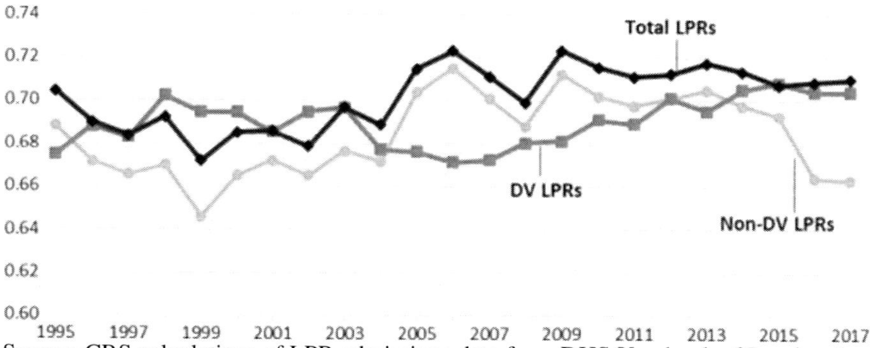

Source: CRS calculations of LPR admissions data from DHS Yearbook of Immigration Statistics, Table 10, various years.

Figure A-1. Entropy Index (Standardized) by LPR Type. FY1995-FY2017.

In: Visas
Editor: Brian A. Shelton

ISBN: 978-1-53619-966-6

Chapter 3

H-2A AND H-2B TEMPORARY WORKER VISAS: POLICY AND RELATED ISSUES*

Andorra Bruno

SUMMARY

Certain foreign workers, sometimes referred to as guest workers, may be admitted to the United States to perform temporary labor under two temporary worker visas: the H-2A visa for agricultural workers and the H-2B visa for nonagricultural workers. The H-2Avisa is not subject to any numerical limitations, while the H-2B visa is subject to a statutory annual cap of 66,000.

H-2A and H-2B workers fill jobs that do not require much formal education. H-2A workers perform seasonal or temporary agricultural labor. They also engage in range herding and livestock production. H-2B workers perform temporary jobs in a variety of fields including landscaping, meat and seafood processing, and construction.

The H-2A and H-2B programs are administered by the Department of Homeland Security (DHS) and the Department of Labor (DOL). These agencies and the Department of State (DOS) have made adjustments, and

* This is an edited, reformatted and augmented version of Congressional Research Service, Publication No. R44849, dated June 9, 2020.

in the case of DHS issued H-2A and H-2B temporary final rules, related to guest worker visas in response to the coronavirus pandemic.

Statutory and regulatory provisions establish processes for bringing in workers under the H-2A and H-2B programs that are intended to protect similarly employed U.S. workers. As an initial step in the process, a prospective H-2Aor H-2B employer must apply for DOL labor certification to ensure that U.S. workers are not available for the jobs in question and that the hiring of foreign workers will not adversely affect the wages and working conditions of U.S. workers. After receiving labor certification, the employer can submit an application, known as a petition, to DHS to bring in foreign workers. If the petition is approved, a foreign worker who is abroad can then go to a U.S. embassy or consulate to apply for an H-2A or H-2B nonimmigrant visa from DOS. If the visa application is approved, the worker is issued a visa that he or she can use to apply for admission to the United States at a port of entry. The final steps are different if the foreign worker is already in the United States; in such a case, there is no visa application.

Over the years, a variety of legislative measures have been put forward concerning foreign temporary agricultural and nonagricultural workers. These have included bills to establish new temporary worker visas for agricultural and nonagricultural workers as well as proposals to change the existing H-2A and H-2B programs. In recent Congresses, the latter proposals have been more common. H-2A-related measures have sought to revise H-2Aprogram requirements on temporary need, wages, U.S. worker recruitment, and housing, among other items. Recent bills on the H-2B visa have focused largely on the annual cap.

The H-2A and H-2B programs—and guest worker programs broadly—strive both to be responsive to legitimate employer needs for temporary labor and to provide adequate protections for U.S. and foreign temporary workers. There is much debate, however, about how to strike the appropriate balance between these goals. Key policy considerations for Congress include the labor market test to determine whether U.S. workers are available for the positions; required wages; and enforcement. The issue of unauthorized workers also arises in connection with guest worker programs.

INTRODUCTION

The United States has a long history of importing foreign temporary workers who are sometimes referred to as guest workers. In the past, guest workers were used to address U.S. worker shortages during times of war.

Notably, the controversial Bracero program, which began during World War II and lasted until 1964, brought several million Mexican agricultural workers into the United States.

Today, the Immigration and Nationality Act (INA)[1] provides for the temporary admission of agricultural and nonagricultural workers to the United States through the H-2A and H-2B visa programs, respectively. H-2A and H-2B workers fill jobs that do not require much formal education. H-2A workers perform seasonal or temporary agricultural labor. They also engage in range herding and livestock production. H-2B workers perform temporary jobs in a variety of fields including landscaping, meat and seafood processing, and construction. The H-2A and H-2B programs, which are subject to detailed recruitment and other requirements, seek to meet the legitimate temporary labor needs of employers while providing protections to U.S. and foreign workers.

The difficulty in balancing the needs of employers and workers in guest worker programs is reflected in ongoing debates about such programs. Some view guest worker programs as helpful to businesses with seasonal needs and "to our long-term economic health" and call for their expansion and simplification.[2] Others see these programs as leaving many participating workers "vulnerable to abuse and retaliation at the hands of employers and their agents."[3]

In response to the Coronavirus Disease 2019 (COVID-19), the Department of State (DOS) suspended routine visa services at all U.S. embassies and consulates as of March 20, 2020.[4] On March 23, 2020, the Department of Homeland Security (DHS) announced that it had reached agreement with Mexico and Canada to "limit all non-essential travel across

[1] Act of June 27, 1952, ch. 477, codified, as amended, at 8 U.S.C. §1101 et seq. The INA is the basis of current immigration law.

[2] See, for example, Isai Chavez, "Guest Worker Programs: What Needs Fixing and Why," E21/Manhat tan Institute for Policy Research, February 26, 2018, https://economics 21.org/html/guest-worker-programs-what-needs-fixing-and-why-2915.html.

[3] See Daniel Costa, "Modern-day Braceros," Working Economics Blog, Economic Policy Institute, March 31, 2017, https://www.epi.org/blog/modern-day-braceros-the-united-states-has-450000-guestworkers-in-low-wage-jobs/.

[4] U.S. Department of State, Bureau of Consular Affairs, "Suspension of Routine Visa Services," March 20, 2020, https://travel.state.gov/content/travel/en/News/visas-news/ suspension-of-routine-visa-services.html.

borders" in an effort to slow further spread of coronavirus.[5] Among the immigration-related issues raised by these actions was the possible impact on the admission to the United States of H-2A temporary agricultural workers and H-2B temporary nonagricultural workers (sometimes referred to collectively as H-2 workers).

In an announcement on March 26, 2020, DOS stated that "the H-2 program is essential to the economy and food security of the United States and is a national security priority" and that the department "intend[s] to continue processing H-2 cases as much as possible, as permitted by post resources and local government restrictions." It further explained that DOS Secretary Mike Pompeo, in consultation with DHS, had "authorized consular officers to expand the categories of H-2 visa applicants whose applications can be adjudicated without an in-person interview."

According to the DOS announcement, "We anticipate the vast majority of otherwise qualified H-2 applicants will now be adjudicated without an interview."[6]

For its part, DHS issued temporary final rules in April 2020 and May 2020 to facilitate the continued employment of H-2A temporary agricultural workers and H-2B temporary nonagricultural workers, respectively, during the COVID-19 national emergency. According to the supplementary information to the H-2A rule, "DHS is taking steps to ensure that the agricultural sector has greater certainty and flexibility to minimize gaps in their H-2A workflow" in view of COVID-19-related travel restrictions, visa processing limitations, and possible H-2A worker unavailability due to illness.[7] The supplementary information to the H-2B rule similarly states that "DHS is taking steps to ensure that employers who

[5] U.S. Department of Homeland Security, "Fact Sheet: DHS Measures on the Border to Limit the Further Spread of Coronavirus," March 23, 2020, https://www.dhs.gov/news/2020/03/23/fact-sheet-dhs-measures-border-limit-further-spread-coronavirus.

[6] U.S. Department of State, Bureau of Consular Affairs, "Important Announcement on H2 Visas," March 26, 2020, https://travel.state.gov/content/travel/en/News/visas-news/important-announcement-on-h2-visas.html (hereinafter cited as "DOS, "Important Announcement on H2 Visas"").

[7] U.S. Department of Homeland Security, "Temporary Changes to Requirements Affecting H–2A Nonimmigrants Due to the COVID–19 National Emergency," 85 *Federal Register* 21739, 21741-21742, April 20, 2020 (hereinafter cited as "2020 DHS H-2A temporary rule").

have needs for temporary nonagricultural workers who provide stability to the nation's food supply chain have greater certainty and flexibility to minimize gaps in the flow of H-2B workers."[8]

This chapter covers the H-2Atemporary agricultural worker program and the H-2B temporary nonagricultural worker program. It explores the statutory and regulatory provisions that govern each program, focusing in particular on the much-debated labor certification process. It also describes 2020 program changes in response to the COVID-19 pandemic. It discusses past and present legislative efforts to reform the H-2A and H-2B programs and to create new guest worker visas, and identifies and analyzes key policy considerations to help inform future congressional action.

OVERVIEW OF H-2A AND H-2B VISAS

The INA enumerates categories of aliens,[9] known as nonimmigrants, who are admitted to the United States for a temporary period of time and specific purpose. Nonimmigrant visa categories are identified by letters and numbers, based on the sections of the INA that authorize them. Among the major nonimmigrant visa categories is the "H" category for temporary workers. It includes H-2A and H-2B visas for guest workers,[10] as well as visas for specialty occupation workers.[11]

The INA, as originally enacted in 1952, authorized an H-2 nonimmigrant visa category for foreign agricultural and nonagricultural workers who were coming temporarily to the United States to perform temporary services (other than those of an exceptional nature requiring distinguished merit and ability) or labor. The 1986 Immigration Reform

---

[8] U.S. Department of Homeland Security, "Temporary Changes to Requirements Affecting H–2B Nonimmigrants Due to the COVID–19 National Emergency," 85 *Federal Register* 28843, 28846, May 14, 2020 (hereinafter cited as "2020 DHS H-2B temporary rule").

[9] An *alien* is defined in the INA as a person who is not a citizen or national of the United States. INA §101(a)(3); 8 U.S.C. §1101(a)(3).

[10] INA §§101(a)(15)(H)(ii)(a), (b); 8 U.S.C. §§1101(a)(15)(H)(ii)(a), (b).

[11] See CRS Report R45040, *Immigration: Nonimmigrant (Temporary) Admissions to the United States*.

and Control Act (IRCA)[12] amended the INA to subdivide the H-2 program into the current H-2Aagricultural worker program and H-2B nonagricultural worker program and to detail the admissions process for H-2A workers. The H-2A and H-2B programs are administered by DHS's U.S. Citizenship and Immigration Services (USCIS) and the Employment and Training Administration (ETA) of the Department of Labor (DOL).

While there are many differences between the H-2A and H-2B programs, the process of bringing in workers under either one entails the same basic steps (see Figure 1). Employers who want to hire workers through either program must first apply to DOL for labor certification. After receiving labor certification, a prospective H-2A or H-2B employer can submit an application, known as a petition, to DHS to bring in foreign workers.

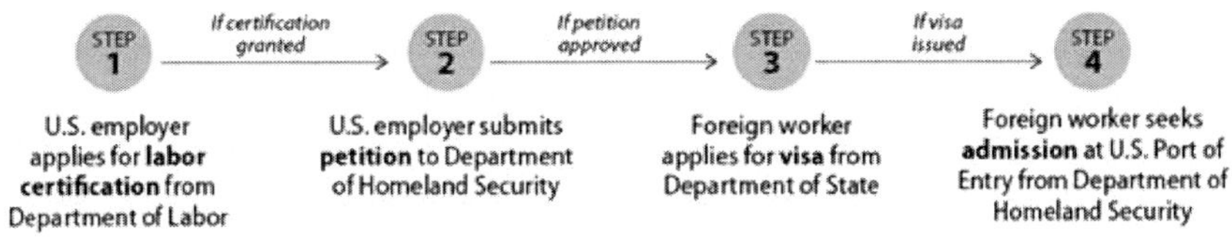

Source: CRS presentation of information from U.S. Department of Homeland Security, U.S. Citizenship and Immigration Services.

Figure 1. Bringing in H-2A and H-2B Workers.

If the petition is approved, foreign workers who are abroad can then go to a U.S. embassy or consulate to apply for an H-2A or H-2B nonimmigrant visa from DOS. As part of the visa process, most applicants must be interviewed, unless the interview requirement is waived.[13] The INA authorizes consular officers to waive nonimmigrant visa interviews in certain cases.[14] It also authorizes the Secretary of State to waive visa

[12] P.L. 99-603, November 6, 1986.

[13] The interview requirements and waiver provisions are enumerated in INA §222(h) (8 U.S.C. §1202(h)). These provisions require interviews for nonimmigrant visa applicants between the ages of 14 and 79, but allow for waivers in certain circumstances.

[14] These include cases in which the consular officer has no indication that the applicant has not complied with U.S. immigration law and regulations, the individual was previously issued a visa of the same type, the individual is applying no more than 12 months after the expiration of the prior visa, and the individual is applying from within his or her

interviews upon a determination that such a waiver is "in the national interest of the United States" or is "necessary as a result of unusual or emergent circumstances."[15] If the visa application is approved, the worker is issued a visa that he or she can use to apply for admission to the United States at a port of entry. If admitted, the H-2Aor H-2B worker can commence employment on the work start date.

The last part of the process is different if the foreign worker who the prospective H-2Aor H-2B employer wants to employ is already in the United States. (There is no visa application step if the beneficiary of the petition is in the United States.) In such a case, the employer requests as part of the petition that the worker be granted an extension of stay (if the worker holds the relevant H-2A or H-2B status) or a change of status/extension of stay (if the worker is in another nonimmigrant status). If the petition is approved, the H-2A or H-2B worker can commence employment on the work start date. DHS temporary final rules, issued in spring 2020 in response to the COVID-19 emergency, enable H-2A workers and H-2B workers to commence employment before petition approval.

---

country of usual residence unless otherwise prescribed in regulations. INA §222(h)(1)(B); 8 U.S.C. §1202(h)(1)(B). In a March 2020 notice to H-2 petitioners, DOS indicated that it would continue to process H-2 cases but needed to modify procedures in light of "the social distancing recommended by health authorities" in response to COVID-19.

DOS stated that it would give processing priority to "returning H-2 workers who are eligible for an interview waiver." It described returning H-2 workers as "applicants whose H-2A or H-2B visas have expired in the last twelve months and are now applying for the same visa classification and did not require a waiver the last time they applied for a visa." An excerpt from one of these letters is available in Ross Courtney, "Coronavirus slows H-2A visas," *Good Fruit Grower*, March 17, 2020.

[15] INA §222(h)(1)(C); 8 U.S.C. §1202(h)(1)(C). DOS's March 26, 2020, H-2 announcement authorized consular officers "if they so choose" to consider as returning workers for purposes of a visa interview waiver H-2 applicants whose prior visas expired in the last 48 months (rather than the normal 12 months) provided that the applicants are applying for the same visa classification and did not require a waiver of ineligibility the last time. See U.S. Department of State, "Important Announcement on H2 Visas." Also see, U.S. Department of State, U.S. Embassy and Consulates in Mexico, "Notice to H2 Agents and Petitioners," March 26, 2020, https://mx.usembassy.gov/notice-to-h2-agents-and-petitioners-march-26-2020/.

Temporary Labor Certification

DOL's ETA administers the labor certification process under the H-2A and H-2B programs. Under both programs, employers submit applications to DOL in which they request certification for a particular number of positions. (See Appendix A for labor certification data for the top states.)

INA provisions on the admission of H-2A workers state that an H-2Apetition cannot be approved unless the petitioner has applied to DOL for certification that

1. there are not sufficient workers who are able, willing, and qualified, and who will be available at the time and at place needed, to perform the labor or services involved in the petition, and
2. the employment of the alien in such labor or services will not adversely affect the wages and working conditions of workers in the United States similarly employed.[16]

There is no equivalent labor certification requirement in statute for the H-2B visa. The INA, however, does contain some related language. For example, it defines an H-2B alien, in relevant part, as an alien "who is coming temporarily to the United States to perform other temporary service or labor if unemployed persons capable of performing such service or labor cannot be found in this country."[17] The H-2B labor certification requirement instead appears in DHS regulations, which state

> The petitioner may not file an H-2B petition unless the United States petitioner has applied for a labor certification with the Secretary of Labor ... and has obtained a favorable labor certification determination.[18]

---

[16] INA §218(a)(1)(A), (B); 8 U.S.C. §1188(a)(1)(A), (B).
[17] INA §101(a)(15)(H)(ii)(b); 8 U.S.C. §1101(a)(15)(H)(ii)(b).
[18] 8 C.F.R. §214.2(h)(6)(iii)(C).

The H-2A and H-2B labor certification requirements are intended to provide job, wage, and working conditions protections to U.S. workers. They are implemented in both programs through a multifaceted labor certification process that requires prospective H-2A and H-2B employers to conduct recruitment for U.S. workers and offer minimum levels of wages and benefits that vary by program.

H-2A AGRICULTURAL WORKER VISA

The H-2A visa allows for the temporary admission of foreign workers to the United States to perform agricultural labor or services of a seasonal or temporary nature. It is governed by provisions in the INA and regulations issued by DHS and DOL. H-2A workers may perform agricultural work, as defined by DOL in regulations and including "agricultural labor" and "agriculture" as these terms are defined in specified laws.[19] H-2A workers may also perform other specified agricultural activities, including the pressing of apples for cider.[20]

Visa Issuances

The H-2A visa program is not subject to a statutory numerical limit and has grown significantly over the last 25 years. One way to measure the H-2Aprogram's growth is to consider changes in the number of H-2A visas issued annually by DOS. The visa application and issuance process occurs after DOL has granted labor certification and DHS has approved the visa petition (see Figure 1). As illustrated in Figure 2, the number of H-2Avisas issued has increased relatively sharply in recent years, with visa issuances

[19] The laws are enumerated in the INA definition of an H-2A worker, INA §§101(a)(15)(H)(ii)(a) (8 U.S.C. §1101(a)(15)(H)(ii)(a)).

[20] The pressing of apples was added to the INA definition of an H-2A worker by the FY2006 Department of Homeland Security Appropriations Act (P.L. 109-90, §536).

more than tripling from FY2011 to FY2019. In FY2019, H-2A visa issuances exceeded 200,000 for the first time in the program's history.[21]

Annual visa issuances provide an approximation of the number of aliens with H-2A status that enter the United States in a given year. However, they are not a precise measure. Among the reasons for this are that not all aliens who are issued H-2A visas necessarily use them to enter the United States, and an alien with an H-2A visa may be denied admission at a U.S. port of entry.

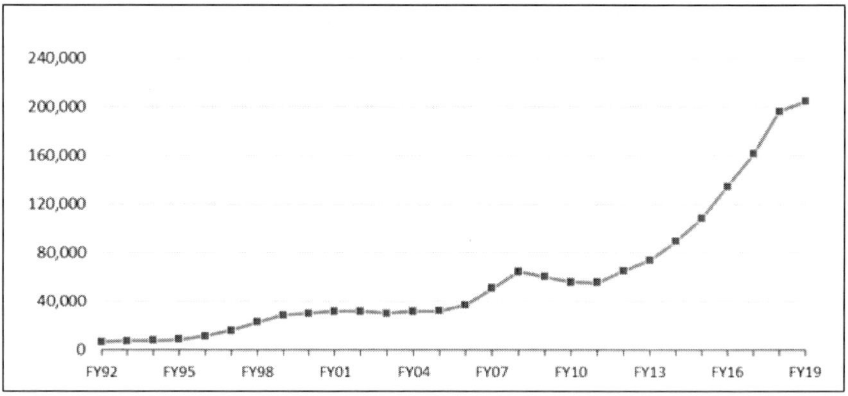

Source: CRS presentation of data from U.S. Department of State, Bureau of Consular Affairs.

Notes: See Appendix C for underlying data.

Figure 2. H-2A Visas Issued, FY1992-FY2019.

With the recent growth in H-2Avisa issuances, questions have arisen about the size of the H-2A visa program relative to the larger agricultural workforce in the United States. Estimates vary depending on how the agricultural workforce is defined and the factors that are taken into account in making the comparison. Based on DOS visa issuance data and DOL data, a 2020 Economic Policy Institute piece by Daniel Costa and Philip Martin estimated that "H-2A workers filled 10% of the roughly one million full-time-equivalent jobs in U.S. crop agriculture" in FY2019.[22] An earlier

[21] See Appendix C for annual H-2A visa issuance data.

[22] Daniel Costa and Philip Martin, *Coronavirus and farmworkers: Farm employment, safety issues, and the H-2A guest worker program*, Economic Policy Institute, March 24,

analysis by Martin found that H-2A workers accounted for "approximately 8 percent of average annual employment on U.S. crop farms" in FY2014.[23] One basic limitation of using annual visa issuance data as a measure of the H-2A workforce is that these data exclude some H-2A workers, such as those who enter the United States on a visa in one fiscal year and then extend their stay into the next fiscal year to perform new employment; such workers would not be included in visa issuance data for the second year.

H-2A Statutory Provisions

The H-2A visa is subject to a set of conditions and rules described in INA §218.[24] As illustrated in Figure 1, prospective H-2A employers must first apply to DOL for labor certification. To approve a labor certification application, DOL must determine that qualified U.S. workers are not available to fill the job openings and that the employment of foreign workers will not adversely affect similarly employed U.S. workers (e.g., by lowering wages).

U.S. worker recruitment is a key component of the H-2Alabor certification process. As required by the INA, the prospective H-2A employer's job offer is circulated through an interstate employment system to recruit qualified U.S. workers. The employer also may be required to

---

2020, https://www.epi.org/publication/coronavirus-and-farmworkers-h-2a/. According to its website, the Economic Policy Institute seeks "to include the needs of low- and middle-income workers in economic policy discussions."

[23] Philip Martin, *Immigration and Farm Labor; From Unauthorized to H-2A for Some?* Migration Policy Institute, August 2017, pp. 8, 15 (footnote 29). Martin's estimates are based on an analysis of DOL Bureau of Labor Statistics data. Another available source of agricultural workforce data is the U.S. Department of Agriculture's National Agricultural Statistics Service (NASS), which reports on the average annual number of hired farm workers in the United States (excluding Alaska). These data are limited for H-2A comparison purposes in that they exclude agricultural service workers, who work on a contract or "fee for service" basis. According to NASS data, the average annual number of hired farm workers in the United States in 2019 was 702,300. U.S. Department of Agriculture, National Agricultural Statistics Service, *Farm Labor*, November 21, 2019.

[24] 8 U.S.C. §1188.

engage in additional recruitment in a "multi-state region of traditional or expected labor supply."[25] INA provisions on the H-2A visa include a fifty percent rule, under which employers are required to hire any qualified U.S. worker who applies for a position during the first half of the work contract under which the H-2Aworkers who are in the job are employed.[26]

Under the INA provisions, DOL cannot require a prospective H-2Aemployer to submit a labor certification application more than 45 days before the employer's date of need for workers. And if the employer has complied with the recruitment and other certification requirements and eligible U.S. workers have not been found to fill the job openings, DOL must issue a labor certification no later than 30 days before the employer's date of need.[27] Among the other statutory labor certification requirements, employers must provide workers with housing in accordance with regulations.

The INA permits the filing of H-2A labor certification applications and petitions by agricultural associations.[28] In addition, it authorizes DOL to take actions, such as imposing penalties, to ensure employer compliance with the terms and conditions of H-2A employment.

---

[25] INA §218(b)(4); 8 U.S.C. §1188(b)(4).

[26] This rule was originally made effective by law for three years beginning in 1987 but remains in place by regulation.

[27] DOL publishes a quarterly report on the H-2A program that includes statistics on application processing. According to the report for the fourth quarter of FY2019 (*H-2A Temporary Agricultural Labor Certification Program - Selected Statistics, FY 2019*), which includes FY2019 full-year data, DOL processed 86.1% of H-2A applications that were complete in a timely fashion (that is, it issued a final determination 30 days before the work start date) in FY2019. The quarterly reports are available on ETA's Office of Foreign Labor Certification (OFLC) Performance Data page.

8 U.S.C. §1188.

INA §218(b)(4); 8 U.S.C. §1188(b)(4).

This rule was originally made effective by law for three years beginning in 1987 but remains in place by regulation.

DOL publishes a quarterly report on the H-2A program that includes statistics on application processing. According to the report for the fourth quarter of FY2019 (*H-2A Temporary Agricultural Labor Certification Program - Selected Statistics, FY 2019*), which includes FY2019 full-year data, DOL processed 86.1% of H-2A applications that were complete in a timely fashion (that is, it issued a final determination 30 days before the work start date) in FY2019. See "Selected Statistics by Program," https://foreign laborcert.doleta.gov/performancedata.cfm#stat.

[28] For purposes of the H-2A program, an agricultural association is a nonprofit or cooperative association of farmers, growers, or ranchers that performs certain functions, such as recruiting or transporting workers.

Separate from the INA, H-2A workers are statutorily eligible for legal assistance by a Legal Services Corporation-funded program on matters arising under workers' specific employment contracts relating to wages, housing, transportation, and other employment rights.[29]

H-2A Regulations

Regulations issued by DHS and DOL implement the INA provisions on the H-2A visa (see Appendix D for additional information on selected H-2A regulations).

DHS Regulations on the H-2A Visa

DHS regulations govern the admission of H-2A workers to the United States.[30] The current DHS rule on the H-2A visa describes its purpose as being "to provide agricultural employers with an orderly and timely flow of legal workers, thereby decreasing their reliance on unauthorized workers, while protecting the rights of laborers."[31]

Under DHS regulations, petitioning H-2A employers must establish that the employment for which they are seeking workers is of a temporary or seasonal nature. In general, the regulations consider work to be of a temporary nature when the employer's need for the worker will last no longer than one year.

DHS regulations limit participation in the H-2A program to nationals of countries designated annually by DHS, with the concurrence of DOS.[32] The regulations also prohibit payments by prospective H-2A workers to

---

[29] 45 CFR §1626.11. The underlying statutory provision is P.L. 99-603, §305.

[30] 8 C.F.R. §214.2(h)(5).

[31] U.S. Department of Homeland Security, "Changes to Requirements Affecting H-2A Nonimmigrants," 73 *Federal Register* 76891, December 18, 2008 (hereinafter cited as "2008 DHSH-2A rule").

[32] DHS published a notice, effective on January 19, 2019, for one year, that identified 84 countries whose nationals are eligible to participate in the H-2A program. See U.S. Department of Homeland Security, "Identification of Foreign Countries Whose Nationals Are Eligible to Participate in the H–2A and H–2B Nonimmigrant Worker Programs," 84 *Federal Register* 133, January 18, 2019. The notice discusses the factors considered in designating eligible countries.

employers, recruiters, or other employment service providers where the payments are a condition of obtaining H-2A employment.

DHS regulations also address an H-2A worker's authorized period of stay. They specify that an H-2A worker can be admitted to the United States up to one week before the start of the approved H-2A petition period in order to travel to the work site and may remain in the country for 30 days after the petition expires in order to prepare to depart or to seek an extension of stay based on a subsequent job offer.[33] An employer can apply to extend an H-2A worker's stay in increments of up to one year, but an alien's total period of stay as an H-2A worker may not exceed three consecutive years. An alien who has spent three years in the United States in H-2A status may not seek an extension of his or her stay or be readmitted to the United States as an H-2A worker until he or she has been outside the country for three months.

In response to the COVID-19 emergency, DHS issued a final rule on April 20, 2020, making temporary changes to some of its H-2Aregulatory requirements that will be in effect until August 18, 2020.[34] The rule enables H-2A workers in the United States who seek to undertake new H-2A employment to begin that work after the employer files a petition, accompanied by a valid labor certification, requesting an extension of stay for the worker (but before the petition is approved). In general, absent this change, the worker could not start the new employment until DHS approved the petition.[35] Under the rule, the H-2A worker would be authorized to start the new employment on the work start date in the filed

---

[33] In March 2020, in response to the COVID-19 pandemic, the U.S. Department of Agriculture (USDA) and DOL announced a partnership to identify workers whose work periods are ending and who may be available to fill positions with U.S. agricultural employers. According to the announcement, "USDA and DOL have identified nearly 20,000 H-2A and H-2B certified positions that have expiring contracts in the coming weeks. There will be workers leaving these positions who could be available to transfer to a different employer's labor certification." U.S. Department of Agriculture, "USDA and DOL Announce Information Sharing to Assist H-2A Employers," March 19, 2020, https://www.usda.gov/media/press-releases/2020/03/19/usda-and-dol-announce-information-sharing-assist-h-2a-employers.

[34] 2020 DHS H-2A temporary rule.

[35] 8 C.F.R. 214.2(h)(2)(i)(D).

petition or the acknowledged petition receipt date, whichever is later, and work for up to 45 days while the petition remains pending.[36]

As noted, an H-2A worker is limited to a three-year maximum period of stay. The rule creates a temporary exception to this limitation. Under the rule, an H-2A petition seeking an extension of stay, accompanied by a valid labor certification, may be approved even if any of the workers requested in the petition either have already been in the United States for three years or would exceed the three-year limit if the extension were approved.

The rule, however, does not modify or waive related DOL regulations. As stated in the supplementary information to the rule, "This final rule proposes no changes to DOL's regulations or to the TLC [temporary labor certification] process, which the employer must undergo to recruit U.S. workers prior to the filing of an H-2A petition with USCIS."[37]

DOL Regulations on H-2A Employment

DOL regulations on the H-2A visa include ETA regulations concerning H-2A labor certification.[38] ETA regulations implement the requirement that before an employer can petition for H-2A workers, the employer must apply for certification that U.S. workers are not available to fill the positions and that the employment of foreign workers will not adversely affect the wages or working conditions of U.S. workers.

ETA regulations detail the process for prospective H-2Aemployers to recruit U.S. workers. The employer must submit a job order containing the terms and conditions of employment to the DOL-funded state workforce agency (SWA)[39] serving the area of intended employment before the

[36] There is a similar permanent regulatory provision that predates the temporary final rule that allows an H-2A worker to begin work with a new petitioning employer before the petition is approved if the employer participates in the E - Verify employment eligibility verification system. 8 C.F.R. §274a.12(b)(21). See 2020 DHS H-2A temporary rule, p. 21742. For information on E-Verify, see CRS Report R40446, *Electronic Employment Eligibility Verification*.

[37] 2020 DHS temporary H-2A rule, p. 21742.

[38] 20 C.F.R. Part 655, Subpart B.

[39] A state workforce agency is a state government agency that receives funds pursuant to the Wagner -Peyser Act (29 U.S.C. §49 et seq.) to administer the state's public labor exchange activities.

employer can submit a labor certification application. The job order becomes the basis for recruiting U.S. workers to fill the employer's openings through an intrastate clearance system. Once the employer submits the labor certification application and job order to ETA and ETA determines that they are complete and comply with applicable requirements, the agency authorizes access to the interstate clearance system and posts the job order on its electronic job registry.[40] ETA also will direct the employer to conduct recruitment by other means, including by contacting former U.S. workers.

H-2A employers must offer and provide required wages and benefits to H-2Aworkers and workers in corresponding employment. Corresponding employment for purposes of the H-2A program is the employment of non-H-2A workers by an employer who has an approved H-2A labor certification in any work included in the job order or in any agricultural work performed by the H-2A workers. H-2Aemployers are required to pay workers the highest of several wage rates (see "Wages" below). Employers must provide a three-fourths guarantee; that is, they must guarantee to offer workers employment for at least three-fourths of the contract period. They must also provide workers with housing, transportation,[41] and other benefits, including workers' compensation insurance.[42]

ETA regulations address circumstances in which, due to natural or manmade catastrophic events beyond the employer's control, an H-2A employer no longer needs the services of a worker. In such a case, the employer may terminate the work contract with DOL approval. However,

---

[40] The registry is available at https://seasonaljobs.dol.gov/jobs.

[41] The transportation requirement covers the H-2A worker's transportation to and from the place of employment at the beginning and end of the work contract period, respectively, and transportation between the worker's living quarters and the worksite.

[42] H-2A workers, like nonimmigrants generally, are not eligible for federally funded public assistance, with the exception of certain emergency services. See CRS Report RL33809, *Noncitizen Eligibility for Federal Public Assistance: Policy Overview*. However, nonimmigrants are generally subject to the provisions of the Affordable Care Act (P.L. 111-148), as amended. See archived CRS Report R43561, *Treatment of Noncitizens under the Affordable Care Act*.

the employer remains obligated to meet certain responsibilities to the worker.[43]

ETA, which is responsible for enforcing H-2Aemployer compliance with obligations related to the labor certification process, may conduct audits of approved labor certification applications.

Under certain circumstances, it may revoke an approved certification or debar an employer from receiving future certifications.

DOL regulations on the H-2A visa also include regulations by the Wage and Hour Division (WHD) concerning enforcement of contractual obligations under the H-2A program.[44] WHD is responsible for enforcing H-2A employer compliance with obligations to H-2A workers and workers in corresponding employment, such as the requirement to offer employment to U.S. workers. The agency is responsible for carrying out investigations, inspections, and law enforcement functions and in appropriate instances, imposing penalties or taking other actions, including debarment.

Range Herding and Livestock Regulations

ETA issued regulations in 2015 on range herding and livestock production that established special standards and procedures for employers applying for labor certification to hire H-2A workers to perform this type of work. These standards and procedures encompass various aspects of the labor certification process, including job order and labor certification

---

[43] These responsibilities include fulfilling a three-fourths guarantee for the period between the contract start date and the termination date. 20 C.F.R. §655.122(o). In a March 2020 FAQ, DOL addressed the application of these DOL H-2A "contract impossibility" regulations and similar DOL H-2B regulations during the COVID-19 pandemic:

"Employers who received temporary labor certification under the H-2A, H-2B, or CW-1 visa programs may request approval from the …[ETA's Office of Foreign Labor Certification] t o terminate work under the job order and/or work contracts before the end date of work due to the impact of the COVID-19 pandemic." U.S. Department of Labor, Employment and Training Administration, Office of Foreign Labor Certification, "COVID-19, Frequently Asked Questions, Round 1," March 20, 2020, p. 7, https://www.foreignlaborcert.doleta.gov/pdf/DOL-OFLC_COVID-19_FAQs_Round%201_03.20.2020.pdf.

[44] 29 C.F.R. Part 501.

application filing, U.S. worker recruitment, wage requirements, and housing standards.[45]

H-2B Nonagricultural Worker Visa

The H-2B visa provides for the temporary admission of foreign workers to the United States to perform temporary nonagricultural service or labor, if unemployed U.S. workers cannot be found. Foreign medical graduates coming to perform medical services are explicitly excluded.

H-2B workers are not limited to a particular set of occupations. Over the years, the H-2B visa has been used to bring in workers to perform a variety of jobs. According to DOL labor certification data, the top H-2B occupation in recent years in terms of the number of positions certified has been landscaping and groundskeeping worker. Other top occupations include forest and conservation worker, maid and housekeeping cleaner, amusement and recreation attendant, and meat, poultry, and fish cutter and trimmer (see Appendix B for data on H-2B labor certifications by occupation).

Visa Issuances

Figure 3 shows H-2B visa issuance data for FY1992 through FY2019.[46] Unlike the uncapped H-2A visa, the H-2B visa is subject to a statutory annual numerical limit of 66,000. For several years (FY2005-

---

[45] U.S. Department of Labor, Employment and Training Administration, "Temporary Agricultural Employment of H – 2A Foreign Workers in the Herding or Production of Livestock on the Range in the United States," 80 *Federal Register* 62958, October 16, 2015 (hereinafter cited as "DOL H-2A herding rule"). Also see U.S. Department of Labor, Employer and Training Administration, Office of Foreign Labor Certification, "2015 Final Rule, Range Herding or Production of Livestock in the United States," factsheet, https://www.foreignlaborcert.doleta.gov/herd_pdf/herder_factsheet.pdf.

[46] There is no precise measure available of the number of aliens with H-2B status that enter the United States in any given year. Visa data provide an approximation but are subject to limitations, including that not all aliens who are issued visas necessarily use them to enter the United States.

FY2007, FY2016), a provision was in effect that exempted certain returning H-2B workers from being counted against the statutory cap. H-2B visa issuances peaked in FY2007, totaling almost twice the cap. The number of H-2Bvisas issued reached a recent low point in FY2009 during the Great Recession. FY2009 was the first year since FY2002 that H-2Bvisa issuances fell below the 66,000 cap. As shown in Figure 3, H-2B visa issuances have followed a generally upward trend since then. For each year from FY2017 to FY2020, Congress has authorized DHS to make additional H-2B visas available (beyond the cap) subject to certain constraints. (For further information about the special H-2B cap provisions, see "Enacted Provisions" below.)

As illustrated in Figure 3, there are several years that H-2B visa issuances exceeded the 66,000 cap when no special H-2B cap provisions were in effect. It is not necessarily clear in such cases whether the H-2B cap was technically exceeded (and if so, by how much) in light of the cap implementation process and other factors (see "Numerical Limits" below).

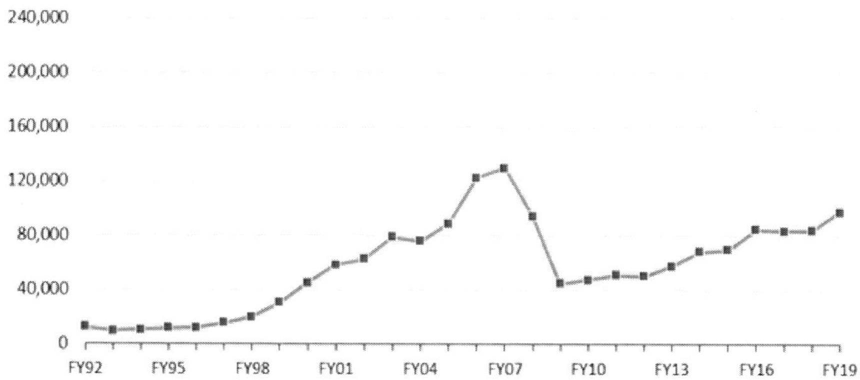

Source: CRS presentation of data from U.S. Department of State, Bureau of Consular Affairs.

Notes: See Appendix C for underlying data. Special cap-related provisions were in effect for FY2005-FY2007 and FY2016-FY2019.

Figure 3. H-2B Visas Issued, FY1992-FY2019.

H-2B Statutory Provisions

The INA does not include a section detailing the conditions and rules applicable to the admission of H-2B workers as it does for H-2Aworkers. It does, however, place some specific requirements on H-2B employers. It requires an employer who dismisses an H-2B worker before the end of his or her period of authorized admission to pay for the worker's return transportation abroad.[47] It also directs DHS to impose a fraud prevention and detection fee on H-2B employers.[48] The INA further authorizes DHS to enforce the conditions of an H-2B petition and allows DHS to delegate this authority to DOL, by agreement.[49] (DHS transferred this enforcement authority to DOL, effective January 18, 2009[50]).

The INA also imposes the aforementioned statutory numerical limit on the H-2B visa, specifying that the total number of aliens who may be issued H-2B visas or otherwise provided H-2B status during a fiscal year may not exceed 66,000. It further specifies that no more than half this total (33,000) may be allocated during the first half of a fiscal year.[51] A statutory provision separate from the INA establishes an H-2B cap-related exception. Enacted as part of the FY2005 Department of Defense Appropriations Act, this provision makes the cap inapplicable to an H-2B

---

[47] INA §214(c)(5); 8 U.S.C. §1184(c)(5).

[48] INA §214(c)(13); 8 U.S.C. §1184(c)(13). H-2B fraud prevention and detection fees are deposited into the Fraud Prevention and Detection Account, which was established in the general fund of the Treasury by INA §286(v) (8 U.S.C. §1356(v)). This account supports activities related to preventing and detecting fraud in the delivery of immigration benefits.

[49] INA §214(c)(14)(A), (B); 8 U.S.C. §1184(c)(14)(A), (B).

[50] See U.S. Department of Labor, Employment and Training Administration and Wage and Hour Division, "Labor Certification Process and Enforcement for Temporary Employment in Occupations Other Than Agriculture or Registered Nursing in the United States (H-2B Workers), and Other Technical Changes," 73 *Federal Register* 78020, 78046, December 19, 2008 (hereinafter cited as "2008 DOL H-2B rule"); U.S. Department of Homeland Security and U.S. Department of Labor, Employment and Training Administration and Wage and Hour Division, "Temporary Non-Agricultural Employment of H–2B Aliens in the United States," 80 *Federal Register* 24041, 24131, April 29, 2015 (hereinafter cited as "2015 DHS/DOL interim final H-2B rule").

[51] INA §§214(g)(1)(B), (g)(10); 8 U.S.C. §§1184(g)(1)((B), (g)(10).

worker employed "as a fish roe processor, a fish roe technician, or a supervisor of fish roe processing."[52]

Temporary H-2B cap-related and other provisions have also been regularly enacted in recent years. For FY2020, language in an omnibus appropriations act provides for the issuance of H-2B visas beyond the statutory cap under certain conditions (see "Enacted Provisions"). DOL appropriations provisions address various DOL H-2B regulations. For FY2020, these provisions define temporary need and the prevailing wage for H-2B purposes, prohibit the use of funds to enact certain regulatory provisions, and allow for the staggered entry of certain H-2B workers (see "DHS/DOL Regulations on H-2B Employment").

In addition, an FY2008 omnibus appropriations act makes H-2B forestry workers eligible, on a permanent basis, for the same Legal Services Corporation-funded legal assistance available to H-2A workers. This legal assistance may be provided to H-2B forestry workers on matters relating to wages, housing, transportation, and other employment rights arising under workers' specific employment contracts.[53]

H-2B Regulations

Regulations issued by DHS and DOL implement the INA provisions on the H-2B visa (see Appendix D for additional information on selected H-2B regulations).

DHS Regulations on the H-2B Visa

DHS regulations govern the admission of H-2B workers to the United States.[54] Under DHS regulations, an H-2B worker can be admitted to the United States up to 10 days before the validity period of the H-2B petition and may remain in the country for 10 days after the petition expires. An employer can apply to extend an H-2B worker's stay in increments of up to

[52] P.L. 108-287, §14006.
[53] P.L. 110-161, Division B, Title V, §540; 45 C.F.R. §1626.11.
[54] 8 C.F.R. §214.2(h)(6).

one year, but an alien's total period of stay as an H-2B worker may not exceed three consecutive years.[55] An H-2B alien who has spent three years in the United States may not seek an extension of stay or be readmitted to the United States as an H-2B worker until he or she has been outside the country for three months.

DHS regulations define *temporary* work for purposes of the H-2B visa. For work to qualify as temporary, the employer must establish that his or her need for the worker will end in the "near, definable future." Additionally, the employer's need for the duties to be performed by the worker must be a one-time occurrence, a seasonal need, a peakload need, or an intermittent need.[56] The employer's need must generally be for a period of one year or less, but, in the case of a one-time occurrence, could last up to three years.

DHS's H-2B regulations limit participation in the H-2B program to nationals of countries designated annually by DHS, with the concurrence of DOS.[57] These regulations also prohibit payments by prospective H-2B workers to employers, recruiters, or other employment service providers where the payments are a condition of obtaining H-2B employment.

As noted above in the discussion of the H-2B statutory provisions, DHS has transferred H-2B enforcement authority to DOL. In accordance with this transfer, DHS regulations provide that

> The Secretary of Labor may investigate employers to enforce compliance with the conditions of a petition and Department of Labor-approved temporary labor certification to admit or otherwise provide status to an H-2B worker.[58]

---

[55] Included in this three-year period is any time an H-2B alien spent in the United States under the "H" (temporary worker) or "L" (temporary intracompany transferee) visa categories.

[56] For definitions of these types of need, see 8 C.F.R. §214.2(h)(6)(ii)(B).

[57] DHS published a notice, effective on January 19, 2019, for one year, that identified 81 countries whose nationals are eligible to participate in the H-2B program. See U.S. Department of Homeland Security, "Identification of Foreign Countries Whose Nationals Are Eligible to Participate in the H–2A and H–2B Nonimmigrant Worker Programs," 84 *Federal Register* 133, January 18, 2019. The notice discusses the factors considered in designating eligible countries.

[58] 8 C.F.R. §214.2(h)(6)(ix).

On May 14, 2020, DHS issued a final rule making temporary changes to some of its H-2B regulatory requirements in response to the COVID-19 emergency. This rule mirrors the H-2Arule issued in April 2020 and similarly provides a 120-day filing period for requesting its flexibilities. The rule does not apply to H-2B workers generally. Instead, it is limited to workers who perform temporary labor "essential to the U.S. food supply chain."[59]

The rule enables H-2B workers in the United States who seek to undertake new H-2B employment to begin that work after the employer files a petition requesting an extension of stay for the worker (but before the petition is approved). The petition must be accompanied by a valid labor certification and an attestation that the worker will be performing work essential to the U.S. food supply chain. In general, absent this change the worker could not start the new employment until DHS approved the petition.[60] Under the rule, the H-2B worker would be authorized to start the new employment on the work start date in the filed petition or the USCIS-acknowledged petition receipt date, whichever is later, and work for up to 60 days while the petition remains pending.[61]

As noted, an H-2B worker is limited to a three-year maximum period of stay. The rule creates a temporary exception to this limitation. Under the rule, an H-2B petition seeking an extension of stay for H-2B workers who are essential to the U.S. food supply chain, which is accompanied by a

---

[59] According to the supplementary information to the rule, this work includes, but is not limited to, "work related to the processing, manufacturing, and packaging of human and animal food; transporting human and animal food from farms, or manufacturing or processing plants, to distributors and end sellers; and the selling of human and animal food through a variety of sellers or retail establishments, including restaurants." 2020 DHS H-2B temporary rule, p. 28846.

[60] 8 C.F.R. 214.2(h)(2)(i)(D).

[61] There is a similar permanent regulatory provision that predates the temporary final rule that allows an H-2A worker to begin work with a new petitioning employer before the petition is approved if the employer participates in the E - Verify employment eligibility verification system. 8 C.F.R. §274a.12(b)(21). Unlike the provision in the temporary final rule that allows the new employment to begin only on the petition work start date and authorizes such employment for up to 45 days, the provision for E-Verify employers enables H-2A workers to begin the new employment immediately, upon DHS receipt of the new H-2A petition, and authorizes employment for up to 120 days. For information on E-Verify, see CRS Report R40446, *Electronic Employment Eligibility Verification*.

valid labor certification, may be approved even if any of the workers requested in the petition either have already been in the United States for three years or would exceed the three-year limit if the extension were approved.

The rule, however, does not modify or waive related DOL regulations. As explained in the supplementary information to the rule, "[T]his temporary final rule does not change applicable regulations pursuant to which employers in the United States must recruit U.S. workers before filing an H–2B petition with USCIS."[62] In addition, the supplementary information states that "DHS is not changing any other H–2B petition requirements or the adjudication process, including the requirement that the H–2B position qualify as temporary services or labor."[63]

DHS/DOL Regulations on H-2B Employment

The 2015 interim final rule on H-2B employment, which includes regulations on H-2B labor certification and enforcement, was issued jointly by DHS and DOL, rather than by DOL alone. This joint issuance came in response to litigation challenging DOL's rulemaking authority with respect to the H-2B program. As noted, the INA does not assign DOL an explicit role in the H-2B visa program. As addressed in the supplementary information to the 2015 rule

> To ensure that there can be no question about the authority for and validity of the regulations in this area, DHS and DOL (the Departments), together, are issuing this interim final rule. By proceeding together, the Departments affirm that this rule is fully consistent with the INA and implementing DHS regulations and is vital to DHS's ability to faithfully implement the statutory labor protections attendant to the program.[64]

Regulations on H-2B labor certification establish a two-part labor certification process with distinct *registration* and *application* phases.[65] In

---

[62] 2020 DHS temporary H-2B rule, p. 28847.
[63] Ibid.
[64] 2015 DHS/DOL interim final H-2B rule, pp. 24045-24046.
[65] 20 C.F.R. Part 655, Subpart A.

the registration phase, DOL must assess an employer's temporary need for H-2B workers. A prospective H-2B employer is required to submit an H-2B registration 120 days to 150 days before the initial date of need for workers and must receive registration approval before filing a labor certification application. A registration approval can be valid for up to three years. (As of the date of this chapter, the registration process is not operational; DOL continues to make determinations about temporary need when it processes labor certification applications.)

Regarding the employer's period of need for workers, the regulations provide that except in cases of a one-time occurrence, labor certification applications with a period of employer need of more than nine months will generally be denied. According to the supplementary information to the 2015 interim final rule, "Recurring temporary needs of more than 9 months are, as a practical matter, permanent positions for which H–2B labor certification is not appropriate." The supplementary information also maintains that "DOL's temporary need period [of nine months] falls comfortably within the parameters of the general 'one year or less' limitation contained in the DHS regulations."[66] The regulations also limit participation of job contractors in the H-2B program to cases in which they can demonstrate their own temporary need for workers, not that of their employer-clients.[67]

During the labor certification application phase, as detailed in the regulations, ETA determines whether U.S. workers are available to fill the labor needs of the employer. Between 75 and 90 days before the employer's date of need for workers, a prospective H-2B employer must concurrently submit a labor certification application to ETA and a job order to the SWA serving the area of intended employment. If ETA determines that the submissions are complete and comply with applicable requirements, it will direct the SWA to place the job order into intrastate

---

[66] 2015 DHS/DOL interim final H-2B rule, p. 24056. Language included in annual DOL appropriations acts since FY2016, however, specifies that the definition of temporary need for H-2B purposes will be that in DHS regulations (i.e., one year or less) (see "Enacted Provisions" for statutory citations).

[67] This restriction reflects a concern that job contractors often have an ongoing, permanent need for workers rather than a temporary need, as statutorily required for the H-2B visa.

and interstate clearance and will post the job order on its electronic job registry to recruit U.S. workers.[68] ETA will also direct the employer to conduct recruitment of U.S. workers, including by contacting former U.S. workers. The employer must continue to accept referrals and applications of U.S. applicants until 21 days before the date of need.

A prospective H-2B employer must indicate the starting and ending dates of the period of need for H-2B workers. If within a season an employer has more than one date of need for workers to perform the same job, the employer must file a separate labor certification application for each date of need. The employer is not allowed to stagger the entry of H-2B workers based on one date of need. There is an exception to this staggered entry prohibition that permits an employer in the seafood industry with an approved H-2B petition to bring in the H-2B workers under that petition any time during the 120 days beginning on the employer's starting date of need. In order to bring in the workers between day 90 and day 120, though, the employer must conduct additional U.S. worker recruitment.[69]

The regulations further require that employers offer and provide required wages and benefits to H-2B workers and workers engaged in corresponding employment. Corresponding employment for purposes of the H-2B program is the employment of non-H-2B workers by an employer that has an approved H-2B labor certification when those workers are performing either substantially the same work included in the job order or substantially the same work performed by the H-2B workers, with exceptions for certain incumbent workers.[70] H-2B employers are required to pay workers the highest of the prevailing wage rate or the federal, state, or local minimum wage.[71] They must offer a three-fourths guarantee (similar to that under the H-2A program) that ensures payment

---

[68] The registry is available at https://seasonaljobs.dol.gov/jobs.

[69] This staggered entry provision has also been included in annual DOL appropriations acts since FY2015 (see "Enacted Provisions" for statutory citations).

[70] Language included in annual DOL appropriations acts since FY2016 prohibits the use of funds to enforce this definition of corresponding employment (see "Enacted Provisions" for statutory citations).

[71] Language included in annual DOL appropriations acts since FY2016 addresses H-2B prevailing wages (see "Enacted Provisions" for statutory citations).

of wages for at least three-fourths of the contract period.[72] Among other benefits, they must pay or reimburse workers for transportation costs (beyond the statutory requirements concerning early dismissal of workers) and visa costs, and they must provide workers with workers' compensation insurance.[73]

As under the H-2A visa program, the regulations address emergency circumstances in which, due to natural or manmade catastrophic events beyond the employer's control, an H-2B employer no longer needs the services of a worker. In such cases, the employer may terminate the job order with DOL approval. However, the employer remains obligated to meet certain responsibilities toward the worker.[74]

Also as under the H-2A program, ETA enforces H-2Bemployer compliance with obligations related to the labor certification process. It may conduct audits of adjudicated labor certification applications. Under

---

[72] Language included in annual DOL appropriations acts since FY2016 prohibits the use of funds to enforce the three - fourths guarantee rule (see "Enacted Provisions" for statutory citations). In a fact sheet originally published in April 2015, following enactment of the FY2016 appropriations act, DOL addressed the prohibitions on enforcing the definitions of the three-fourths guarantee and corresponding employment. DOL took the position that the FY2016 appropriations riders "did not vacate these regulatory provisions, and they remain in effect, thus imposing a legal duty on H-2B employers, even though the Department will not use any funds to enforce them until such time as the rider may be lifted." U.S. Department of Labor, Wage and Hour Division, *Fact Sheet #78E: Job Hours and the Three-Fourths Guarantee under the H-2B Program*, April 2015 (as updated), https://www.dol.gov/sites/dolgov/files/WHD/legacy/files/whdfs78e.pdf.

[73] H-2B workers, like nonimmigrants generally, are not eligible for federally funded public assistance, with the exception of certain emergency services. See CRS Report RL33809, *Noncitizen Eligibility for Federal Public Assistance: Policy Overview*. However, nonimmigrants are generally subject to the provisions of the Affordable Care Act (P.L. 111-148), as amended. See archived CRS Report R43561, *Treatment of Noncitizens under the Affordable Care Act*.

[74] These responsibilities include fulfilling a three-fourths guarantee for the period between the contract start date and the termination date. 20 C.F.R. §655.20(g). In a March 2020 FAQ, DOL addressed the application of these DOL H-2B "impossibility of fulfillment" regulations and similar DOL H-2A regulations during the COVID-19 pandemic: "Employers who received temporary labor certification under the H-2A, H-2B, or CW-1 visa programs may request approval from the ...[ETA's Office of Foreign Labor Certification] to terminate work under the job order and/or work contracts before the end date of work due to the impact of the COVID-19 pandemic." U.S. Department of Labor, Employment and Training Administration, Office of Foreign Labor Certification, "COVID-19, Frequently Asked Questions, Round 1," March 20, 2020, p. 7, https://www.foreignlaborcert.doleta.gov/pdf/DOL-OFLC_COVID-19_FAQs_Round%201_03.20.2020.pdf.

certain circumstances, it may revoke an approved certification or debar an employer from receiving future certifications.

WHD also has enforcement responsibility under the H-2B visa program, which is detailed in regulations.[75] It enforces the rights of H-2B workers and workers in corresponding employment and the employer's obligations to H-2B and U.S. workers, such as whether employment was offered to U.S. workers. WHD is responsible for carrying out investigations, inspections, and law enforcement functions as well as, in appropriate instances, imposing penalties or taking other actions, including debarment.

LEGISLATIVE ACTIVITY

Since the 1990s, a variety of legislative proposals have been put forward concerning foreign temporary agricultural and nonagricultural workers. Some of these proposals have been introduced in Congress as stand-alone bills, while others have been part of larger immigration or other measures. While most have seen no legislative action, a number of guest worker-related provisions and bills have been considered and, in some cases, enacted into law.

Major guest worker reform legislation was considered in the 113th Congress. The Senate passed a comprehensive immigration reform bill that would have established new temporary agricultural and nonagricultural worker visas, reformed the H-2B visa, and phased out the H-2A visa.[76] In addition, the House Judiciary Committee reported a bill in the 113th Congress to establish a new H-2C agricultural worker visa to replace the H-2A visa.[77]

---

[75] 29 C.F.R. Part 503.

[76] See archived CRS Report R43097, *Comprehensive Immigration Reform in the 113th Congress: Major Provisions in Senate-Passed S. 744*.

[77] See archived CRS Report R43161, *Agricultural Guest Workers: Legislative Activity in the 113th Congress*.

While some Members have continued to put forward legislation to establish new temporary worker visas for agricultural and nonagricultural workers,[78] guest worker bills introduced in recent years have more commonly proposed changes to the existing visa programs. For example, recent bills on the H-2B visa have focused largely on the statutory annual cap. They include proposals to establish a permanent exemption from the H-2B cap for H-2B returning workers and to create new exemptions from the cap for H-2B workers performing certain types of work.[79]

Bills on the H-2A visa introduced in recent Congresses would variously change existing H-2A requirements concerning temporary need, wages, U.S. worker recruitment, and housing, among other items.[80] One such bill—the Farm Workforce Modernization Act (H.R. 5038)—passed the House in the 116th Congress.

H.R. 5038, as passed by the House, would make significant changes to the H-2A visa. With respect to required wages, it would revise one of the applicable wage rates, the adverse effect wage rate (see "Wages"). It would establish a six-year Portable H–2A Visa Pilot Program to enable a limited number of H-2A workers to perform agricultural labor for employers who would not need to file H-2A petitions. It would also allow DHS to approve petitions for H-2A workers to perform year-round agricultural work, subject to an initial annual numerical limitation of 20,000 (see "Temporary or Seasonal Nature of Work" for related discussion).[81]

---

[78] See, for example, H.R. 4760 (Division A, Title II), as introduced and considered on the House floor, in the 115th Congress. H.R. 4760 would have established a new H-2C visa for temporary agricultural workers. (It was one of several bills considered on the House or the Senate floor in June 2018 that included provisions on unauthorized childhood arrivals. House floor action on H.R. 4760 is discussed in CRS Report R45995, *Unauthorized Childhood Arrivals, DACA, and Related Legislation*.) Also see S. 2827, as introduced in the 114th Congress, which proposed a new H-2C visa for nonagricultural workers.

[79] See, for example, H.R. 798 and H.R. 2658, as introduced in the 116th Congress.

[80] See, for example, H.R. 60, H.R. 1778, and H.R. 3740, as introduced in the 116th Congress.

[81] In addition to making changes to the H-2A program, H.R. 5038 would establish a legalization program for unauthorized agricultural workers and would require agricultural employers to participate in an employment eligibility verification program modeled on E-Verify.

Enacted Provisions Since 2015

Since the 114th Congress, provisions on the H-2B visa have been regularly enacted as part of appropriations measures. One set of such provisions concerns certain H-2B regulations related to DOL labor certification. Language included in DOL appropriations acts for each year from FY2016 to FY2020 addresses the H-2B prevailing wage, requires use of the DHS regulatory definition of H-2B temporary need (i.e., one year or less), and prohibits the use of funds to enforce the definition of corresponding employment and the three-quarters guarantee rule (see "Wages" and "DHS/DOL Regulations on H-2B Employment").[82] In addition, DOL appropriations acts for each year from FY2015 to F2020 include "staggered entry" provisions that give employers in the seafood industry with approved H-2B petitions additional time (beyond the approved start date) to bring in workers (see "DHS/DOL Regulations on H-2B Employment").[83]

A second set of appropriations provisions concerns the H-2B statutory cap. H-2B cap relief has taken two different forms in recent years. For FY2016, Congress enacted an H-2B returning worker exemption that provided that a returning H-2B worker who had been counted against the 66,000 cap in FY2013, FY2014, or FY2015 would not be counted again in FY2016.[84] For FY2017, FY2018, FY2019, and FY2020, Congress enacted a different type of H-2B cap-related provision.[85] These provisions

---

[82] P.L. 114-113, Division H, Title I, §112, §113 (FY2016); P.L. 115-31, Division H, Title I, §112, §113 (FY2017); P.L. 115-141, Division H, Title I, §112, §113 (FY2018); P.L. 115-245, Division B, Title I, §111, §112 (FY2019); P.L. 116-94, Division A, Title I, §110, §111 (FY2020).

[83] P.L. 113-235, Division G, Title I, §108 (FY2015); P.L. 114-113, Division H, Title I, §111 (FY2016); P.L. 115-31, Division H, Title I, §111 (FY2017); P.L. 115-141, Division H, Title I, §111 (FY2018); P.L. 115-245, Division B, Title I, §110 (FY2019); P.L. 116-94, Division A, Title I, §109 (FY2020). For additional information about the staggered entry provision, see CRS Report R44306, *The H-2B Visa and the Statutory Cap*.

[84] P.L. 114-113, Division F, Title V, §565. H-2B returning worker provisions were also enacted for FY2005, FY2006, and FY2007, but not in appropriations measures. See CRS Report R44306, *The H-2B Visa and the Statutory Cap*.

[85] P.L. 115-31, Division F, Title V, §543 (FY2017); P.L. 115-141, Division M, Title II, §205 (FY2018); P.L. 116-6, Division H, Title I, §105 (FY2019); P.L. 116-94, Division I, Title I, §105 (FY2020).

authorized DHS, after consultation with DOL, to make additional H-2B visas (beyond the 66,000 cap) available in a fiscal year, subject to certain constraints, upon a determination that the needs of American businesses could not be satisfied with available U.S. workers. DHS rules implementing these provisions made 15,000 additional H-2B visas available annually for FY2017 and FY2018, and 30,000 additional H-2B visas available for FY2019.[86] For FY2020, DHS had planned to issue a rule making 35,000 additional H-2B visas available, but announced on April 2, 2020, that it was putting that rule on hold.[87]

POLICY CONSIDERATIONS

Guest worker programs generally try to achieve two goals simultaneously: to be responsive to legitimate employer needs for temporary labor and to provide adequate protections for U.S. and foreign temporary workers. DOL explicitly addressed the idea of balancing the needs of employers and workers in the supplementary information accompanying a 2011 proposed rule on the H-2B visa:

> Although the Department still seeks to maintain an efficient system, it has in this new rule struck a balance between reducing processing times and protecting U.S. worker access to these job opportunities.[88]

The balancing of broad guest worker program goals is reflected, in practice, in the particular provisions that H-2A and H-2B proposals include

---

[86] For additional information about the FY2017, FY2018, and FY2019 statutory provisions and related implementing rules, see CRS Report R44306, *The H-2B Visa and the Statutory Cap*.

[87] According to the tweet announcing the change, "DHS's rule on the H-2B cap is on hold pending review due to present economic circumstances. No additional H-2B visas will be released until further notice." Quoted in Suzanne Monyak, "DHS Halts Extra Guestworker Visas As Unemployment Jumps," Law360, April 2, 2020.

[88] U.S. Department of Labor, Employment and Training Administration and Wage and Hour Division, "Temporary Non-Agricultural Employment of H–2B Aliens in the United States," 76 *Federal Register* 15129, 15133, March 18, 2011 (hereinafter cited as "2011 DOL proposed H-2B rule") (see Appendix D).

on a range of component policy considerations, such as program administration, the labor market test, and wages, among others.

Program Administration

Under the H-2A and H-2B programs, DOL makes determinations on labor certification applications, and DHS adjudicates nonimmigrant visa petitions (see Figure 1). Under the INA, as explained, prospective H-2A employers must apply to DOL for labor certification. The INA does not require DOL labor certification for the H-2B visa. Rather, it makes general reference to "consultation with appropriate agencies of the Government" as part of the process of adjudicating petitions for "H" and other specified nonimmigrants.[89] The requirement for H-2B labor certification by DOL is established by regulation. The supplementary information accompanying the current 2015 DHS/DOL interim final rule on H-2B employment includes the following rationale for DOL's labor certification role:

> DOL is the appropriate government agency with expertise in labor questions and historic and specific expertise in addressing labor protection questions related to the H–2B program. This advice helps DHS fulfill its statutory duty to determine, prior to approving an H–2B petition, that unemployed U.S. workers capable of performing the relevant service or labor cannot be found in the United States.[90]

Over the years, regulatory and legislative proposals have sought to establish new agency roles in administering guest worker programs. For example, H-2B rules proposed in 2005 by DHS and DOL would have eliminated DOL's labor certification role in the interest of efficiency. Under this proposal, which was ultimately withdrawn in the face of opposition, employers would have applied directly to DHS for H-2B workers and would have included certain labor attestations with their

---

[89] INA §214(c)(1); 8 U.S.C. §1184(c)(1).
[90] 2015 DHS/DOL interim final H-2B rule, p. 24045.

applications.[91] Under some more recent proposals for new guest worker programs, such as that included in H.R. 4760, as considered on the House floor in the 115th Congress, employers likewise would have applied directly to DHS.[92]

H.R. 4760 also envisioned a new role for the U.S. Department of Agriculture (USDA) in its proposed agricultural worker program. USDA would have been charged with ensuring employer compliance with program requirements. Some past and present legislative measures to reform the H-2A program have proposed reassigning DOL's administrative responsibilities to USDA.[93]

Labor Market Test

Fundamental questions about any guest worker program include if and how it tests the labor market to determine whether U.S. workers are available for the job opportunities in question. Under both the H-2A and H-2B programs, employers interested in hiring foreign workers must first go through the process of labor certification. Intended to protect job opportunities for U.S. workers, labor certification entails a determination by DOL about whether qualified U.S. workers are available to perform the needed work and whether the hiring of foreign workers will adversely affect the wages and working conditions of similarly employed U.S. workers.

---

91 See U.S. Department of Homeland Security, "Petitions for Aliens To Perform Temporary Nonagricultural Services or Labor (H–2B)," 70 *Federal Register* 3984, January 27, 2005; U.S. Department of Labor, Employment and Training Administration and Wage and Hour Division, "Post -Adjudication Audits of H-2B Petitions in All Occupations Other Than Excepted Occupations in the United States," 70 *Federal Register* 3993, January 27, 2005. Under this proposal, DOL would have conducted post-certification audits.

92 H.R. 4760, Division A, Title II. The temporary agricultural worker program provisions in H.R. 4760 were also included in H.R. 4092, as ordered to be reported in the 115th Congress.

93 See, for example, H.R. 5795, as introduced in the 116th Congress, and H.R. 281 and H.R. 641, as introduced in the 115th Congress.

Recruitment is the primary method used to determine U.S. worker availability. While there is widespread agreement on the goals of labor certification, the process itself has been criticized for being cumbersome, slow, expensive, and ineffective in protecting U.S. workers.

The nature of the labor market test was a main difference between the DOL H-2A and H-2B rules issued by the George W. Bush Administration in 2008 and the rules issued by the Obama Administration in 2010 and 2015, which are now in effect. The 2008 DOL rules for both programs changed the traditionally supervised labor certification process into an attestation-based certification process (see Appendix D). In the supplementary information to its 2008 proposed H-2A rule, DOL cited criticism of the labor certification process as "complicated, time-consuming, and requiring the considerable expenditure of resources by employers." It further stated that its proposals "to re-engineer the H–2A program processing" will "simplify the process by which employers obtain a labor certification while maintaining, and even enhancing, the Department's substantial role in ensuring that U.S. workers have access to agricultural job opportunities."[94]

Current regulations on H-2A and H-2B employment return to a supervised, certification-based model of labor certification (see "DOL Regulations on H-2A Employment" and "DHS/DOL Regulations on H-2B Employment" above). A key argument made in support of this change concerned the need to restore protections for U.S. and foreign workers. For example, a 2011 DOL proposed H-2B rule stated

> [T]here are insufficient worker protections in the current attestation-based model in which employers merely assert, and do not demonstrate, that they have performed an adequate test of the U.S. labor market and one which is in accordance with the regulations.[95]

---

[94] U.S. Department of Labor, Employment and Training Administration and Wage and Hour Division, "Temporary Agricultural Employment of H–2A Aliens in the United States; Modernizing the Labor Certification Process and Enforcement," 73 *Federal Register* 8538, 8542, February 18, 2008.

[95] 2011 DOL proposed H-2B rule, p. 15132 (see Appendix D).

Legislative guest worker proposals continue to incorporate various forms of labor attestation. In some cases, they seek to replace existing labor certification requirements with labor attestation requirements, while generally retaining the current two-stage process in which employers first test the labor market and then, after receiving certification, petition for guest workers.[96] Other measures represent a greater departure from the current system in proposing to eliminate the current labor certification application step and to incorporate labor attestation requirements into the process of petitioning for guest workers.[97]

Wages

To prevent adverse effects on similarly employed U.S. workers, the H-2A and H-2B programs require employers to offer wages at or above specified levels. The particular wage requirements, which vary by program, are in regulation.[98] Under the H-2A program, employers must pay their workers the highest of the federal or applicable state minimum wage rate, the applicable prevailing wage rate,[99] the adverse effect wage rate (AEWR),[100] or the agreed-upon collective bargaining wage rate. Under the H-2B program, employers must pay their workers the highest of the federal, state, or local minimum wage or the prevailing wage rate.

Wage requirements have been a key area of controversy about the H-2A and H-2B programs. The 2015 DHS/DOL interim final rule on H-2B wages was issued following years of court challenges and congressional objections to earlier regulations.[101] Regarding H-2B wage requirements,

---

[96] See, for example, H.R. 281, as introduced in the 115th Congress.

[97] See, for example, S. 792, as introduced in the 115th Congress.

[98] 20 C.F.R. §655.120, §655.12(l) (H-2A); 20 C.F.R. §655.20(a) (H-2B).

[99] In general, the prevailing wage rate is the average wage paid to similarly employed workers in an occupation in an area of intended employment.

[100] The AEWR is equal to the annual weighted average hourly wage for field and livestock workers combined in a state or region, as published annually by the U.S. Department of Agriculture.

[101] U.S. Department of Homeland Security and U.S. Department of Labor, Employment and Training Administration and Wage and Hour Division, "Wage Methodology for the Temporary Non-Agricultural Employment H–2B Program," 80 *Federal Register*

provisions included in annual DOL appropriations acts since FY2016 mandate that the prevailing wage for H-2B purposes be the greater of the actual wage paid by the employer to other employees with similar experience and qualifications for the position in the same location, or the prevailing wage level for the occupational classification in the applicable geographic area. The appropriations language further requires DOL to accept a private wage survey for determining the prevailing wage unless "the methodology and data in the provided survey are not statistically supported" (see "Enacted Provisions" for statutory citations).

Policy differences about H-2Awage requirements center on the AEWR; the H-2A visa is the only nonimmigrant visa subject to it. A single AEWR is set annually for each state or region based on data from USDA's Farm Labor Survey.[102] Farm labor advocates have argued that the AEWR is necessary to protect U.S. agricultural workers from a possible depression of wages resulting from the hiring of foreign workers. Employers have long maintained that the AEWR results in inflated wage rates.

Legislative proposals over the years to reform the H-2Aprogram or establish new agricultural guest worker programs have often included provisions to eliminate the use of the AEWR or effectively redefine it. In the 116th Congress, House-passed H.R. 5038 proposes to calculate separate AEWRs for individual occupational classifications, preferably by state or region if such data are reported.[103] The bill also includes provisions to limit

---

24145, April 29, 2015 (hereinafter cited as "2015 DHS/DOL final H-2B wage rule"). For a discussion of the controversy surrounding this rule, see pp. 24146 -24154. The content of this rule is beyond the scope of this chapter.

[102] For 2020, the AEWR ranges from $11.71 for Alabama, Georgia, and South Carolina, to $15.83 for Oregon and Washington State. The 2020 AEWRs for all states are available in U.S. Department of Labor, Employment and Training Administration, "Labor Certification Process for the Temporary Employment of Aliens in Agriculture in the United States: 2020 Adverse Effect Wage Rates for Non-Range Occupations," 84 *Federal Register* 69774, December 19, 2019.

[103] A 2019 DOL proposed rule on H-2A employment would revise the H-2A wage requirements to similarly establish AEWRs by agricultural occupation, although the particulars of the AEWR changes in the proposed rule and House - passed H.R. 5038 differ. The proposed rule would also modify the methodology used to determine H-2A prevailing wages. U.S. Department of Labor, Employment and Training Administration and Wage and Hour Division, "Temporary Agricultural Employment of H–2A Nonimmigrants in the United States," 84 *Federal Register* 36168, July 26, 2019. For information about other components of the proposed rule, see Appendix D.

annual AEWR increases and decreases. A fact sheet on H.R. 5038 describes the impact of moving to a system of occupation-specific AEWRs: "This will ensure that wage requirements better reflect the real-world wages paid to specific types of workers. Some workers would see higher wages (machine operators), while others would see lower wages (crop workers)."[104]

Temporary or Seasonal Nature of Work

The H-2A and H-2B programs are, by definition, limited to temporary or seasonal work.[105] They are intended to meet employers' temporary—and not permanent—needs for labor when U.S. workers cannot be found.

This "temporary or seasonal" requirement places restrictions on both programs. With respect to the H-2A program, it means that the program cannot be used to meet employers' year-round agricultural labor needs absent a statutory provision. There is a long-standing exception to this year-round restriction for herding on the range.[106] Legislation in recent

---

[104] See *Farm Workforce Modernization Act*, https://lofgren.house.gov/sites/lofgren.house.gov/files/Bipartisan%20Farm%20Workforce%20Modernization%20Act%20-%20One%20Pager.pdf.

[105] The INA definition of the H-2A nonimmigrant category generally requires the agricultural work to be "of a temporary or seasonal nature" (INA §101(a)(15)(H)(ii)(a); 8 U.S.C. §1101(a)(15)(H)(ii)(a)), and the INA definition of the H-2B nonimmigrant category requires the performance of nonagricultural "temporary service or labor" (INA §101(a)(15)(H)(ii)(b); 8 U.S.C. §1101(a)(15)(H)(ii)(b)). In the case of both the H-2A and H-2B visas, this temporary nature-of-the-work requirement is separate from and in addition to the requirement that workers must be coming for a temporary period of time.

[106] Herding activities are not mentioned in the INA definition of the H-2A nonimmigrant category. However, according to DOL, the inclusion of herding, specifically sheepherding, in the H-2A program has a statutory basis: "Sheepherders … owe their inclusion in the program to a statutory provision dating back to the 1950s. That legislative inclusion was implicitly ratified in [the Immigration Reform and Control Act of 1986]." See U.S. Department of Labor, Employment and Training Administration and Wage and Hour Division, "Temporary Agricultural Employment of H-2A Aliens in the United States," 75 *Federal Register* 6884, 6891, February 12, 2010 (hereinafter cited as "2010 DOL H-2A rule"). For many years, DOL sub-regulatory guidance (special procedures) governed the labor certification process for occupations in sheep and goat herding and range production of livestock. In 2 015, DOL published a final

Congresses has sought to include dairy industry activities—most of which are excluded from the H-2Aprogram as being year-round—in the H-2A program by amending INA provisions of the H-2A visa.[107] Other legislative proposals would more broadly amend the statutory definition of the H-2A visa to eliminate the requirement that H-2A nonimmigrants perform work "of a temporary or seasonal nature."[108] H.R. 5038, as passed by the House in the 116th Congress, takes a more incremental approach. It would permit a limited number of H-2A workers (initially capped at 20,000 per year) to perform year-round employment, with a set aside for dairy work.

Under the H-2B program, as described, the employer's need for the duties to be performed by the worker must be a one-time occurrence, seasonal need, peakload need, or intermittent need. Some proposals in past Congresses would have broadened the H-2B visa from a category restricted to temporary need to one covering "short-term" labor.[109] This change, which was not enacted, would have permitted H-2B workers to fill a wider range of job openings.

Numerical Limits

A numerical cap provides a means, separate from program requirements, of limiting the number of foreign workers who can be admitted annually in a visa category. The H-2Avisa is not numerically limited. The H-2B program, by contrast, is statutorily capped at 66,000 annually. Certain H-2B petitions are exempt from the cap, such as petitions filed for current H-2B workers who are seeking an extension of stay, a change of employer, or a change in the terms of employment and petitions

---

rule to establish a single set of regulations for H-2A employment in these occupations (see "Range Herding and Livestock Regulations").

[107] See, for example, H.R. 1778, as introduced in the 116th Congress.

[108] See, for example, H.R. 60, as introduced in the 115th Congress.

[109] See, for example, S. 1918, as introduced in the 109th Congress.

filed for fish roe workers and supervisors (see "H-2B Statutory Provisions").[110]

Annual numerical limitations on the H-2B visa and other capped temporary worker visas are implemented by DHS at the petition stage. Under DHS regulations

> When calculating the numerical limitations ... for a given fiscal year, USCIS will make numbers available to petitions in the order in which the petitions are filed. USCIS will make projections of the number of petitions necessary to achieve the numerical limit of approvals, taking into account historical data related to approvals, denials, revocations, and other relevant factors. USCIS will monitor the number of petitions (including the number of beneficiaries requested when necessary) received and will notify the public of the date that USCIS has received the necessary number of petitions (the "final receipt date").[111]

In other words, in a given fiscal year USCIS accepts the number of petitions it estimates will result in the appropriate number of foreign workers receiving a visa or otherwise obtaining status under a particular temporary worker visa program. USCIS has described the inherent challenges in this system in connection with the H-2B visa

> It can be difficult to estimate in advance how many beneficiaries of an H-2B petition approved by USCIS will actually seek H-2B status or eventually be issued an H-2B visa by the Department of State (DOS).[112]

If USCIS accepts more petitions than necessary, the H-2B cap can be exceeded. In at least one year (FY2015), however, USCIS initially

---

[110] For additional information, see CRS Report R44306, *The H-2B Visa and the Statutory Cap.*

[111] 8 C.F.R. §214.2((h)(8)(ii)(B).

[112] U.S. Department of Homeland Security, U.S. Citizenship and Immigration Services, "USCIS to Reopen H-2B Cap for the Second Half of Fiscal Year 2015," June 5, 2015, https://www.uscis.gov/news/alerts/uscis-reopen-h-2b-cap-second-half-fiscal-year-2015.

accepted too few petitions and had to briefly reopen the window for accepting cap-subject H-2B petitions.[113]

In years when the demand for H-2B visas exceeds the supply, there is pressure to admit additional H-2B workers. Temporary statutory provisions have been enacted to allow for the admission of additional H-2B workers (beyond the 66,000 cap) every year since FY2016 (see "Enacted Provisions" above). These provisions permit the admission of increased numbers of H-2B workers, while leaving the statutory annual 66,000 limit in place.

Treatment of Family Members

The INA allows for the admission to the United States of the spouses and minor children of foreign workers on H-2A, H-2B, and other "H" visas who are accompanying or following to join the worker. These family members are issued H-4 visas and do not count against the numerical cap, if any, on the relevant temporary worker visa (such as the H-2B visa). Allowing for the admission of guest workers' spouses and minor children enables families to stay together. On the other hand, this practice has been faulted for decreasing incentives for guest workers to return home after their authorized period of stay. Some legislative proposals to establish new guest worker programs would have explicitly prohibited family members from accompanying or following to join principal aliens.[114]

Enforcement

Another set of considerations relates to enforcement of the terms of guest worker programs. With respect to the H-2A program, the INA broadly authorizes the Secretary of Labor to

---

[113] See CRS Report R44306, *The H-2B Visa and the Statutory Cap*.

[114] See, for example, H.R. 4760 (Division A, Title II), as introduced in the 115th Congress.

> take such actions, including imposing appropriate penalties and seeking appropriate injunctive relief and specific performance of contractual obligations, as may be necessary to assure employer compliance with terms and conditions of employment.[115]

More limited language added to the INA in 2005 applies to the H-2B program. These provisions authorize the Secretary of Homeland Security to impose administrative remedies and to deny certain petitions filed by an employer if the Secretary finds "a substantial failure to meet any of the conditions of the [H-2B] petition" or "a willful misrepresentation of a material fact in such petition."[116] As discussed, the Secretary of Homeland Security has delegated this enforcement authority to the Secretary of Labor in accordance with an agreement between the two agencies. The Secretary of Labor subsequently delegated this authority to WHD, which is now responsible for assuring employer compliance with the terms and conditions of H-2B employment.[117]

Another enforcement-related question concerns what type of mechanism, if any, ensures that guest workers do not remain in the United States beyond their authorized period of stay and become part of the unauthorized population. Among the related regulatory provisions currently in effect are provisions establishing notification requirements for H-2A and H-2B employers. DHS regulations on the H-2A visa and the H-2B visa require petitioners to notify DHS within two work days when an H-2Aor H-2B worker fails to report at the start of the employment period, absconds[118] from the worksite, or is terminated prior to completion of the work, or when the work for which H-2A or H-2B workers were hired is

---

[115] INA §218(g)(2); 8 U.S.C. §1188(g)(2).

[116] INA §214(c)(14)(A); 8 U.S.C. §1184(c)(14)(A).

[117] U.S. Department of Labor, Office of the Secretary, Secretary's Order 01 –2014, 79 *Federal Register* 77527, December 24, 2014. For an evaluation of federal enforcement of H-2A and H-2B program laws and regulations, see U.S. Government Accountability Office, *H-2A and H-2B Visa Programs: Increased Protections Needed for Foreign Workers*, GAO-15-154, March 2015.

[118] *Absconding* is defined as not reporting for work for five consecutive work days without the employer's consent. 8 C.F.R. §§214.2(h)(5)(vi)(E), (h)(6)(i)(F)(2).

completed early.[119] In the case of the H-2B visa, DHS explained the purpose of these notification requirements as enabling the agency

> to keep track of H–2B workers while they are in the United States and take appropriate enforcement action where DHS determines that the H–2B workers have violated the terms and conditions of their nonimmigrant stay.[120]

Other suggestions that have been offered to help ensure that temporary workers depart at the end of their authorized period of stay include involving the workers' home countries in guest worker programs. Another idea is to create an incentive for foreign workers to leave the United States at the appropriate time by, for example, withholding earnings or otherwise setting aside a sum of money for each worker that would only become available once the worker returned home.[121]

Unauthorized Workers

The H-2A and H-2B visa programs account for a fraction of all the workers in the United States performing the type of agricultural and nonagricultural work covered by these visas. Unauthorized workers comprise a sizeable percentage of workers in some related industries and occupations. For example, according to Pew Research Center estimates, unauthorized workers held about a quarter of farming jobs and 15% of construction jobs in 2016.[122]

Policymakers have periodically considered establishing a statutory mechanism to grant permanent immigration status to unauthorized or

---

[119] 8 C.F.R. §§214.2(h)(5)(vi)(B)(1), (h)(6)(i)(F)(1).

[120] U.S. Department of Homeland Security, "Changes to Requirements Affecting H-2B Nonimmigrants and Their Employers," 73 *Federal Register* 78104, 78116, December 19, 2008 (hereinafter cited as "2008 DHS H-2B rule").

[121] See, for example, H.R. 4760 (Division A, Title II), as introduced in the 115th Congress.

[122] Jeffrey S. Passel and D'Vera Cohn, *U.S. Unauthorized Immigrant Total Dips to Lowest Level in a Decade*, Pew Research Center, November 27, 2018. The report estimates that in 2016 there were 7.8 million unauthorized aliens in the civilian labor force, representing 4.8% of the total.

authorized guest workers. Historically, these discussions have focused on agricultural workers, and in some past and present legislative measures, guest worker reform provisions have been paired with programs to grant permanent immigration status. For example, along with its agricultural guest worker provisions, the comprehensive immigration reform bill passed by the Senate in 2013 proposed a two-stage agricultural worker legalization program, through which farm workers who had performed a requisite amount of agricultural work and satisfied other requirements could have obtained legal temporary resident status (termed "blue card" status). After meeting additional agricultural work and other requirements, these workers could have applied for lawful permanent resident (LPR) status. (Unauthorized workers and H-2A workers would have been eligible for this program.)[123]

More recently, in the 116th Congress, House-passed H.R. 5038 would establish a two-stage legalization program for unauthorized agricultural workers to first obtain legal temporary certified agricultural worker (CAW) status and then LPR status, subject to work and other requirements at each stage. Alternatively, H.R. 5038 would permit workers to remain in CAW status indefinitely (without ever applying for LPR status) provided they continued to perform a requisite amount of agricultural work annually. This "indefinite temporary status" option distinguishes H.R. 5038 from the 2013 Senate bill and other past agricultural legalization measures that treated the legal temporary status as a way station to LPR status and limited how long an individual could remain in that temporary status. In addition, H.R. 5038 includes provisions not included in earlier agricultural legalization measures to enable an H-2A worker who had performed a threshold amount of H-2Awork in each of 10 years to self-petition for LPR status.

---

[123] Sections 2211-2212 of S. 744, as passed by the Senate in the 113th Congress. For further information about this proposal and other proposals, see archived CRS Report R43161, *Agricultural Guest Workers: Legislative Activity in the 113th Congress*.

CONCLUSION

Many policymakers assert that the H-2A and H-2B visa programs are not adequately meeting employers' labor needs and/or are not adequately protecting U.S. and foreign workers, although their particular criticisms vary widely. In past years, proposed solutions have taken the form of reforms to the H-2A and H-2B visas as well as new guest worker visa programs. In the current climate, pursuing reforms to existing visa programs seems to be the course more policymakers are likely to follow. It remains unclear whether and how the COVID-19 pandemic may affect future guest worker-related legislative efforts.

APPENDIX A. H-2A AND H-2B CERTIFICATIONS BY STATE

Table A-1. Top 10 states granted H-2A labor certifications: FY2018 and FY2019
Rankings based on number of positions certified

	FY2018		**FY2019**	
Ranking	State	Positions Certified	State	Positions Certified
1	Georgia	32,364	Florida	33,598
2	Florida	30,462	Georgia	29,480
3	Washington	24,862	Washington	26,226
4	North Carolina	21,794	California	23,321
5	California	18,908	North Carolina	21,605
6	Louisiana	10,079	Louisiana	10,816
7	Michigan	8,359	Michigan	9,096
8	New York	7,634	Kentucky	8,315
9	Kentucky	7,604	New York	8,104
10	Arizona	7,497	South Carolina	6,082
	Total, All States	242,762	Total, All States	257,667

Source: CRS presentation of data from U.S. Department of Labor, Employment and Training Administration, Office of Foreign Labor Certification, *H-2A Temporary Agricultural Labor Certification Program - Selected Statistics, FY 2018*, and *H-2A Temporary Agricultural Labor Certification Program - Selected Statistics, FY 2019.*

Table A-2. Top 10 states granted H-2B labor certifications: FY2018 and FY2019
Rankings based on number of positions certified

	FY2018		**FY2019**	
Ranking	State	Positions Certified	State	Positions Certified
1	Texas	20,443	Texas	16,106
2	Florida	10,690	Colorado	6,943
3	Colorado	7,556	Florida	5,768
4	Louisiana	5,341	North Carolina	5,074
5	Pennsylvania	5,216	Pennsylvania	5,006
6	Virginia	5,173	Louisiana	4,924
7	North Carolina	5,129	Alaska	4,892
8	South Carolina	4,984	New York	4,590
9	New York	4,579	Virginia	4,165
10	Maryland	4,439	Maryland	4,022
	Total, All States	147,592	Total, All States	150,465

Source: CRS presentation of data from U.S. Department of Labor, Employment and Training Administration, Office of Foreign Labor Certification, *H-2B Temporary Non-Agricultural Labor Certification Program - Selected Statistics, FY 2018*, and *H-2B Temporary Non-Agricultural Labor Certification Program - Selected Statistics, FY 2019 EOY.*

APPENDIX B. H-2B CERTIFICATIONS BY OCCUPATION

In FY2019, DOL approved 7,377 H-2B labor certification applications. As part of these applications, DOL approved 150,465 requests for H-2B positions.

Typically, a majority of H-2B requests certified by DOL are for workers in a few occupations. In FY2019, as shown in Table B-1, 79% of certified positions were in 10 occupations. One occupation, landscaping & groundskeeping worker, accounted for 44% of the total number of H-2B positions certified.

Table B-1. Number of certified H-2B positions by occupation, FY2019

Ranking	Occupation	Number of Workers Certified	Percentage of Total Workers Certified	Cumulative Percentage
1	Landscaping & groundskeeping worker	66,151	44.0%	44.0%
2	Forest & conservation worker	11,283	7.5%	51.5%
3	Maid & housekeeping cleaner	9,869	6.6%	58.1%
4	Meat, poultry & fish cutter and trimmer	8,486	5.6%	63.7%
5	Amusement & recreation attendant	8,014	5.3%	69.0%
6	Waiter & waitress	4,104	2.7%	71.7%
7	Construction laborer	3,369	2.2%	73.9%
8	Cook, restaurant	3,299	2.2%	76.1%
9	Laborer & Material Mover	2,274	1.5%	77.6%
10	Nonfarm animal caretaker	2,226	1.5%	79.1%
	Other	31,390	20.9%	100.0%
	Total	150,465	100.0%	

Source: CRS presentation of data from U.S. Department of Labor, Employment and Training Administration, Office of Foreign Labor Certification, *H-2B Temporary Non-Agricultural Labor Certification Program - Selected Statistics, FY 2019 EOY.*

APPENDIX C. H-2A AND H-2B VISA ISSUANCES

Table C-1. Number of H-2A and H-2B visas issued, FY1992-FY2019

Fiscal Year	H-2A Visas Issued	H-2B Visas Issued
1992	6,445	12,552
1993	7,243	9,691
1994	7,721	10,400
1995	8,379	11,737
1996	11,004	12,200
1997	16,011	15,706
1998	22,676	20,192
1999	28,568	30,642
2000	30,201	45,037
2001	31,523	58,215
2002	31,538	62,591
2003	29,882	78,955

Fiscal Year	H-2A Visas Issued	H-2B Visas Issued
2004	31,774	76,169
2005	31,892	89,135
2006	37,149	122,541
2007	50,791	129,547
2008	64,404	94,304
2009	60,112	44,847
2010	55,921	47,403
2011	55,384	50,826
2012	65,345	50,009
2013	74,192	57,600
2014	89,274	68,102
2015	108,144	69,684
2016	134,368	84,627
2017	161,583	83,600
2018	196,408	83,774
2019	204,801	97,623

Source: CRS presentation of data from U.S. Department of State, Bureau of Consular Affairs.

APPENDIX D. SUPPLEMENTARY INFORMATION ON H-2A AND H-2B REGULATIONS

H-2A Rules

The H-2A visa program is governed mainly by a DHS final rule issued in 2008 and a DOL final rule issued in 2010. A 2019 DOL final rule made some additional changes to the labor certification process. A2019 DOL proposed rule would make major changes to the certification process. In addition, a 2020 DHS final rule makes temporary changes to some DHS regulatory requirements in response to the COVID-19 emergency (for a discussion of these 2020 temporary changes, see "DHS Regulations on the H-2A Visa").

Background

In 2008, during the George W. Bush Administration, DHS and DOL published final rules to significantly amend their respective H-2A regulations.[124] The agencies issued these rules to streamline the H-2A program in the aftermath of unsuccessful congressional efforts to enact comprehensive immigration reform legislation with guest worker provisions.

The DOL rule was controversial. Prior to its issuance, the H-2Alabor certification process had been a fully supervised certification-based process, in which federal or state officials reviewed an employer's actual efforts or documentation to ensure compliance with program requirements. The 2008 rule replaced this supervised process with an attestation-based process, in which prospective H-2A employers had to attest in their applications, under threat of penalties, that they complied with H-2A program requirements.

Under the Obama Administration, the 2008 DHS rule was retained, but the 2008 DOL rule was replaced with a new H-2A final rule issued in 2010. In the supplementary information accompanying the proposed version of this replacement rule, DOL cited concerns about employer noncompliance with program requirements under the 2008 rule. It explained the need for new rulemaking, in part, as follows

> The Department, upon due consideration, believes that the policy underpinnings of the 2008 Final Rule, e.g., streamlining the H–2A regulatory process to defer many determinations of program compliance until after an Application has been fully adjudicated, do not provide an adequate level of protection for either U.S. or foreign workers.[125]

The 2010 DOL H-2A final rule reversed changes made by the 2008 rule to the H-2A labor certification process and reestablished the type of compliance-demonstration process that had been in effect prior to the 2008 rule.

---

[124] 2008 DHS H-2A rule; U.S. Department of Labor, Employment and Training Administration and Wage and Hour Division, "Temporary Agricultural Employment of H-2A Aliens in the United States; Modernizing the Labor Certification Process and Enforcement," 73 *Federal Register* 77110, December 18, 2008.

[125] U.S. Department of Labor, Employment and Training Administration and Wage and Hour Division, "Temporary Agricultural Employment of H-2A Aliens in the United States," 74 *Federal Register* 45906, 45908, September 4, 2009.

2019 DOL Final and Proposed Rules

A 2019 DOL H-2A rule made a few changes to the labor certification process.[126] It eliminated a regulatory requirement that a prospective H-2A employer advertise its job opportunity in a print newspaper as part of its required recruitment activities. At the same time, it added a new regulatory provision allowing the ETA officer making a determination on an H-2A labor certification application, where appropriate, to direct the SWA to notify organizations that provide employment and training services about the job opportunity. Under the rule, DOL also enhanced the publicly available electronic job registry (https://seasonaljobs.dol.gov/jobs) where it posts approved H-2A job orders to recruit U.S. workers.[127]

A 2019 DOL proposed rule would make more fundamental changes to the H-2Aprogram.[128] It would further amend ETA regulations on the labor certification process and would amend WHD regulations on the enforcement of H-2Aemployers' contractual obligations. Among the major regulatory changes included in the rule, DOL proposes to revise the methodologies used to determine two wage rates relevant to the H-2A program: the AEWR and the prevailing wage rate (see "Wages"). The rule would also expand the definition of *agriculture* for H-2A purposes to encompass reforestation and pine straw activities.

Under the proposed rule, H-2A employers would be permitted to stagger the entry of H-2A workers, allowing them to bring the workers into the United States at any time during the first 120 days after the date of need in the approved labor certification.[129] DOL also proposes to replace the existing fifty percent rule with a new 30-day rule. As discussed, the

---

[126] U.S. Department of Labor, Employment and Training Administration and Wage and Hour Division, "Modernizing Recruitment Requirements for the Temporary Employment of H–2A Foreign Workers in the United States," 84 *Federal Register* 49439, September 20, 2019.

[127] As explained in the supplementary information to the rule, "[DOL] will enhance the functional capabilities of this registry so that it also serves as a job search website that broadly advertises and disseminates H–2A job opportunities to U.S. workers." Ibid, p. 49444.

[128] U.S. Department of Labor, Employment and Training Administration and Wage and Hour Division, "Temporary Agricultural Employment of H–2A Nonimmigrants in the United States," 84 *Federal Register* 36168, July 26, 2019.

[129] A staggered entry provision that applies to H-2B employers in the seafood industry is discussed in "DHS/DOL Regulations on H-2B Employment."

fifty percent rule requires an H-2A employer to hire any qualified U.S. worker who applies for a position during the first half of the work contract under which the H-2Aworkers who are in the job are employed.

Under DOL's replacement 30-day rule, an H-2A employer would be required to hire any qualified U.S. worker who applies for a job until 30 calendar days after the employer's first date of need on the approved labor certification. Special requirements would apply to employers who stagger the entry of H-2A workers.

H-2B Rules

The H-2B visa program is governed mainly by a DHS final rule issued in 2008 and a DHS/DOL interim final rule issued in 2015. A DHS/DOL final rule issued in 2015 revised the methodology for calculating prevailing wage rates under the H-2B program. In addition, a DHS/DOL rule issued in 2019 made some changes to the H-2B labor certification process.[130] Also, a 2020 DHS final rule makes temporary changes to some DHS regulatory requirements in response to the COVID-19 emergency (for a discussion of these 2020 temporary changes, see "DHS Regulations on the H-2B Visa").

Background

Mirroring regulatory actions taken on the H-2A program, DHS and DOL under the George W. Bush Administration published final rules to significantly amend their respective H-2B regulations in 2008. Under the DOL H-2B rule, which streamlined the labor certification process, determinations about H-2B program compliance were made only after a labor certification application had been adjudicated.

---

[130] U.S. Department of Labor, Employment and Training Administration and Wage and Hour Division, "Modernizing Recruitment Requirements for the Temporary Employment of H–2B Foreign Workers in the United States," 84 *Federal Register* 62431, November 15,2019.

The Obama Administration retained the DHS H-2B rule but wanted to replace the DOL rule. To that end, DOL published a new H-2B proposed rule in 2011. In this proposed rulemaking, DOL took the position that the 2008 rule did not provide sufficient protections for U.S. or foreign workers. It further described problems of noncompliance

> [I]n the first year of the operation of the attestation-based system our experience indicates that employers are attesting to compliance with program obligations with which they have not complied, and that employers do not appear to be recruiting, hiring and paying U.S. workers, and in some cases the H-2B workers themselves, in accordance with established program requirements.[131]

DOL issued an H-2B final rule in 2012 that required employers to show compliance with recruitment and other requirements in advance of DOL making a determination on the labor certification application.[132] This rule, however, never became operative due to court action. A key issue in the litigation was whether DOL had the authority to promulgate regulations for the H-2B program (see "DHS/DOL Regulations on H-2B Employment"). In April 2015, DOL and DHS jointly issued two H-2B rules: an interim final rule on H-2B employment that was "virtually identical" to the DOL 2012 final rule,[133] and a companion final rule on prevailing wage rates under the H-2B program.

2019 DOL Final Rule

A 2019 DHS/DOL H-2B final rule made changes to the H-2B labor certification process that were analogous to some of the changes the 2019 DOL H-2A final rule made to the H-2A certification process.[134] Like the

---

[131] 2011 DOL proposed H-2B rule, p. 15132.

[132] U.S. Department of Labor, Employment and Training Administration and Wage and Hour Division, "Temporary Non-Agricultural Employment of H-2B Aliens in the United States," 77 *Federal Register* 10038, February 21, 2012.

[133] 2015 DHS/DOL interim final H-2B rule, p. 24043.

[134] U.S. Department of Labor, Employment and Training Administration and Wage and Hour Division, "Modernizing Recruitment Requirements for the Temporary Employment of H–2B Foreign Workers in the United States," 84 *Federal Register* 62431, November 15, 2019.

H-2A rule, the 2019 H-2B rule eliminated a regulatory requirement that a prospective H-2A employer advertise its job opportunity in a print newspaper. DOL also indicated that it would post H-2B job opportunities on the same expanded electronic job registry used to advertise H-2A jobs, as discussed above.

In: Visas
Editor: Brian A. Shelton

ISBN: 978-1-53619-966-6

Chapter 4

TEMPORARY WORK VISA HOLDERS IN THE UNITED STATES, BY THE NUMBERS*

Doug Rand and Lindsay Milliken

The Trump administration is expected to unveil an executive action in the near future that would significantly restrict temporary ("nonimmigrant") work visa categories, potentially including:

- H-1B visas for skilled "specialty occupation" workers
- H-2B visas for nonagricultural seasonal workers
- H-4 visas for the spouses or children of H-1B and H-2B visa holders (among others)
- J-1 visas for exchange visitors
- J-2 visas for the spouses or children of J-1 visa holders
- L-1 visas for employees of multinational companies
- L-2 visas for the spouses or children of L-1 visa holders

* This is an edited, reformatted and augmented version of Federation of American Scientists Publication, dated June 12, 2020.

- F visas for those international students staying in the United States after graduation to gain on-the-job training with a U.S. employer through the Optional Practical Training (OPT) program

While there are multiple public data sets available from the Department of Homeland Security (DHS) and the Department of State (DOS) relevant to these visa categories, they are unfortunately not sufficient to answer these basic questions with great precision:

- How many individuals enter the country each year, for the first time, using each of these visa categories?
- How many individuals are already in the United States at any given moment, having previously entered using each of these visa categories?

Our goal below is to synthesize the relevant data and clearly present what it can—and cannot—reveal about the number of individuals potentially impacted by work visa restrictions.

WHO IS ARRIVING FROM ABROAD?

It is the job of the State Department to issue the visas that allow individuals abroad to travel to the United States for work and other purposes.

The State Department provides a simple tally of the number of visas issued each fiscal year, in each category (see Table 1). Unfortunately, these numbers do not reflect the actual number of people who arrive in the United States, nor do they reflect the actual number of new temporary workers arriving in the United States.

In some circumstances, an individual living abroad who is issued a visa may save that visa until the next fiscal year, or may not end up traveling to the United States at all. To make things more complicated, this visa issuance data also includes individuals living in the United States who travel abroad briefly and simply need a visa to return here.

For example, it would not be accurate to say that 188,123 H-1B visa holders newly arrived in the United States in Fiscal Year 2019—the real number could be higher or (more likely) significantly lower.

Table 1. Number of nonimmigrant visas issued abroad by State Dept.

Visa Type	For Principal Workers or Dependents	2015	2016	2017	2018	2019
H-1B	Workers	172,748	180,057	179,049	179,660	188,123
H-2B	Workers	69,684	84,627	83,600	83,774	97,623
H-4	Dependents	124,484	131,051	136,393	130,814	125,999
J-1	Workers	374,829	380,120	383,165	382,219	391,561
J-2	Dependents	42,289	40,408	39,354	39,580	38,282
L-1	Workers	164,604	165,178	163,432	153,099	157,708
L-2	Dependents	86,067	85,872	85,254	78,711	80,720

The Department of Homeland Security provides separate data on how many people enter the United States at border crossings and ports of entry, but this includes multiple re-entries by individuals who may go back and forth more than once in a given year. Because this data can be so misleading, we do not present it here.

How Many Temporary Workers Are in the United States?

Tallying the number of temporary visa holders currently working in the United States is also surprisingly complicated.

Most of the time, this process starts with a U.S. employer filing a petition with U.S. Citizenship and Immigration Services (USCIS) to sponsor a worker under a particular visa category. This petition is called Form I-129.

Table 2 includes the total number of I-129 petitions approved by USCIS each fiscal year. However, these numbers mix together workers who are currently abroad and those who are already in the United States. Some of these petitions are for a worker filling a job for the first time, but others include extensions of a current job, reapplications for those changing jobs, or even just changing the location of a job. Some individuals may have more than one active petition at a time. Moreover, in the L-1 category, these numbers do not reflect the "blanket" petitions approved by USCIS that allow direct visa applications at consular posts abroad, without individual petition adjudication by USCIS. Therefore it is impossible to figure out, from this data alone, how many workers are actually in the United States.

The same is true for Form I-539, which is mostly used by spouses and children of primary workers to extend or change immigration status from one temporary category to another. This includes, but is by no means limited to, H-4 and L-2 visa holders.

Table 2. Total number of nonimmigrant forms approved by USCIS

Form Type	2015	2016	2017	2018	2019
I-129					
H-1B only	288,501	357,195	373,342	334,945	389,362
H-2B only	5,144	5,992	5,860	5,883	7,358
L-1 only	33,454	34,058	35,680	29,533	29,335
I-539	146,340	207,866	180,899	187,913	--

(This chart was drawn from USCIS I-129 data and I-539 data found in the All USCIS Application and Petition Form Types quarterly reports.)

How Many People Are Using Optional Practical Training (OPT)?

Students who are on an F-1 visa have the opportunity to apply for the Optional Practical Training (OPT) program to stay in the United States after graduation. OPT allows for on-the-job training with a U.S. company in a relevant field for up to one year.

Those who participate in the STEM OPT extension program must have received a qualifying bachelor's degree or higher in a science, technology, engineering, and math (STEM) field from an accredited U.S. institution of higher education. STEM OPT participants also receive training for one year in a relevant field under standard OPT, plus they are eligible for a 24-month extension after their first year is completed (for a total of three years). Immigration and Customs Enforcement (ICE) administers OPT approvals and its most recent data can be found in Tables 3a and 3b below.

Table 3a. Authorized employment start dates, by calendar year

	2015	2016	2017	2018
OPT	99,323	137,570	152,681	145,564
STEM OPT	27,493	41,782	64,481	69,650
Total SEVIS IDs w/ OPT	126,509	171,593	204,633	200,162

Table 3b. Employment authorizations issued, by calendar year

	2015	2016	2017	2018
Regular OPT + STEM OPT	159,298	190,683	218,998	208,065

(This chart was drawn from the ICE Student and Exchange Visitor Program (SEVP) database.)

Table 3a shows, according to ICE, the total number of annual OPT and STEM OPT "authorizations with employment start dates during an indicated calendar year and a [sic] employer name." This is presumably the number of individuals who are authorized to work in a given year and who actually end up going to work for a particular employer. (ICE provides no explanation as to why the numbers for OPT and STEM OPT do not add up to the totals listed in the third row above.)

Table 3b shows, according to ICE, the "number of students issued an EAD [employment authorization document] for OPT or STEM OPT." This is presumably the number of individuals receiving a work permit in a given calendar year, whether or not they end up going to work for a particular employer. (ICE does not provide a breakdown between OPT and STEM OPT.)

How Many J-1 Visa Holders Are in the United States?

Table 4. Number of J-1 program participants by calendar year

Program	2016	2017	2018
Au Pair	19,233	20,353	20,678
Camp Counselor	22,991	24,868	24,919
Intern	25,202	26,075	26,112
Physician*	2,623	2,830	2,738
Professor and Research Scholar	37,445	36,363	35,627
Short-Term Scholar	19,928	19,730	18,885
Specialist	1,327	1,354	1,350
Summer Work Travel	101,054	104,921	104,512
Teacher	2,662	2,867	3,252
Trainee	10,751	10,885	10,857
Total	243,216	250,246	246,192

* The Physician category was renamed in 2018 and became the Alien Physician category. (This data comes from the DOS J-1 Facts and Figures site.)

J-1 cultural exchange visas are managed by the State Department and used for short-term, often summer-long, work assignments in many different categories, such as au pairs, professors, research scholars, and camp counselors. The State Department provides data on the number of J-1 program participants in the U.S. for 2016 through 2018 as seen below in Table 4.

Because of the COVID-19 pandemic, as of early March all exchange visitor programs, including the ones listed above, were paused until further notice. For the participants in summer programs, this means that they likely did not arrive in the U.S. before the pause was announced.

How Much Are H-1B Workers Paid?

The Trump administration's executive order may put restrictions on H-1B visa holders below a certain income threshold. Table 5 shows the number of H-1B workers who earn above the 75th percentile in each major occupational group, based on USCIS data; overall, 25 percent earned a salary of at least $110,000 in fiscal year 2017. Unfortunately, USCIS has not yet published reports with more updated information.

Table 5. Annual compensation of all H-1B workers by occupation in FY 2017

Occupations	Total Visa Holders Reported	75th Salary Percentile	Total at or Above 75th Percentile
Computer-related occupations	254,590	109,000	63,648
Occupations in architecture, engineering, and surveying	29,210	113,000	7,303
Occupations in administrative specializations	20,544	115,000	5,136
Occupations in education	18,685	80,000	4,671
Occupations in medicine and health	14,883	198,000	3,721
Occupations in mathematics and physical sciences	6,869	115,000	1,717
Occupations in life sciences	5,054	81,000	1,264
Managers and officials not elsewhere classified	4,284	143,000	1,071
Miscellaneous professional, technical, and managerial occupations	3,635	145,000	909

Table 5. (Continued)

Occupations	Total Visa Holders Reported	75th Salary Percentile	Total at or Above 75th Percentile
Occupations in social sciences	2,993	120,000	748
Occupations in art	1,982	88,000	496
Occupations in law and jurisprudence	947	188,000	237
Occupations in writing	345	84,000	86
Miscellaneous	265	69,000	66
Occupations in museum, library, and archival sciences	139	97,000	35
Occupations in entertainment and recreation	104	69,000	26
Occupations in religion and theology	61	66,000	15
Sale promotion occupations	7	78,000	2
Occupations unknown	1,075	100,000	269
Total	365,672	110,000	91,418

(This chart is drawn from USCIS' report, Characteristics of H-1B Specialty Occupation Workers.)

How Many H-4 Visa Holders Are Working in the United States?

Skilled workers with H-1B visas are authorized to work in the United States, but their spouses (who have "H-4" visas) do not receive work permits solely by virtue of being a dependent of a primary worker. In 2015, a new regulation made it possible for these spouses to apply for a work permit, during the typically years-long wait for their families to obtain permanent residency after receiving an approved green card petition.

Most of these H-4 workers are Indian, female, and highly educated.

Based on the most recent data provided by USCIS, a total of 120,514 H-4 visa holders successfully applied for a new work permit between May

26, 2015 (the effective date of the new regulation) and March 29, 2019. Not all of these individuals are necessarily employed at present, however.

OTHER ESTIMATES

DHS provides an annual estimate of the number of nonimmigrants residing in the United States, and its most recent estimate applies to Fiscal Year 2016:

Table 6. Number of nonimmigrants residing in the U.S. in FY 2016

Type of nonimmigrant	Number of residents
Temporary workers and trainees	1,100,000
Students	870,000
Exchange visitors	240,000

(Data drawn from DHS' March 2018 Population Estimates report.)

While these estimates are no doubt reliable, they are not fine-grained enough to help with the present task of estimating the impact of restricting a particular visa category. DHS includes a wide range of categories in "temporary workers" (including but not limited to H-1B, H-2B, H-4, L-1, and L-2), but not individuals with work permits under the Optional Practical Training program, who are lumped together with all other "students" on F-1 visas. "Exchange visitors" includes all J-1 and J-2 visa holders, with no distinction among the very different exchange programs (au pairs, summer workers, medical professionals, etc.).

Because of the difficulty in obtaining accurate statistics from government agencies, there are relatively few studies that attempt to provide an educated guess of how many temporary work visa holders are in the United States. The Economic Policy Institute (EPI) published one such study, summarized in Table 7 below.

Table 7. Estimated number of temporary foreign workers in the U.S. in FY 2013

Visa Category	Total number of workers
H-2A	74,859
H-2B	94,919
H-1B	460,749
J-1	215,866
J-2	8,243
L-1	311,257
L-2	38,952
O-1/O-2	29,894
F-1 (OPT)	139,155
TN	50,000
EPI Total	1,423,894

(Chart gleaned from EPI's 2017 report, Temporary Foreign Workers by the Numbers.)

With the caveat that EPI tends to be a vocal critic of temporary work visas, its methodology in this study is not unreasonable. A great deal has changed in immigration policy since 2013, however, so it is important to note that the numbers above likely do not reflect the reality today.

Conclusion

As outlined above, the Department of Homeland Security and the State Department do not provide sufficiently detailed data to determine precisely how many people would be affected by new restrictions on various temporary work visa programs. Depending on the details of the Trump administration's anticipated executive actions, however, the number of people directly affected could be in the hundreds of thousands.

APPENDIX A - RELEVANT REPORTS

Cato Institute

- The facts about the L-1 visa program - June 2020
- Facts about the summer work and travel program - May 2020
- The facts about Optional Practical Training (OPT) for foreign students - May 2020
- 100% of H-1B employers pay market wages - 78% pay more – May 2020
- Research provides no basis for pandemic travel bans - April 2020
- H-2A visas for agriculture: The complex process for farmers to hire agricultural guest workers - March 2020
- Temporary protected status and immigration to the United States - January 2019
- The political impact of immigration: Evidence from the United States - September 2018
- The association between immigration and labor market outcomes in the United States - January 2016

National Foundation for American Policy

- H-1B denial rates and numerical limits as indicators of current restrictions - May 2020
- The impact of H-1B visa holders on the U.S. workforce - May 2020
- State Department immigrant and temporary visa declines and refusals in FY2019 - March 2020
- H-1B approved petitions and denial rates for FY 2019 - February 2020
- The impact of Administration policies on immigration levels and labor force growth - February 2020

- International students, STEM OPT, and the U.S. STEM workforce - March 2019
- H-1B visas by the numbers: 2017-18 - April 2018
- International students and STEM OPT - October 2017

Niskanen Center

- Ten policy briefs to better understand the U.S. immigration system - September 2019
- Optional Practical Training (OPT) and international students after graduation - March 2019
- Niskanen immigration policy brief: H-2A temporary agricultural worker visas - January 2018
- Niskanen immigration policy brief: CONRAD 30 J-1 visa waiver program - July 2017
- Immigration reform catalog: 20 changes to improve U.S. immigration policy - May 2017
- Research paper: The legislative history of state-based guest worker programs - May 2017
- Niskanen report: Americans favor new immigrant workers - June 2015
- H-1Bs don't replace U.S. workers: Employment rises in top H-1B fields as H-1Bs enter - April 2015.

Pew Research Center

- Americans' immigration policy priorities: Divisions between - and within - the two parties - November 2019
- Far more immigration cases are being prosecuted criminally under Trump Administration - September 2019
- Facts on U.S. immigrants, 2017 - June 2019

- Key facts about U.S. immigration policies and proposed changes - May 2019
- Majority of Americans continue to say immigrants strengthen the U.S. - January 2019
- Majority of U.S. public supports high-skilled immigration - January 2019
- Number of foreign college graduates staying in U.S. to work climbed again in 2017, but growth has slowed - July 2018
- Number of foreign college students staying and working in U.S. after graduation surges - May 2018
- New foreign student enrollment at U.S. colleges and universities doubled since Great Recession - November 2017
- Salaries have risen for high-skilled foreign workers in U.S. on H-1B visas - August 2017
- Key facts about the U.S. H-1B visa program - April 2017

Summary of Economic Benefits of L-1, H-1B, OPT and H-4

- Business community letter with links to economic studies and statistics – May 2020.

In: Visas
Editor: Brian A. Shelton
ISBN: 978-1-53619-966-6

Chapter 5

THE H-2B VISA AND THE STATUTORY CAP*

Andorra Bruno

SUMMARY

The Immigration and Nationality Act (INA) of 1952, as amended, enumerates categories of foreign nationals, known as nonimmigrants, who are admitted to the United States for a temporary period of time and a specific purpose. One of these nonimmigrant visa categories— known as the H-2B visa—is for temporary nonagricultural workers.

The H-2B visa allows for the temporary admission of foreign workers to the United States to perform nonagricultural labor or services of a temporary nature if unemployed U.S. workers are not available. Common H-2B occupations include landscaping worker, housekeeper, and amusement park worker.

The H-2B program is administered by the U.S. Department of Homeland Security's (DHS's) U.S. Citizenship and Immigration Services (USCIS) and the U.S. Department of Labor's (DOL's) Employment and Training Administration. DOL's Wage and Hour Division also has certain concurrent enforcement responsibilities. The H-2B program operates mainly under regulations issued by DHS in 2008 on H-2B

* This is an edited, reformatted and augmented version of Congressional Research Service Publication No. R44306, updated February 26, 2020.

requirements, by DHS and DOL jointly in 2015 on H-2B wages, and by DHS and DOL jointly in 2015 and 2019 on H-2B employment.

Bringing workers into the United States under the H-2B program is a multiagency process involving DOL, DHS, and the Department of State (DOS). A prospective H-2B employer must apply to DOL for labor certification. Approval of a labor certification application reflects a finding by DOL that there are not sufficient U.S. workers who are qualified and available to perform the work and that the employment of foreign workers will not adversely affect the wages and working conditions of U.S. workers who are similarly employed.

If granted labor certification, an employer can file a petition with DHS to bring in the approved number of H-2B workers. If the petition is approved, a foreign worker overseas who the employer wants to employ can go to a U.S. embassy or consulate to apply for an H-2B nonimmigrant visa from DOS. If the visa application is approved, the worker is issued a visa that he or she can use to apply for admission to the United States at a port of entry. H-2B workers can be accompanied by eligible spouses and children.

H-2B Annual Numerical Limitations

By law, the H-2B visa is subject to an annual numerical cap. Under the INA, the total number of individuals who may be issued H-2B visas or otherwise provided with H-2B nonimmigrant status in any fiscal year may not exceed 66,000. USCIS is responsible for implementing the H-2B cap, which it does at the petition receipt stage. Spouses and children accompanying H-2B workers are not counted against the H-2B cap. In addition, certain categories of H-2B workers are exempt from the cap. Among these categories are current H-2B workers who are seeking an extension of stay, change of employer, or change in the terms of their employment.

Employer demand for H-2B workers has varied over the years. In recent years, demand has exceeded supply, and special provisions have been enacted to make additional H-2B visas available. For FY2016, a temporary statutory provision exempted certain H-2B workers from the cap. It applied to H-2B workers who had been counted against the cap in any one of the three prior fiscal years and would be returning as H-2B workers in FY2016. For FY2017, FY2018, FY2019, and FY2020, a different type of H-2B cap-related provision authorized DHS to issue additional H-2B visas (above the cap) subject to specified conditions.

INTRODUCTION

FY2020 is the fifth year in a row that Congress has enacted a special provision to allow for the issuance of H-2B visas beyond the annual statutory cap of 66,000 in response to high levels of employer demand for the visa. For FY2016, Congress exempted certain H-2B workers from the statutory cap. For the four most recent fiscal years (FY2017-FY2020), Congress has authorized the Department of Homeland Security (DHS) to make additional H-2B visas available subject to certain conditions. For FY2017 and FY2018, DHS used this authority to make an additional 15,000 H-2B visas available each year. For FY2019, DHS made an additional 30,000 H-2B visas available. As of the date of this chapter, DHS has not yet exercised this authority for FY2020.

H-2B NONAGRICULTURAL WORKER VISA

The Immigration and Nationality Act (INA) of 1952, as amended,[1] enumerates categories of aliens,[2] known as nonimmigrants, who are admitted to the United States for a temporary period of time and a specific purpose. Nonimmigrant visa categories are identified by letters and numbers, based on the sections of the INA that established them. Among the major nonimmigrant visa categories is the "H" category for temporary workers. Included in this category is the H-2B visa for temporary nonagricultural workers.[3]

---

[1] Act of June 27, 1952, ch. 477, codified at 8 U.S.C. §1101 *et seq.* The INA is the basis of current immigration law.

[2] *Alien* is the term used in the INA to describe any person who is not a U.S. citizen or national.

[3] INA §101(a)(15)(H)(ii)(b), 8 U.S.C. §1101(a)(15)(H)(ii)(b).

The H-2B program allows for the temporary admission of foreign workers to the United States to perform nonagricultural labor or services of a temporary nature if unemployed U.S. workers are not available. H-2B workers perform a wide variety of jobs. Top H-2B occupations in recent years have included landscaping worker, forest worker, housekeeper, amusement park worker, and meat cutter. By regulation, participation in the H-2B program is limited to designated countries, and DHS publishes a list of eligible countries each year.[4]

Bringing workers into the United States under the H-2B program is a multiagency process involving the U.S. Department of Labor (DOL), DHS, and the Department of State (DOS). The program itself is administered by DHS's U.S. Citizenship and Immigration Services (USCIS) and DOL's Employment and Training Administration (ETA). DOL's Wage and Hour Division (WHD) also has certain concurrent enforcement responsibilities. The H-2B program operates mainly under regulations issued by DHS in 2008 on H-2B requirements, by DHS and DOL jointly in 2015 on H-2B wages, and by DHS and DOL jointly in 2015 and 2019 on H-2B employment.[5]

For work to qualify as temporary under the H-2B visa, the employer's need for the duties to be performed by the worker must "end in the near, definable future" and must be a one-time occurrence, a seasonal need, a

[4] For 2020, nationals of 81 countries are eligible to participate in the H-2B program. For a list of these countries, see U.S. Department of Homeland Security, "Identification of Foreign Countries Whose Nationals Are Eligible To Participate in the H–2A and H–2B Nonimmigrant Worker Programs," 85 *Federal Register* 3067, January 17, 2020.

[5] U.S. Department of Homeland Security, "Changes to Requirements Affecting H-2B Nonimmigrants and Their Employers," 73 *Federal Register* 78104, December 19, 2008; U.S. Department of Homeland Security and U.S. Department of Labor, Employment and Training Administration, "Temporary Non-Agricultural Employment of H–2B Aliens in the United States," 80 *Federal Register* 24042-24144, April 29, 2015 (hereinafter cited as the 2015 DHS- DOL rule on H-2B employment); U.S. Department of Homeland Security and U.S. Department of Labor, Employment and Training Administration, Wage and Hour Division, "Modernizing Recruitment Requirements for the Temporary Employment of H–2B Foreign Workers in the United States," 84 *Federal Register* 62431- 62447, November 15, 2019; U.S. Department of Homeland Security and U.S. Department of Labor, Employment and Training Administration, "Wage Methodology for the Temporary Non-Agricultural Employment H–2B Program," 80 *Federal Register* 24146- 24190, April 29, 2015.

peak load need, or an intermittent need.[6] The employer's need for workers generally must be for a period of one year or less, but in the case of a one-time occurrence, can be for up to three years.

In order to bring H-2B workers into the United States, an employer must first receive labor certification from DOL. An interim final rule on H-2B employment that was issued jointly by DHS and DOL in April 2015 establishes a new registration requirement as a preliminary step in the labor certification process; once it is implemented, prospective H-2B employers would demonstrate their temporary need to DOL through this registration process before submitting a labor certification application. (As of the date of this chapter, however, DOL continues to make determinations about temporary need during the processing of labor certification applications.)[7]

At the same time that the employer submits the labor certification application to DOL, the employer must submit a job order to the state workforce agency (SWA) serving the area of intended employment. The job order is used to recruit U.S. workers. The employer also must conduct its own recruitment.

In order to grant labor certification to an employer, DOL must determine that (1) there are not sufficient U.S. workers who are qualified and available to perform the work, and (2) the employment of foreign workers will not adversely affect the wages and working conditions of U.S. workers who are similarly employed. To prevent an adverse effect on U.S. workers, H-2B employers must offer and provide required wages and benefits to H-2B workers and workers in corresponding employment.[8] H-2B employers must pay their workers the highest of the prevailing wage

---

[6] 8 C.F.R. §214.2(h)(6)(ii)(B).

[7] According to the supplementary information to the 2015 rule, a future "announcement in the Federal Register ... will provide the public with notice of when DOL will initiate the registration process." 2015 DHS-DOL rule on H-2B employment, p. 24052.

[8] *Corresponding employment* is defined in DOL regulations as "the employment of workers who are not H–2B workers by an employer that has a certified H–2B Application for Temporary Employment Certification when those workers are performing either substantially the same work included in the job order or substantially the same work performed by the H–2B workers," with exceptions for certain incumbent workers. 20 C.F.R. §655.5. Language included in DOL appropriations acts since FY2016 prohibits the use of funds to enforce this definition of corresponding employment. P.L. 114-113, Div. H, Title I, §113 (FY2016); P.L. 115-31, Div. H, Title I, §113 (FY2017); P.L. 115-141, Div. H, Title I, §113 (FY2018); P.L. 115-245, Div. B, Title I, §112 (FY2019); P.L. 116-94, Div. A, Title I, §111 (FY2020).

rate or the federal, state, or local minimum wage. They must provide a "three-fourths guarantee"; that is, they must guarantee to offer workers employment for at least three-fourths of the contract period.[9] H-2B employers also must pay worker visa fees and certain worker transportation costs. H-2B employers are not required to provide health insurance coverage.[10]

After receiving labor certification, a prospective H-2B employer can submit an application, known as a petition, to DHS to bring in foreign workers. If the foreign workers are already in the United States, the employer can request a change of status to H-2B status on the petition. In the typical case, however, the workers are abroad. If the petition is approved, they can visit a U.S. embassy or consulate to apply for H-2B nonimmigrant visas from DOS. If the visa applications are approved, the workers are issued visas that they can use to apply for admission to the United States at a port of entry. H-2B workers can be accompanied by eligible spouses and children, who are issued H-4 visas.[11]

An alien's total period of stay as an H-2B worker may not exceed three consecutive years. An H- 2B alien who has spent three years in the United States may not seek an extension of stay or be readmitted to the United States as an H-2B worker until he or she has been outside the country for at least three months.

The INA grants enforcement authority with respect to the H-2B program to DHS, but allows for the delegation of that authority to DOL.[12] DHS has delegated that authority to DOL, and now DOL's WHD has responsibility for enforcing compliance with the conditions of an H-2B petition and temporary labor certification.

---

[9] Language included in DOL appropriations acts since FY2016 prohibits the use of funds to enforce the three-fourths guarantee rule. P.L. 114-113, Div. H, Title I, §113 (FY2016); P.L. 115-31, Div. H, Title I, §113 (FY2017); P.L. 115- 141, Div. H, Title I, §113 (FY2018); P.L. 115-245, Div. B, Title I, §112 (FY2019); P.L. 116-94, Div. A, Title I, §111 (FY2020).

[10] H-2B workers, like nonimmigrants generally, are not eligible for federally funded public assistance, with the exception of Medicaid emergency services. See CRS Report RL33809, *Noncitizen Eligibility for Federal Public Assistance: Policy Overview*. Nonetheless, they may be eligible for coverage through a health insurance exchange. See archived CRS Report R43561, *Treatment of Noncitizens Under the Affordable Care Act*.

[11] H-4 visas are for the spouses and children of H-1B, H-1B-1, H-2A, H-2B, or H-3 visa holders.

[12] INA §214(c)(14), 8 U.S.C. §1184(c)(14).

Seafood Industry Staggered Entry Provision

As part of the labor certification process, prospective H-2B employers must indicate the starting and ending dates of their period of need for H-2B workers. According to the supplementary information to the 2015 DHS-DOL interim final rule on H-2B employment: "An application with an accurate date of need will be more likely to attract qualified U.S. workers to fill those open positions, especially when the employer conducts recruitment closer to the actual date of need."[13] If within a season an employer has more than one date of need for workers to perform the same job, the employer must file a separate labor certification application for each date of need. The employer is not allowed to stagger the entry of H-2B workers based on one date of need.

There is an exception to this prohibition on the staggered entry of H-2B workers, however, that applies to employers in the seafood industry. First enacted as part of the Consolidated Appropriations Act, 2014,[14] and subsequently incorporated into the 2015 DHS-DOL interim final rule on H-2B employment,[15] this provision permits an employer in the seafood industry with an approved H-2B petition to bring in the H-2B workers under that petition any time during the 120 days beginning on the employer's starting date of need. In order to bring in the workers between day 90 and day 120, though, the employer must conduct additional U.S. worker recruitment. This provision has been reenacted in DOL appropriations acts for each year from FY2015 through FY2020.[16]

---

[13] 2015 DHS-DOL rule on H-2B employment, p. 24060.

[14] P.L. 113-76, Div. H, Title I, §113.

[15] See 20 C.F.R. §655.15(f).

[16] P.L. 113-235, Div. G, Title I, §108 (FY15); P.L. 114-113, Div. H, Title I, §111 (FY2016); P.L. 115-31, Div. H, Title I, §111 (FY2017); P.L. 115-141, Div. H, Title I, §111 (FY2018); P.L. 115-245, Div. B, Title I, §110 (FY2019); P.L. 116-94, Div. A, Title I, §109 (FY2020).

NUMERICAL LIMITATIONS

The H-2B program is subject to an annual statutory numerical limit. Under the INA, as amended by the Immigration Act of 1990, the total number of aliens who may be issued H-2B visas or otherwise provided with H-2B nonimmigrant status in any fiscal year may not exceed 66,000.[17] Since FY2006 there also has been a cap of 33,000 on the number of aliens subject to H-2B numerical limits who may enter the United States on an H-2B visa or be granted H-2B status during the first six months of a fiscal year.[18] This INA amendment, enacted as part of the REAL ID Act of 2005, effectively divided the annual H-2B cap of 66,000 into two semiannual caps of 33,000, respectively covering work in the first and second halves of the fiscal year.[19]

The intent of the semiannual caps was to establish "a fair allocation of visas." As explained in introductory remarks on a related Senate bill that included this same provision: "We reserve half of the visas for the winter and half for the summer. Allocating visas ensures that, until a long-term solution is reached, all employers will have an equal chance of getting the workers that they need."[20] In practice, however, in times of high demand for H-2B workers, employers whose start dates of need fall late in a semiannual period may not have a chance to get workers. In a 2018 report, prepared in response to a congressional reporting requirement, DHS provided Congress with options to improve late season access to H-2B workers. Among the options presented were moving from semiannual to quarterly H-2B caps and giving preferential access to H-2B visas to employers in industries determined to be in the national interest.[21]

---

[17] INA §214(g)(1)(B), 8 U.S.C. §1184(g)(1)(B). The Immigration Act of 1990 is P.L. 101-649. Section 205(a) of that law established the H-2B cap of 66,000.

[18] INA §214(g)(10), 8 U.S.C. §1184(g)(10).

[19] The REAL ID Act of 2005 is Division B of P.L. 109-13. The provision establishing the 33,000 semiannual cap is Div. B, Title IV, §405. If the 33,000 cap is not reached for the first half of the fiscal year, the unused numbers are made available for the second half of the fiscal year.

[20] Senator Barbara Mikulski, introductory remarks in the Senate on the Save Our Small and Seasonal Businesses Act of 2005 (S. 352), *Congressional Record*, daily edition, vol. 151 (February 10, 2005), pp. S1280-S1281.

[21] U.S. Department of Homeland Security, *Options for Reforming the H-2B Visa Program and Improving Late Season Employers' Access to Workers*, June 7, 2019. The reporting

Not all categories of H-2B workers are subject to the statutory cap. Certain categories are exempt, including the following:

- current H-2B workers seeking an extension of stay, change of employer, or change in the terms of employment;
- H-2B workers previously counted toward the cap in the same fiscal year;
- fish roe processors, fish roe technicians, and/or supervisors of fish roe processing;[22] and
- H-2B workers performing labor in the U.S. territories of the Commonwealth of the Northern Mariana Islands (CNMI) and/or Guam until December 31, 2029.

As noted, spouses and children who are accompanying H-2B workers are issued H-4 visas and, as such, are not counted against the H-2B cap.

Special H-2B Cap-Related Provisions

Legislation is regularly introduced in Congress concerning the H-2B cap. In the 116th Congress, one such bill—the Labor, Health and Human Services, Education, Defense, State, Foreign Operations, and Energy and Water Development Appropriations Act, 2020 (H.R. 2740), as passed by the House—proposed to replace the current semiannual allocation of H-2B visas, as described above, with a type of quarterly allocation. In addition, in quarters in which requests for H-2B workers by employers (whose petitions met the requirements for approval) exceeded the availability of visas, H-2B visas would have been allocated proportionally among these employers.[23]

---

requirement can be found in U.S. Congress, House Committee on Appropriations, *Consolidated Appropriations Act, 2018*, committee print, 115th Cong., 2nd sess. (Washington: GPO, 2018), p. 996.

[22] P.L. 108-287, Title X, Chap. 4, §14006.

[23] In the language of the bill, in quarters with excess demand, "the Secretary [of DHS] shall ensure that each such petition is approved for a minimum number of visas, which shall be

Several measures have been enacted since 2005 to provide for the issuance of H-2B visas or granting of H-2B status beyond the statutory cap. The enacted provisions have been of two main types.

Returning Worker Exemption

The INA was amended during the 109th Congress to add a provision establishing a temporary exemption from the H-2B statutory cap for certain H-2B returning workers. The provision, initially in effect for FY2005 and FY2006, exempted from the cap H-2B returning workers who had been counted against the cap in any one of the three prior fiscal years.[24] This H-2B returning worker provision was subsequently extended for FY2007,[25] and expired at the end of that fiscal year.[26] An H-2B returning worker exemption of the same type was reinstated for FY2016. It provided that an H-2B returning worker who had been counted against the statutory cap in FY2013, FY2014, or FY2015 would not be counted again in FY2016.[27] Multiple bills were introduced in the 115th Congress to enact temporary or permanent H-2B returning worker exemptions from the statutory cap.[28] At least one H-2B returning worker bill has been introduced in the 116th Congress as of the date of this chapter.[29]

Provision Authorizing Additional H-2B Visas

For FY2017, FY2018 and FY2019, a different type of H-2B cap-related provision was enacted. For each of these years, provisions in year-end omnibus appropriations laws authorized DHS to make additional H-2B visas available beyond the statutory cap after consultation with DOL and

calculated based on the ratio between the total number of visas requested by such employers and the total number of visas available." H.R. 2740, Division A, Title V, §525, as passed by the House. Other H-2B cap-related bills introduced in the 116th Congress include H.R. 798, H.R. 2658, and S. 135.

[24] P.L. 109-13, Div. B, Title IV, §402.

[25] P.L. 109-364, Div. A, Title X, §1074.

[26] For a discussion of legislative efforts to reenact an H-2B returning worker exemption in the 110th Congress, see archived CRS Report RL34204, *Immigration Legislation and Issues in the 110th Congress* (available to congressional clients upon request).

[27] P.L. 114-113, Div. F, Title V, §565.

[28] There were a variety of proposals. See, for example, H.R. 1941, H.R. 2004, H.R. 4207, S. 792, and S. 3125, as introduced in the 115th Congress.

[29] See H.R. 798, as introduced in the 116th Congress.

"upon the determination that the needs of American businesses cannot be satisfied" with available U.S. workers. Under these provisions, the number of additional aliens who could receive H-2B visas each year was limited to "not more than the highest number of H–2B nonimmigrants who participated in the H–2B returning worker program in any fiscal year in which returning workers were exempt from such numerical limitation."[30] As discussed below, DHS and DOL jointly published final rules to implement the FY2017, FY2018, and FY2019 provisions.

The FY2020 Consolidated Appropriations Act, enacted on December 20, 2019, includes a provision of the same type for FY2020. Using the same language as its predecessors, the FY2020 provision authorizes DHS, after consultation with DOL and "upon the determination that the needs of American businesses cannot be satisfied" with available U.S. workers, to make additional H-2B visas available for FY2020 up to a maximum of "the highest number of H–2B nonimmigrants who participated in the H–2B returning worker program in any fiscal year in which returning workers were exempt from such numerical limitation."[31] As of the date of this chapter, DHS and DOL have not issued a rule implementing the FY2020 provision. For comparison purposes, there was a two- to three-month gap between the enactment of the FY2017, FY2018, and FY2019 statutory provisions and DHS issuance of the associated implementing rules.

FY2017 Provision

In July 2017, DHS and DOL jointly published a final rule to implement the FY2017 provision.[32] The rule temporarily amended DHS regulations on the H-2B visa to state that for FY2017, DHS "has authorized up to an additional 15,000 aliens who may receive H–2B

[30] P.L. 115-31, Div. F, Title V, §543 (FY2017); P.L. 115-141, Div. M, Title II, §205 (FY2018); P.L. 116-6, Div. H, Title I, §105 (FY2019).

[31] P.L. 116-94, Div. I, Title I, §105.

[32] U.S. Department of Homeland Security and U.S. Department of Labor, Employment and Training Administration, "Exercise of Time-Limited Authority To Increase the Fiscal Year 2017 Numerical Limitation for the H–2B Temporary Nonagricultural Worker Program," 82 *Federal Register* 32987, July 19, 2017.

nonimmigrant visas."[33] In the supplementary information to the rule, DHS explained that the statutory provision applied only to H-2B workers entering the United States on visas and not to aliens in the United States who were seeking a change of status to H-2B status.[34]

The statutory definition of the maximum authorized number (i.e., "the highest number of H–2B nonimmigrants who participated in the H–2B returning worker program in any fiscal year") can be interpreted in different ways, as DHS acknowledged in the supplementary information to the rule. However, the agency determined that 64,716 was the most appropriate maximum number of additional H-2B visas authorized under the special FY2017 provision, this being "the number of beneficiaries covered by H–2B returning worker petitions that were approved for FY 2007."[35]

The supplementary information to the rule included the following explanation for limiting the FY2017 numerical increase to 15,000:

> Most recently, in FY 2016, 18,090 returning workers were approved for H–2B petitions, despite Congress having reauthorized the returning worker program with more than three- quarters of the fiscal year remaining. Of those 18,090 workers authorized for admission, 13,382 were admitted into the United States or otherwise acquired H–2B status [T]he Secretary, in consideration of the statute's reference to returning workers, determined that it would be appropriate to use these recent figures as a basis for the maximum numerical limitation under section

[33] See 8 C.F.R. §214.2 (h)(6)(x)(A) (effective July 19, 2017, through September 30, 2017) in ibid. p. 32998.

[34] Ibid. p. 32989 (footnote 11).

[35] Ibid. p. 32988 (footnote 4). In the supplementary information to its subsequent rules implementing the FY2018 and FY2019 statutory provisions, DHS likewise maintained that 64,716 was the most appropriate maximum number of visas that it was authorized to make available. Others, however, take the position that 69,320 is the most appropriate maximum number authorized by the statutory language. This higher figure represents the number of visas issued to returning H-2B workers in FY2007, according to publicly available State Department data. See, for example, the comments of an executive in the landscaping industry in Janet H. Cho, "Area Employers Complain about Tightened Temp Visas," *Plain Dealer*, October 7, 2018, p. F1. State Department data on visa issuances to H-2B returning workers (available for FY2005-FY2007) can be found at https://travel.state.gov/content/dam/visas/Statistics/ FY09Annual Report_TableXVI_B.pdf.

543. This rule therefore authorizes up to 15,000 additional H–2B visas (rounded up from 13,382) for FY 2017.[36]

In addition, in implementing the statutory provision, DHS decided to limit eligibility for the additional H-2B workers to certain U.S. businesses. Under the FY2017 rule, the prospective H- 2B employer must submit to DHS, along with the H-2B petition, a new attestation form "evidencing that without the ability to employ all of the H–2B workers requested on the petition... its business is likely to suffer irreparable harm (that is, permanent and severe financial loss)."[37]

FY2018 Provision

In May 2018, DHS and DOL jointly published a final rule to implement the FY2018 H-2B cap- related provision.[38] The FY2018 rule, which is similar to the FY2017 rule, temporarily amended DHS H-2B regulations to state that for FY2018, DHS had authorized the issuance of up to 15,000 additional H–2B visas.[39] In supplementary information to the FY2018 rule, DHS explained its decision to authorize up to 15,000 additional visas despite the fact that all 15,000 additional visas authorized in FY2017 were not used.

Out of a maximum of 15,000 supplemental H–2B visas for FY 2017, a total of 12,294 beneficiaries were approved for H–2B classification [T]he Secretary has determined that it is appropriate to authorize 15,000 additional visas again, as employers will have a longer period in which to submit their petitions due to the earlier publication date of this rule, thereby

---

[36] Ibid. p. 32990.

[37] See 8 C.F.R. §214.2 (h)(6)(x)(B)(2) (effective July 19, 2017, through September 30, 2017) in ibid. p. 32998.

[38] U.S. Department of Homeland Security and U.S. Department of Labor, Employment and Training Administration, "Exercise of Time-Limited Authority To Increase the Fiscal Year 2018 Numerical Limitation for the H–2B Temporary Nonagricultural Worker Program," 83 *Federal Register* 24905, May 31, 2018.

[39] See temporary 8 C.F.R. §214.2 (h)(6)(x)(A) (effective May 31, 2018, through September 30, 2018) in ibid. p. 24917. In the supplementary information to the FY2018 rule, DHS explained that the statutory provision applied only to H-2B workers entering the United States on visas and not to aliens in the United States who were seeking a change of status to H-2B status. Ibid. p. 24908 (footnote 14).

allowing for the possibility of more petitions being filed this fiscal year than in FY 2017.[40]

The FY2018 rule also included the same language as the FY2017 rule requiring an employer petitioning for supplemental visas to submit an attestation along with the H-2B petition evidencing that without the ability to employ all the requested H–2B workers the employer's business would likely suffer irreparable harm.

FY2019 Provision

In May 2019, DHS and DOL jointly published a final rule to implement the FY2019 provision.[41] The FY2019 rule temporarily amended DHS H-2B regulations to state that for FY2019, DHS has authorized the issuance of up to 30,000 additional H–2B visas.[42] As it did in the supplementary information to the FY2017 and FY2018 rules, DHS clarified in the supplementary information to this rule that the FY2019 provision only authorized DHS to increase the number of H-2B visas; it did not cover individuals in the United States changing to H-2B status.[43]

The supplementary information to the FY2019 rule, consistent with the supplementary information to the FY2017 and FY2018 rules, indicated that the most appropriate maximum number of additional H-2B visas authorized under the statutory provision was 64,716.[44] DHS explained its decision to allow 30,000 supplemental visas as follows:

> In setting the number of additional H–2B visas to be made available during FY 2019, DHS considered this number [i.e., 64,716], overall indications of increased need, and the time remaining in FY 2019, and

---

[40] Ibid. p. 24908.

[41] U.S. Department of Homeland Security and U.S. Department of Labor, Employment and Training Administration, "Exercise of Time-Limited Authority To Increase the Fiscal Year 2019 Numerical Limitation for the H–2B Temporary Nonagricultural Worker Program," 84 *Federal Register* 20005, May 8, 2019.

[42] See 8 C.F.R. §214.2 (h)(6)(x)(B)(*2*)(*ii*)) (effective May 8, 2019, through September 30, 2019) in ibid. p. 20020.

[43] DHS stated in the supplementary information that the supplemental cap was limited to workers who obtained visas abroad and then sought admission to the United States. See ibid. p. 20009 (footnote 17).

[44] The supplementary information to the FY2019 rule states, "The highest number of H–2B returning workers approved was 64,716 in FY2007." Ibid. p. 20009.

> determined that it would be appropriate to limit the supplemental cap to approximately half of the highest number for returning workers, or up to 30,000.[45]

Like its FY2017 and FY2018 predecessors, the FY2019 rule required an employer petitioning for supplemental visas to submit an attestation along with the H-2B petition evidencing that without the ability to employ all the requested H–2B workers the employer's business would likely suffer irreparable harm.

In addition, the FY2019 rule imposed a limitation not applicable under the FY2017 and FY2018 rules. Under the FY2019 rule, an employer could request supplemental visas only for H-2B workers "who have been issued an H–2B visa or otherwise granted H–2B status in Fiscal Years 2016, 2017, or 2018."[46] DHS offered the following rationale for limiting the additional visas to H-2B returning workers:

> Such workers (i.e., those who recently participated in the H–2B program) have previously obtained H– 2B visas and therefore been vetted by DOS, would have departed the United States after their authorized period of stay as generally required by the terms of their nonimmigrant admission, and therefore may obtain their new visas through DOS and begin work more expeditiously.[47]

The supplementary information to the rule highlighted the importance, in particular, of returning workers' proven "willingness to return home after they have completed their temporary labor or services or their period of authorized stay."[48] It stated:

> The returning workers condition therefore provides a basis to believe that H–2B workers under this cap increase will likely return home again

[45] Ibid. p. 20009.
[46] See 8 C.F.R. §214.2 (h)(6)(x)(B)(*2*)(*ii*)) (effective May 8, 2019, through September 30, 2019) in ibid. p. 20020. This language does not require the workers to have been counted against the H-2B cap in any of the three years, unlike the previous statutory returning worker provisions (see "Returning Worker Exemption"). See ibid. p. 20007 (footnote 11).
[47] Ibid. p. 20008.
[48] Ibid.

after another temporary stay in the United States. That same basis does not exist for non-returning workers, not all of whom have a track record of returning home. Although the returning worker requirement limits the flexibility of employers, the requirement provides an important safeguard, which DHS deems paramount.[49]

Implementation of H-2B Numerical Limits

USCIS is responsible for implementing numerical limits on temporary worker visas (including the H-2B visa), which it does at the petition receipt stage. Under DHS regulations:

> When calculating the numerical limitations ... USCIS will make numbers available to petitions in the order in which the petitions are filed. USCIS will make projections of the number of petitions necessary to achieve the numerical limit of approvals, taking into account historical data related to approvals, denials, revocations, and other relevant factors. USCIS will monitor the number of petitions (including the number of beneficiaries requested when necessary) received and will notify the public of the date that USCIS has received the necessary number of petitions (the "final receipt date") If the final receipt date is any of the first five business days on which petitions subject to the applicable numerical limit may be received (i.e., if the numerical limit is reached on any one of the first five business days that filings can be made), USCIS will randomly apply all of the numbers among the petitions received on any of those five business days.[50]

In one recent fiscal year, the final receipt date announced by USCIS ended up being too early. For FY2015, USCIS announced on April 2,

---

[49] Ibid.

[50] 8 C.F.R. §214.2(h)(8)(ii)(B). For a discussion of USCIS implementation of the H-2B cap over the years, see U.S. Department of Homeland Security, U.S. Citizenship and Immigration Services, *H-2B Usage and Recommendations*, Fiscal Year 2016 Report to Congress, July 22, 2016, https://www.dhs.gov/sites/default/files/publications/U.S.%20Citizenship%20and%20Immigration%20Services%20-%20H-2B%20Usage%20and%20Recommendations.pdf.

2015, that March 26, 2015, was the final receipt date for new H-2B petitions. The agency had accepted about 3,900 H-2B petitions for FY2015 through March 26, 2015, which it believed to be sufficient to reach the annual 66,000 cap. In early June 2015, however, USCIS announced that it would reopen the H-2B cap for the second half of FY2015 and accept additional petitions for new H-2B workers. It offered the following public explanation:

> USCIS continues to work in collaboration with DOS to monitor the issuance of H-2B visas and has determined that as of June 5, 2015, DOS received fewer than the expected number of requests for H-2B visas. A recent analysis of DOS H-2B visa issuance and USCIS petition data reveals that the number of actual H-2B visas issued by DOS is substantially less than the number of H-2B beneficiaries seeking consular notification listed on cap- subject H-2B petitions approved by USCIS. In light of this new information, USCIS has determined that there are still available H-2B visa numbers remaining for the second half of the FY15 cap.[51]

Following a brief reopening, USCIS announced that June 11, 2015, was the final receipt date for new H-2B worker petitions for FY2015.

Since FY2015, the semiannual cap of 33,000 has been reached in each half of the fiscal year.

Employer demand has been particularly strong for H-2B visas for the second half of the fiscal year (for employment beginning April 1 to September 30), with the final receipt date for new H- 2B worker petitions falling in March in FY2017[52] and in February in FY2018, FY2019, and FY2020.[53] Since FY2018, in particular, the scale of employer requests for

---

[51] U.S. Department of Homeland Security, U.S. Citizenship and Immigration Services, archived content, "USCIS to Reopen H-2B Cap for the Second Half of Fiscal Year 2015," news alert, June 5, 2015, http://www.uscis.gov/news/alerts/uscis-reopen-h-2b-cap-second-half-fiscal-year-2015.

[52] U.S. Department of Homeland Security, U.S. Citizenship and Immigration Services, "USCIS Reaches the H-2B Cap for Fiscal Year 2017," news alert, March 16, 2017, https://www.uscis.gov/news/alerts/uscis-reaches-h-2b-cap-fiscal- year-2017.

[53] U.S. Department of Homeland Security, "DHS Announces Additional Visas for Foreign Workers to Assist American Businesses at Risk of Failing," press release, May 31, 2018,

H-2B workers has triggered DOL and DHS to implement special procedures.

FY2018

Until FY2018, the final receipt date for H-2B petitions had never fallen within the first five days of filing and, thus, the random selection process (lottery) described in the DHS regulatory provision in the preceding section had never been required.[54] That changed with petition filings by employers seeking to hire H-2B workers for the second half of FY2018, which began on April 1, 2018. DOL was also impacted by the high level of employer demand for H-2B workers for the second half of FY2018 since an employer must receive labor certification from DOL before filing an H-2B petition.

DOL Labor Certification Applications

In accordance with H-2B regulations, January 1, 2018, was the first date that employers could submit H-2B temporary labor certifications to DOL requesting a work start date of April 1, 2018. On January 1, 2018, DOL received about 4,498 applications requesting an April 1, 2018, start date; those applications covered 81,008 workers. In response, DOL announced a process change.

It indicated in a Federal Register notice that it would not begin releasing certified H–2B applications, which employers need in order to petition USCIS for H-2B workers (see "H-2B Nonagricultural Worker Visa"), until February 20, 2018, and on that date, it would issue such

---

https://www.dhs.gov/news/2018/05/31/dhs-announces- additional-visas-foreign-workers-assist-american-businesses-risk; U.S. Department of Homeland Security, U.S. Citizenship and Immigration Services, "H-2B Cap Reached for FY 2019," news alert, February 22, 2019, https://www.uscis.gov/news/alerts/h-2b-cap-reached-fy-2019; U.S. Department of Homeland Security, U.S. Citizenship and Immigration Services, "H-2B Cap Reached for Second Half of FY2020," news alert, February 26, 2020, https://www.uscis.gov/news/alerts/h-2b-cap-reached-second-half-fy2020.

[54] By contrast, lotteries have been regularly held under the separate H-1B visa for professional specialty workers. For information about the H-1B visa, see CRS Report R43735, *Temporary Professional, Managerial, and Skilled Foreign Workers: Policy and Trends*.

certified applications in order of receipt.[55] DOL offered the following explanation for adopting this procedure:

> This process change will allow employers who filed promptly on January 1, 2018, sufficient time to meet regulatory requirements, including the recruitment and hiring of qualified and available U.S. workers, thus preserving the sequential order of filing that took place on January 1, 2018, to the extent possible.[56]

DHS Petitions

On March 1, 2018, USCIS announced that in the first five business days of accepting H-2B petitions for the second half of FY2018, it had received petitions requesting about 47,000 cap- subject H-2B workers, more than could be accommodated under the 33,000 limitation for the second half of FY2018. It further reported that it had conducted a lottery on February 28, 2018, to randomly select a sufficient number of these petitions to meet the statutory cap.[57]

As discussed, on May 31, 2018, USCIS published a final rule authorizing the issuance of up to 15,000 additional H–2B visas for FY2018. In the first five business days of accepting petitions under this supplemental cap, USCIS received petitions for more beneficiaries than the number of H-2B visas available. As a result, it conducted a second FY2018 H-2B lottery on June 7, 2018, to randomly select a sufficient number of petitions to meet the supplemental cap.[58]

---

[55] U.S. Department of Labor, Employment and Training Administration, "Labor Certification Process for the Temporary Employment of Aliens in Non-Agricultural Employment in the United States," 83 *Federal Register* 3189, January 23, 2018.

[56] Ibid. p. 3190.

[57] U.S. Department of Homeland Security, U.S. Citizenship and Immigration Services, "USCIS Completes Random Selection Process for H-2B Visa Cap for Second Half of FY 2018," news release, March 1, 2018, https://www.uscis.gov/news/news-releases/uscis-completes-random-selection-process-h-2b-visa-cap-second-half-fy- 2018-0.

[58] U.S. Department of Homeland Security, U.S. Citizenship and Immigration Services, "USCIS Completes Lottery for Temporary Increase in FY 2018 H-2B Cap," news alert, June 11, 2018, https://www.uscis.gov/news/alerts/uscis-completes-lottery-temporary-increase-fy-2018-h-2b-cap.

FY2019

Employer demand for H-2B workers for the second half of FY2019 reached new heights.

DOL Labor Certification Applications

January 1, 2019, was the first day that employers could file H-2B labor certification applications for the second half of FY2019. On January 2, 2019, DOL announced that due to high demand its iCERT online application filing system had "experienced a system disruption" on January 1, 2019, that prevented some employers from submitting their H-2B certification applications: "Within the first five minutes of opening the semi-annual H-2B certification process on January 1, 2019, the U.S. Department of Labor iCERT system had an unprecedented demand for H-2B certifications with more than 97,800 workers requested in pending applications for the 33,000 available visas."[59] When the system re-opened on January 7, 2019, it "handled the submission of approximately 4,749 H-2B applications covering more than 87,900 workers positions for an April 1, 2019, start date of work within the first one hour of operation."[60] This experience led DOL to announce additional process changes for FY2020, as described below.

DHS Petitions

On February 19, 2019, the first day of accepting H-2B petitions for the second half of FY2019, USCIS announced that it had received petitions for more H-2B workers than there were remaining H-2B numbers under the

---

[59] U.S. Department of Labor, Employment and Training Administration, Office of Foreign Labor Certification, Announcements, "January 2, 2019. Important Announcement Regarding the Availability of the iCERT System for H- 2B Program Filings," https://www.foreign laborcert.doleta.gov/.

[60] U.S. Department of Labor, Employment and Training Administration, Office of Foreign Labor Certification, Announcements, "January 7, 2019. OFLC Issues Status Update on the iCERT System," https://www.foreignlaborcert.doleta.gov/.

FY2019 cap. On February 21, 2019, USCIS conducted a lottery to randomly select a sufficient number of petitions to meet the cap.[61]

FY2020

DOL implemented new processing procedures for FY2020 in anticipation of continued high numbers of H-2B labor certification application submissions.

DOL Labor Certification Applications

In February 2019, in light of its experience with H-2B submissions in January 2019 and the resulting unanticipated "burdens" placed on "its electronic filing system, network infrastructure, and staff resources," DOL announced new H-2B temporary labor certification application processing changes for FY2020.[62] It indicated that beginning with H-2B certification applications for the first half of FY2020, it would randomly order and assign for processing all applications submitted within designated groups. The first group would consist of applications requesting the earliest start date of work (e.g., October 1, 2019, for the first half of FY2020) and filed during the first three calendar days of the filing period (which begins on July 3, 2019, for the first half of FY2020). DOL maintained that this new process "balances employers' interest in utilizing the H- 2B program with OFLC's [DOL's Office of Foreign Labor Certification's] interest in ensuring that access to its filing system is equitable and occurs with no user disruption."[63]

These new DOL procedures took effect on July 3, 2019, the earliest filing date for the first half of FY2020. In the first three filing days, DOL received 493 H-2B labor certification applications requesting a work start date of October 1, 2019. These applications covered 12,098 worker

---

[61] U.S. Department of Homeland Security, U.S. Citizenship and Immigration Services, "H-2B Cap Reached for FY 2019," news alert, February 22, 2019, https://www.uscis.gov/news/alerts/h-2b-cap-reached-fy-2019.

[62] U.S. Department of Labor, Employment and Training Administration, "Selection Procedures for Reviewing Applications Filed by Employers Seeking Temporary Employment of H-2B Foreign Workers in the United States," 84 *Federal Register* 7399, 7401, March 4, 2019.

[63] Ibid. pp. 7401-7402.

positions, less than the 33,000 semiannual H-2B allotment for the first half of FY2020. DOL assigned all the applications to Group A for processing.[64]

During the first three filing days for the second half of FY2020 (January 2-4, 2020), DOL received 5,677 H-2B labor certification applications requesting the earliest work start date of April 1, 2020. These applications covered 99,362 worker positions. DOL randomly assigned these applications to assignment groups in accordance with its new procedures. It reported that Group A included a sufficient number of workers to reach the 33,000 allotment for the second half of FY2020. It also indicated that it had randomly assigned the remaining applications to four other groups (Groups B-E), each including no more than 20,000 worker positions.[65] DOL has published a list of all the H-2B labor certification applications requesting a work start date of April 1, 2020, that were submitted January 2-4, 2020, with their group assignments.[66]

DHS Petitions

USCIS announced that as of February 18, 2020, it had received petitions for more H-2B workers than there were remaining H-2B numbers under the FY2020 cap. On February 20, 2020, the agency conducted a lottery to randomly select a sufficient number of petitions to meet the cap.[67]

---

[64] U.S. Department of Labor, Employment and Training Administration, Office of Foreign Labor Certification, Announcements, "July 15, 2019. OFLC Announces List of Randomized H-2B Applications Submitted July 3-5 for Employers Seeking H-2B Workers Starting October 1, 2019," https://www.foreignlaborcert.doleta.gov/.

[65] U.S. Department of Labor, Employment and Training Administration, Office of Foreign Labor Certification, Announcements, "January 6, 2020. OFLC Conducts Randomization Process on H-2B Applications Requesting an April 1, 2020, Work Start Date," and "January 8, 2020. OFLC Publishes List of Randomized H-2B Applications Submitted January 2-4 for Employers Seeking H-2B Workers Starting April 1, 2020," both available at https://www.foreignlaborcert.doleta.gov/.

[66] The list, which is in alphabetical order by employer name and includes the worksite state, can be found at https://foreignlaborcert.doleta.gov/pdf/Disclosure%20of%20H- 2B%20Applications%20Group%20Assignment%201.8.2020.pdf.

[67] U.S. Department of Homeland Security, U.S. Citizenship and Immigration Services, "H-2B Cap Reached for Second Half of FY2020," news alert, February 26, 2020, https://www.uscis.gov/news/alerts/h-2b-cap-reached-second-half- fy2020.

Data on Grants of H-2B Status

In any year, most, but not all, foreign nationals who obtain H-2B status acquire that status through admission to the United States on H-2B visas. Those who obtain H-2B status but are not issued visas include H-2B workers who are admitted to the United States without visas (mostly Canadians) and individuals who change to H-2B status while in the United States.[68] Regarding the latter category, USCIS data show that between FY2009 and FY2018, the number of individuals who were approved for a change to H-2B status ranged from about 110 (in FY2017) to about 470 (in FY2010).[69]

H-2B Visa Issuances

Figure 1 provides data on H-2B visa issuances from FY1992 through FY2018. These data offer one way to measure the growth of the H-2B program over the years. As explained above, the visa application and issuance process occurs after DOL has granted labor certification and DHS has approved the visa petition.

As illustrated in Figure 1, the number of H-2B visas issued generally increased from FY1992 until FY2007, when H-2B visa issuances reached a highpoint of 129,547 (see the Appendix for yearly visa issuance data). H-2B visa issuances fell after FY2007 with the start of the economic recession, but, as shown in Figure 1, have generally been increasing since FY2009.

---

[68] Individuals in these categories are counted against the H-2B cap. Note, however, that a Canadian H-2B worker admitted without a visa may cross the U.S. border multiple times while working for an employer on the basis of an H- 2B petition, but is only counted against the H-2B cap on the first U.S. admission.

[69] U.S. Department of Homeland Security, U.S. Citizenship and Immigration Services, *Characteristics of H-2B Nonagricultural Temporary Workers …*, FY2009-FY2018; U.S. Department of Homeland Security, U.S. Citizenship and Immigration Services, *H-2B Nonagricultural Temporary Worker Visa and Status …*, FY2009-FY2017. Reports available from USCIS at https://www.uscis.gov/tools/reports-studies/reports-and-studies.

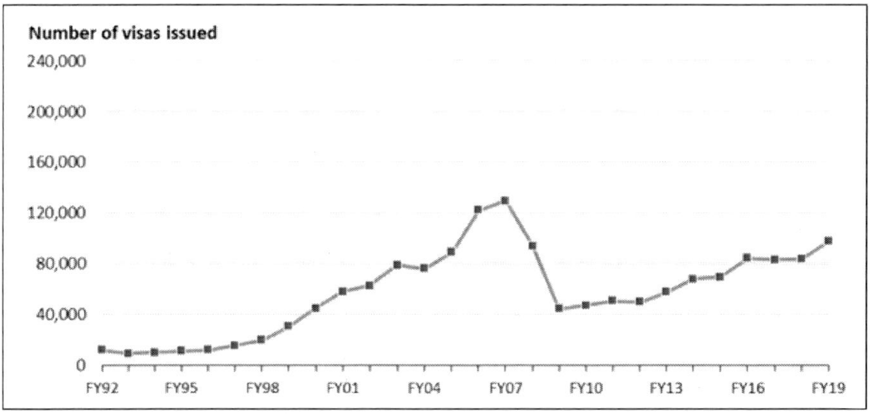

Source: CRS presentation of data from U.S. Department of State, Bureau of Consular Affairs.

Figure 1. H-2B Visas Issued, FY1992-FY2019.

In FY2005-FY2007 and FY2016-FY2019, as discussed, temporary provisions established exceptions to the statutory annual cap of 66,000. In some other years in which visa issuances surpassed 66,000, it seems reasonable to assume that the H-2B cap was exceeded given the magnitude of the numbers.[70]

Conclusion

With employer demand for H-2B visas exceeding supply, H-2B admissions and the statutory cap are once again receiving attention from policymakers. While previous Congresses considered broad immigration reform bills that included proposals for new temporary worker programs to address any perceived shortfalls in the supply of foreign workers, any legislative efforts to address the numerical limitations on nonagricultural guest workers in the near term seem likely to be focused on the existing H-2B program.

[70] It should be noted, however, that for various reasons not all visas issued during a fiscal year necessarily count against that year's cap or, in some cases, any year's cap.

Appendix. H-2B Visa Issuances

Table A-1. Number of H-2B visas issued, FY1992-FY2019

Fiscal Year	H-2B Visas Issued
1992	12,552
1993	9,691
1994	10,400
1995	11,737
1996	12,200
1997	15,706
1998	20,192
1999	30,642
2000	45,037
2001	58,215
2002	62,591
2003	78,955
2004	76,169
2005	89,135
2006	122,541
2007	129,547
2008	94,304
2009	44,847
2010	47,403
2011	50,826
2012	50,009
2013	57,600
2014	68,102
2015	69,684
2016	84,627
2017	83,600
2018	83,774
2019	97,623

Source: CRS presentation of data from U.S. Department of State, Bureau of Consular Affairs.

Note: For various reasons, not all visas issued during a fiscal year necessarily count against that year's cap or, in some cases, any year's cap.

In: Visas
Editor: Brian A. Shelton

ISBN: 978-1-53619-966-6

Chapter 6

EB-5 Immigrant Investor Visa*

Holly Straut-Eppsteiner

Summary

Under the Immigration and Nationality Act (INA), there are five categories of employment-based visas in the permanent immigration system. The EB-5 immigrant investor visa, the fifth employment preference immigrant visa category, was created in 1990 to benefit the U.S. economy through job creation and foreign capital investment. It provides lawful permanent residence (LPR status) to foreign nationals who invest $1,800,000 or more, or $900,000 or more in a rural area or an area with high unemployment (referred to as targeted employment areas [TEAs]), in a new commercial enterprise (NCE) in the United States and create or preserve at least 10 jobs. Approximately 10,000 visas annually, 7.1% of all employment-based visas, are allotted to immigrant investors and their family members. The majority (80% in FY2019) of EB- 5 visas are issued to investors from Asia, with 46% issued to Chinese-origin investors in FY2019.

The EB-5 visa grants foreign national investors conditional residence status. After approximately two years, the foreign national must apply to

* This is an edited, reformatted and augmented version of Congressional Research Service Publication No. R44475, Updated January 26, 2021.

remove the conditionality (i.e., adjust to full-LPR status). If the foreign national has met the visa requirements (i.e., invested the required money and created the required jobs), he/she will receive full LPR status. If the foreign national has not met the requirements or does not apply to have the conditional LPR status removed, his or her conditional status is terminated, and, generally, the foreign national is required to leave the United States, or will be placed in removal proceedings.

In 1992, Congress established the Regional Center (Pilot) Program, which created an additional pathway in the EB-5 visa category. Regional centers are "any economic unit, public or private, which [are] involved with the promotion of economic growth, including increased export sales, improved regional productivity, job creation, and increased domestic capital investment." The program allows investors to pool their investment in a regional center to fund a project in a specific geographic area. The Regional Center Program now accounts for nearly all EB-5 visas (96% in FY2019). Unlike the standard EB-5 visa category, which does not expire, funding for the Regional Center Program requires reauthorization. In recent years, funding has been appropriated through a series of continuing resolutions.

A 2019 Department of Homeland Security (DHS) regulation implemented major changes to the EB-5 program, including increases to the minimum investment amounts, changes to the TEA designation process, and allowing petitioners to retain the priority dates of approved EB-5 petitions for subsequent EB-5 petitions. These changes addressed some longstanding concerns about the EB-5 program. Nevertheless, the EB-5 visa continues to be the subject of ongoing policy debates. Proponents contend that providing visas to foreign investors benefits the U.S. economy through economic growth and job creation. Opponents argue that the visa allows wealthy individuals to buy their way into the United States and have highlighted instances of fraud and threats to national security associated with the EB-5 program. Some have moved to eliminate it entirely.

Compared with other immigrant visas, the EB-5 visa presents additional risks of fraud. Such risks are associated with difficulty verifying that investors' funds are obtained lawfully and with the visa's potential for large monetary gains, which could motivate individuals to take advantage of investors and make the visa susceptible to the appearance of favoritism. U.S. Citizenship and Immigration Services (USCIS) has reported improvements in fraud detection but also states it is restricted by statutory limitations. EB-5 stakeholders have voiced concerns over the delays in processing EB-5 applications and possible effects on investors and time sensitive projects as well as uncertainty generated by the short-term reauthorizations of the Regional Center Program, the most common pathway for EB-5 visas.

OVERVIEW

The EB-5 Immigrant Investor Program was created through the Immigration Act of 1990 (P.L. 101-649) and is administered by the Immigrant Investor Program Office (IPO) within U.S. Citizenship and Immigration Services (USCIS). "EB-5" is the fifth of five permanent, employment-based (EB) visa preference categories under the Immigration and Nationality Act (INA).[1] Congress created the EB-5 visa category to attract new foreign capital investment to the United States and generate employment.[2] The program provides individual foreign national investors and their derivatives (i.e., family members)[3] lawful permanent residence (LPR status)[4] in the United States when they invest a specified amount of capital in a new commercial enterprise (NCE) that creates at least 10 jobs.[5]

In general, individuals receiving EB-5 visas are granted a conditional residence status. After approximately two years, they must apply to remove the conditionality from their residency status. If they have met the visa requirements (i.e., invested and sustained the required money and created the required jobs), they receive full LPR status. If a foreign national investor has not met the requirements or does not apply to have the conditional status removed, his or her conditional LPR status is terminated, and, generally, the foreign national is required to leave the United States, or will be placed in removal proceedings.

Some Members of Congress contended during discussions around the creation of the visa that potential immigrants would be "buying their way in" to the United States. Others maintained that the program's

---

[1] Immigration and Nationality Act (INA) §203(b)(5). For more on the employment preference immigration system, see CRS Report R42866, *Permanent Legal Immigration to the United States: Policy Overview*.

[2] See INA §203(b)(5); 8 U.S.C. §1153(b)(5).

[3] Spouses and children who accompany or later follow qualifying or principal immigrants are referred to as derivative immigrants. For the purposes of EB-5, a derivative refers to spouses and unmarried children less than 21 years of age.

[4] An LPR is a foreign national who has been admitted to live permanently in the United States and possibly to become a citizen when those requirements are met.

[5] Under certain circumstances, the preservation of existing jobs can count towards the job creation. 8 C.F.R. 204.6(j)(4)(ii).

requirements would protect its integrity.[6] The Senate Judiciary Committee report on the originating legislation stated that it "is intended to provide new employment for U.S. workers and to infuse new capital into the country, not to provide immigrant visas to wealthy individuals."[7]

In 1992, Congress created the Regional Center Program,[8] an additional pathway for foreign national investors to obtain an EB-5 visa. By investing through a regional center, foreign national investors are subject to different requirements pertaining to the measure of job creation, and are unlikely to be involved in the management of the commercial enterprise. Unlike the standard EB- 5 visa category, which does not expire, the Regional Center Program is temporary and is currently authorized through June 30, 2021. Although it is temporary, the Regional Center Program has become the primary pathway for EB-5 investors since 2008 and now accounts for nearly all EB-5 investments.

Typically, there are 140,000 total employment-based visas made available each fiscal year, with 7.1% of that total (approximately 10,000) allocated to EB-5 investors and their derivatives.

However, 261,500 employment-based visas have been allocated for FY2021[9]—an all-time high[10]—18,567 of which would be allocated to EB-5. Of the EB-5 visas, Congress has specifically allocated 3,000 visas for entrepreneurs investing in targeted employment areas (TEA) and 3,000 for those participating in the Regional Center Program each year.[11]

A 2019 Department of Homeland Security (DHS) federal regulation made the most substantive modifications to the EB-5 program since the Regional Center Program was introduced. The EB-5 Immigrant Investor Program Modernization regulation made three major changes to the

---

[6] For debate on this issue, see 136 *Congressional Record* S7768-75 (July 12, 1990).

[7] S.Rept.101-55, p. 21.

[8] As enacted in 1992 (P.L. 102-395 §610), the program was known as the Regional Center Pilot Program. In recent reauthorizations, it has been referred to as the Regional Center Program.

[9] U.S. Department of State, *Visa Bulletin for October 2020*, https://travel.state.gov/content/dam/visas/Bulletins/ visabulletin october2020.pdf.

[10] This surplus is the result of unused family-based visas in 2020, which, under the INA, are reallocated to the employment preference category in the next fiscal year.

[11] INA §203(b)(5) and §203 note. Note that a regional center's defined area may be in a TEA, so the set asides are not mutually exclusive.

program (also see the "EB-5 Immigrant Investor Program Modernization" section):

1. For the first time, DHS increased the minimum required investment amounts for EB-5 projects, which had been unchanged since 1990, from $1,000,000 to $1,800,000 for non-TEA projects and from $500,000 to $900,000 for investments in TEAs. In addition, the regulation sets a schedule for adjustments for inflation every five years, starting from the November 21, 2019 effective date.
2. The regulation changed the process by which TEAs are determined, making DHS exclusively responsible for determining which geographies may qualify as high unemployment areas and removing states' authority to do so.
3. The regulation allows petitioners to retain the priority dates of EB-5 petitions approved for classification for subsequent EB-5 petitions.[12]

Some of these changes—particularly, the first two—have been met with objection from industry stakeholders.[13]

Although this recent federal regulatory action has addressed some of the concerns about the EB-5 program, there are additional concerns that Congress may consider. For example, some Members have frequently raised concerns about fraud in the program,[14] including possible national security concerns.[15] Thus, Congress may choose to evaluate the oversight of the EB-5 category and the fraud detection mechanisms used during EB-

[12] Department of Homeland Security, "EB-5 Immigrant Investor Program Modernization," 84 *Federal Register* 35750, July 24, 2019.

[13] Ibid.

[14] U.S. Government Accountability Office (GAO), *Immigrant Investor Program: Additional Actions Needed to Better Assess Fraud Risks and Report Economic Benefits*, GAO-15-696, August 2015.

[15] Prepared Statement by Senator Chuck Grassley, Senate Judiciary Committee Chairman, in U.S. Congress, Senate Committee on the Judiciary, *Citizenship for Sale: Oversight of the EB-5 Investor Visa Program,* hearing, 115th Cong., 2nd sess., June 19, 2018. https://www.judiciary.senate.gov/grassley-statement-at-hearing-on-citizenship-for-sale- oversight-of-the-eb-5-investor-visa-program.

5 adjudications, and the authority delegated to USCIS to sanction or terminate regional centers based on evidence of fraud or national security risks.

The temporary nature of the Regional Center Program has also been a concern among lawmakers and stakeholders. The program has been by far the most common pathway for investors obtaining EB-5 visas for more than a decade. Nevertheless, it is technically a pilot program that must be periodically reauthorized by Congress, leading to uncertainty and unpredictability (currently, the program is authorized through June 30, 2021). Other issues include processing delays and the need for more data collection.

This chapter begins with a discussion of the EB-5 visa's requirements and an overview of the Regional Center Program. It then provides information on the EB-5 application (petition) process, admissions, economic impacts of the visa, and summarizes the EB-5 Immigrant Investor Program Modernization regulation. Next, the report reviews policy issues surrounding the visa and the Regional Center Program, including application processing, fraud and security risks, data collection, and implications of the Coronavirus Disease 2019 (COVID-19) pandemic. As of the date of this chapter, aside from reauthorization of the Regional Center Program, Congress has not passed legislation related to the EB-5 program. At the conclusion of the report, the Appendix provides tables of acronyms and forms referenced throughout the report.

EB-5 Investor Program Requirements

EB-5 visa requirements for foreign investors include the investment of capital into a new commercial enterprise and resulting job creation. Currently, investors have two available pathways to gain lawful permanent resident (LPR) status through the EB-5 visa: the standard visa and the Regional Center Program. As noted earlier, the overwhelming majority of investors invest through the Regional Center Program.[16] Both pathways require the same amount of capital to be invested and minimum number of jobs to be created.

Minimum investment amounts, for either the standard pathway or the Regional Center Program, depend on whether investors choose to invest in a TEA. Most investors choose to invest in TEAs, which have minimum investments that are 50% lower than the standard pathway. The standard pathway typically is the only one in which some investors choose not to invest in a TEA—nearly all Regional Center Program investments are made in TEAs. Other differences between the two pathways include the measure of job creation and the role of the investor in the enterprise.

Investment of Capital

Currently, to qualify for the EB-5 visa, petitioners must invest in an NCE a minimum of $1,800,000, or $900,000 in a TEA. After previously remaining unchanged since 1990 (at $1,000,000 or $500,000 in a TEA), the 2019 EB-5 modernization regulation requires that these amounts be adjusted for inflation, as measured by the Consumer Price Index for All Urban Consumers (CPI-U), every five years.[17] The entire investment must be at risk for the purpose of generating a return.[18]

[16] In FY2019, approximately 96% of investors entered through the Regional Center Program.

[17] 8 C.F.R. §204.6.

[18] *At risk* means immigrant investors cannot be guaranteed the return of any part of their investment or a rate of return on their investment. There must be a risk of loss and chance for gain. The investor may receive a return on the investment during or after the conditional residence period, as long as before or during the conditional residence period or before required jobs are created the return is not a portion of the principal investment and was not guaranteed to the investor. U.S. Department of Homeland Security, U.S. Citizenship and Immigration Services, *EB-5 Adjudications Policy*, Policy Memorandum PM-602-0083, Washington, DC, May 30, 2013.

What is a Targeted Employment Area (TEA)?

A TEA is defined under statute as either a rural area or an area experiencing high unemployment of at least 150% of the national average. Rural areas are areas outside Metropolitan Statistical Areas (MSAs), as designated by the Office of Management and Budget, or areas outside of cities and towns with populations of 20,000, based on the most recent decennial census. High unemployment areas in which the New Commercial Enterprise (NCE) is principally doing business, may include MSAs, counties within MSAs, counties in which a city or town with a population of 20,000 or more is located, or cities and towns with populations of 20,000 or more that are located outside of MSAs. These geographies must meet the 150% or greater unemployment threshold. High unemployment areas may also include areas based on census tract designations. A 2019 Department of Homeland Security (DHS) rule change removed states' authority to designate high unemployment areas, placing the authority directly with U.S. Citizenship and Immigration Services (USCIS). Under the regulation, a high unemployment area calculation in multiple census tracts must be based on the unemployment rate of the census tract or contiguous census tracts in which the NCE is principally doing business and may also include directly adjacent census tracts. In these cases, the 150% unemployment determination is based on the weighted average for unemployment rates in those tracts.

A New Commercial Enterprise (NCE)

A commercial enterprise is "any for-profit activity formed for the ongoing conduct of lawful business," such as a sole proprietorship, partnership, holding company, joint venture, corporation, business trust, or other publicly or privately owned entity.[19] A new commercial enterprise is one established after November 29, 1990. If the commercial enterprise was established before November 29, 1990, the immigrant investor's capital must have been used to expand or restructure/reorganize the enterprise.[20]

[19] 8 C.F.R. §204.6(e).

[20] For more information, see 8 C.F.R. §204.6(h).

Applicants are also allowed to invest funds in troubled businesses.[21] The immigrant investor must be engaged in the management of the commercial enterprise through policy formation, daily managerial responsibilities, or direct management.[22]

Job Creation

In order to meet the requirements for the EB-5 visa, the foreign national's investment capital in the new commercial enterprise must create a minimum of 10 jobs.[23] The EB-5 visa has three different measures of job creation.

1. If an immigrant invests in a troubled business, directly or through a regional center, he/she can show preservation of jobs for at least two years, in lieu of creating new jobs.[24]
2. Investments made in an NCE in a non-regional center context must create 10 jobs within the NCE. (Such jobs are called direct or payroll jobs.)
3. For NCEs located within a regional center, the 10 new jobs required can be created directly or indirectly (i.e., employees not working directly for the commercial enterprise).[25]

---

[21] A troubled business is one that has been in existence for at least two years and has experienced a net loss equal to or at least 20% of its net worth in the 12- or 24-month period prior to the immigrant investor's filing of Form I-526, *Petition by Alien Entrepreneur*. 8 C.F.R. §204.6(e).

[22] According to a USCIS policy memorandum, "if the foreign national investor is a limited partner and the limited partnership agreement provides the investor with certain rights, powers, and duties normally granted to limited partners under the Uniform Limited Partnership Act, the immigrant investor will be considered sufficiently engaged in the management of the new commercial enterprise." U.S. Department of Homeland Security, U.S. Citizenship and Immigration Services, *EB-5 Adjudications Policy*, Policy Memorandum PM-602-0083, Washington, DC, May 30, 2013; p. 12.

[23] The position must be full-time, meaning at least 35 hours a week, and be held by a qualifying employee (U.S. citizen, LPR, or other work-authorized migrant), meaning an individual legally able to work in the United States. Jobs are also expected to last two years and cannot be intermittent, temporary, seasonal, or transient in nature. 8 C.F.R. §204.6(j)(4).

[24] 8 C.F.R. §204.6(j)(4)(ii).

REGIONAL CENTER PROGRAM

The Regional Center Program was originally authorized in the Departments of Commerce, Justice, and State, the Judiciary, and Related Agencies Appropriations Act in 1992.[26] Since its creation, the program has been reauthorized several times.[27] Since 2015, reauthorization of the Regional Center Program has occurred primarily through short-term continuing resolutions. The program was established as a pilot to achieve the economic growth and job creation goals of the immigrant investor statute[28] by encouraging immigrants to invest in commercial enterprises located within public or private economic units known as *regional centers*. In order to receive investment from foreign nationals wishing to obtain EB-5 status, a regional center must be designated as such by USCIS. Regional centers are intended to provide a coordinated focus of foreign investment on a particular project or projects by pooling investments across multiple investors[29] (see section entitled "What is a Regional Center?" for a detailed discussion).

The Regional Center Program differs from the standard EB-5 visa[30] in three ways (*Table 1*). First, although both pathways require individual investors to create at least 10 jobs, in the regional center context indirect

---

[25] Indirect jobs are held outside of the NCE but are created as a result of it. For example, they can include persons employed by the producers of materials/inputs for the immigrant investor's enterprise. "Reasonable" economic methodologies must be used to demonstrate indirect job creation. 8 C.F.R. §204.6 (m)(l)(7).

[26] P.L. 102-395 §610 (October 6, 1992).

[27] Section 116 of P.L. 105-119 extended the Regional Center Program's reauthorization from 5 years to 7 years, and Section 402 of P.L. 106-396 further extended it to 10 years. Section 548 of P.L. 108-156 extended the program to FY2008, Section 548 of P.L. 111-83 extended it to FY2012, and Section 1 of P.L. 112-176 extended it through FY2015. Section 131 of P.L. 114-53 extended the program to December 11, 2015; P.L. 114-96 extended it to December 16, 2015; and P.L. 114-100 extended it to December 22, 2015. Division F, Section 575 of P.L. 114-113 extended the program to September 30, 2016.

[28] 8 U.S.C. §1153(b)(5) and 8 U.S.C. §1153 note.

[29] Pooled investments can also include investments from non EB-5 investors, such as U.S. citizens.

[30] *Standard EB-5 visa* refers to investors that obtain an EB-5 visa through the regular EB-5 visa process rather than by investing in a regional center. Individuals using either pathway, the standard EB-5 visa or the Regional Center Program, can obtain an EB-5 visa. USCIS refers to the standard EB-5 visa as the basic EB-5 program.

job creation[31] may be counted instead of or in addition to direct job creation. Second, unlike with the standard EB-5 visa, foreign nationals investing in a regional center are unlikely to be involved in the management and daily activities of the commercial enterprise. Third, the EB-5 visa category is permanent, while the Regional Center Program is temporary.

Table 1. Comparison of the two EB-5 pathways

Standard EB-5 Visa	Regional Center Program
Required capital investment is $1.8 million, or $900,000 in a targeted employment area.	Same.
Foreign national receives conditional LPR status and after approximately two years must apply to have the conditions removed or leave the country.	Same.
To have the conditions removed, the immigrant investor must, among other requirements, show that he/she created or can be expected to create within a reasonable time 10 full-time jobs for U.S. citizens, LPRs, or other work-authorized aliens. Employment must be *direct* (i.e., employees working for the commercial enterprise).[a]	Same but the employment can be *indirect* (i.e., employees not working for the commercial enterprise).
Investor *tends to be* involved in daily operations of enterprise.	Investor *tends not to be* involved in the daily operation of the enterprise.
Visa category is permanent; does not expire.	Program is temporary; set to expire June 30, 2021.

Source: CRS analysis of Immigration and Nationality Act Section 203(b)(5) and Section 610 of P.L. 102-395.

Foreign nationals may invest in any of the regional centers currently approved by USCIS to qualify for their conditional LPR status.[32]

[31] Indirect job creation refers to jobs a regional center estimates to create indirectly through revenues generated from increased exports, improved regional productivity, job creation, or increased domestic capital investment.

[32] For a list of approved regional centers, see U.S. Citizenship and Immigration Services, *Immigrant Investor Regional Centers,* http://www.uscis.gov/working-united-states/permanent-workers/employment-based-immigration-fifth-preference-eb-5/immigrant-

Investments may be both within a regional center and a TEA. Although a regional center does not have to be in a TEA, almost all foreign nationals applying for EB-5 status invest with regional centers whose defined boundaries constitute a TEA.[33]

What is a Regional Center?

Regional centers are defined as "any economic unit, public or private, which is involved with the promotion of economic growth, including increased export sales, improved regional productivity, job creation, and increased domestic capital investment."[34] More simply, the term *regional center* refers to an entity (often a limited partnership or a limited liability corporation) where investment from multiple foreign nationals and non-EB-5 investors (e.g., U.S. citizens) can be pooled to fund a broad range of projects.[35] Regional centers often rely on third-party intermediaries to recruit immigrant investors.[36]

Regional centers can be privately owned, publicly owned (operated by a city, county, state, or economic development agency), or a public-private partnership.[37] There are many different models for regional centers. For

---

investor-regional-centers. There is no citizenship requirement to file for regional center designation with USCIS.

[33] The Regional Center designation requires that applicants show how their proposed program will focus on a geographic region; promote economic growth through increased export sales, if applicable; promote improved regional productivity; create a minimum of 10 jobs directly or indirectly per investor; increase domestic capital investment; be promoted and publicized to prospective investors; have a positive impact on the regional or national economy through increased household earnings; and generate a greater demand for business services, utilities maintenance and repair, and construction jobs both in and around the center. 8 C.F.R. §204.6(m)(3).

[34] 8 C.F.R. §204.6 (e).

[35] In addition, approximately 20% of those receiving LPR status from an investment under the standard EB-5 category are involved in pooled investments. CRS conversation with staff from USCIS' Immigrant Investor Program Office, April 8, 2016.

[36] Audrey Singer and Camille Galdes, *Improving the EB-5 Investor Visa Program: International Financing for U.S. Regional Economic Development*, Brookings-Rockefeller, Project on State and Metropolitan Innovation, February 2014.

[37] For a discussion of regional center public-private partnerships, see Lazaro Zamora and Theresa Cardinal Brown, *EB- 5 Program: Success, Challenges, and Opportunities for States and Localities*, Bipartisan Policy Center, Washington, DC, September 2015.

example, in the lending model, the NCE is a lending entity that provides loans to those (i.e., U.S. citizens) seeking funding for business activities, such as new construction or expansions of their operations.[38] Regional centers can also use an equity model, where pooled EB-5 investments are used to purchase equity stakes in a project company (i.e., job- creating entity). In addition, regional centers have been created for direct investment to build a variety of projects, such as hotels, a ski resort, convention centers, arenas, and retail and mixed use developments. Certain state[39] and local governments have also established their own regional centers or public-private partnerships (e.g., City of Dallas Regional Center and Philadelphia Authority for Industrial Development).

Since the inception of the Regional Center Program in 1992, the number of USCIS-approved regional centers has increased substantially across the United States. In FY2007, there were 11 approved regional centers.[40] As of December 2020, there were 674 approved regional centers. However, not all regional centers have received investment from foreign nationals wishing to immigrate under the EB-5 visa category.

The proportion of immigrant investors using regional centers, specifically those in a TEA, has been increasing, especially since FY2007. Since FY2008, immigrants investing in regional centers and their family members (derivatives) have represented by far the largest proportion of EB-5 visas issued and adjustments of status, representing 96% in FY2019. Figure 1 displays the distribution of EB-5 grantees investing over the past 10 years through (1) the standard program (not in a TEA), (2) the standard program in a TEA, and (3) a regional center. Because nearly all regional

---

[38] The growth of and preference for the loan model may be driven by the fact that many investors' primary motive is to qualify for LPR status and recover their investment. Jeanne Calderon and Gary Friedland, *EB-5 Capital Project Database: Revisited and Expanded*, NYU Stern School of Business, Center for Real Estate Finance Research, New York, NY, March 29, 2016, p. 9.

[39] Currently, there are no active state-run regional centers. USCIS terminated Vermont's regional center in 2018.

[40] U.S. Citizenship and Immigration Services, *Number of Approved EB5 Regional Centers Fiscal Year(s): 2007 – 2012,* https://www.uscis.gov/sites/default/files/USCIS/Resources/Reports%20and%20Studies/Immigration%20Forms%20Data/Employment-based/I526_I924_I829_performancedata_qtr43.pdf.

center investors invest in a TEA, the figure does not include separate non-TEA and TEA categories for regional centers.

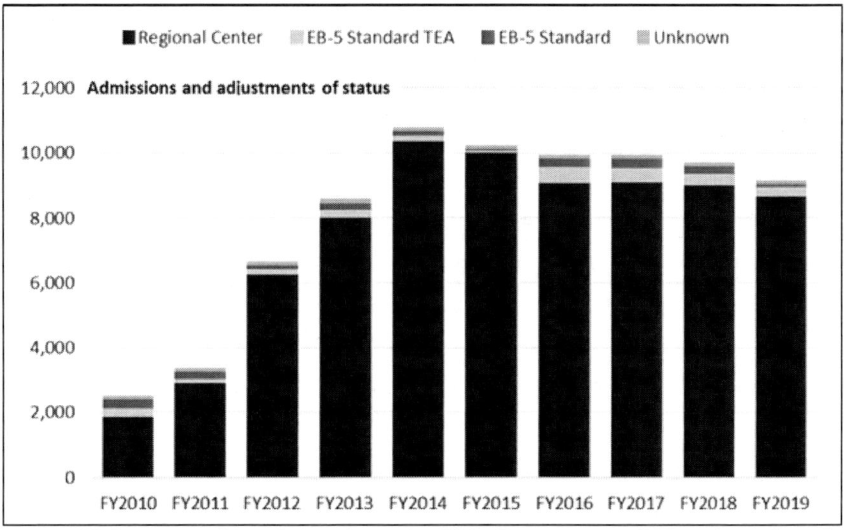

Source: CRS presentation of data from the U.S. Department of Homeland Security, Yearbook of Immigration Statistics, Table 7, multiple fiscal years.

Notes: Admissions include principal investors and derivative family members (spouses and children). EB-5 Standard represents those receiving EB-5 visa classification on the basis of investment in a non-TEA area that is not associated with a regional center. EB-5 Standard TEA represents those who have received EB-5 visa classification through investment in a targeted employment area (TEA) that is not associated with a regional center. Regional Center represents those who received EB-5 visa classification based on investment in a regional center in both TEAs and non-TEAs. CRS presents those receiving EB-5 visa classifications based on investment in TEA and non-TEA regional center projects together because the number of visa numbers issued based on investment in non-TEA regional center projects was relatively low. Unknown represents admissions whose categories have been withheld by DHS.

Figure 1. Immigrant Investor (EB-5) Admissions and Adjustments of Status, FY2010-FY2019.

Each year, regional centers must apply for re-certification by USCIS and provide evidence of promoting economic growth to remain eligible for the EB-5 program. In 2017, USCIS began conducting compliance reviews to verify the information provided in regional centers' initial applications (Form I-924) and annual certifications (Form I-924A) by reviewing records and evidence, performing site inspections, and interviewing personnel.[41]

USCIS may terminate a regional center's participation in the EB-5 program if it fails to submit required information to USCIS or fails to demonstrate that it continues to promote economic growth.[42] After receiving a Notice of Intent to Terminate from USCIS, regional centers have 30 days to submit evidence opposing the ground(s) alleged in the notice. During this period, the regional center may continue to operate. If the designation is terminated, USCIS will provide a Notice of Termination. Terminated regional centers may appeal decisions but may not solicit, generate, or promote investors or investments while their cases are under appeal. Investors with conditional LPR status who have invested in a new commercial enterprise associated with a regional center that USCIS has removed from the program may still demonstrate compliance with EB-5 program requirements to maintain their status.

As of December 2020, USCIS listed 532 regional centers terminated from their participation in the EB-5 program since 2008.[43] Seventy-three percent of those centers were terminated since FY2018. A USCIS analysis of regional center terminations in 2017 showed that about 58% were terminated for failing to promote economic growth, 40% were terminated for failing to file the required I-924A, and two regional centers elected to withdraw from the program.[44]

---

[41] "USCIS Launches EB-5 Regional Center Audit Program," *Thomson Reuters Practical Law Labor & Employment* (blog), March 22, 2017, https://content.next.westlaw.com/Document/Ia8a7571c0e4511e798dc8b09b4f043e0/View/FullText.html?transitionType=Default&contextData=(sc.Default).

[42] 8 C.F.R. §204.6(m)(6).

[43] For a list of terminated regional centers, see U.S. Citizenship and Immigration Services, *Terminated Regional Centers,* http://www.uscis.gov/working-united-states/permanent-workers/employment-based-immigration-fifth-preference-eb-5/eb-5-immigrant-investor-process/terminated-regional-centers.

[44] Responses to Questions for the Record by L. Francis Cissna, USCIS Director, in U.S. Congress, Senate Committee on the Judiciary, *Citizenship for Sale: Oversight of the EB-5 Investor Visa Program*, hearing, 115th Cong., 2nd sess., June 19, 2018. https://www.judiciary.senate.gov/imo/media/doc/Cissna%20Responses%20to%20QFRs%20(Public).pdf.

In 2017, DHS published an Advance Notice of Proposed Rulemaking (ANPRM) regarding regulatory changes it was considering for the Regional Center Program.[45] The ANPRM sought public comment on improving the regional center designations process, a requirement for centers to file exemplar project requests, "continued participation" requirements to maintain designations, and termination processes. An Notice of Proposed Rulemaking (NPRM) has not yet been published in the *Federal Register*.

THE EB-5 PETITION PROCESS

The EB-5 petition process, which is largely administered by the USCIS Immigrant Investor Program Office, requires various steps before an individual can obtain full (i.e., unconditional) LPR status.

The first step of the process is filing USCIS Form I-526, *Immigrant Petition by Alien Investor* and paying the $3,675 filing fee. The petitioner must prove that he/she meets the requirements for EB-5 classification, including that the capital being invested came from a legitimate source, and that he/she has presented a valid business plan or showed that the investment will go to a USCIS- certified regional center.

I-526 petition receipts increased substantially between 2010 and 2015, growing more than six- fold. The program grew in the wake of the 2008 financial crisis, which increased demand for EB- 5 capital as an alternative funding source, particularly for real estate development projects.[46] Filings remained high through FY2017, and then dropped substantially in FY2018

[45] Department of Homeland Security, *The EB-5 Immigrant Investor Regional Center,* at https://www.reginfo.gov/ public/do/eAgendaViewRule?pubId=201910&RIN=1615-AC11.

[46] Testimony of Jeanne Calderon, NYU Stern School of Business Clinical Associate Professor, in U.S. Congress, House Committee on the Judiciary, *Is the Investor Visa Program an Underperforming Asset?*, hearing, 114th Cong., 1st sess., February 11, 2016, at https://docs.house.gov/meetings/JU/JU00/20160211/104454/HHRG-114-JU00-Wstate-CalderonJ-20160211.pdf.

and FY2019 (*Figure 2*). Some observers have associated the decrease with the growing backlog of pending EB-5 petitions.[47]

I-526 filings from FY2020 reflect an expected surge prior to the November 2019 implementation of increased required investment amounts (see "EB-5 Immigrant Investor Program Modernization") followed by a decline in filings.[48] USCIS received 4,254 petitions in the first quarter of FY2020; subsequently, I-526 receipts dropped to 21 in the second quarter and 40 in the third quarter.[49] In addition to increases to the minimum investment amounts, reduced I-526 filings during FY2020 may also be associated with impacts from the COVID-19 pandemic (see the "COVID-19 and the EB-5 Program" section) and long wait times for investors from certain countries (see the "Application and Petition Processing" section).[50]

USCIS experienced a growing backlog of pending I-526 petitions through FY2017 (*Figure 2*), which then declined after the Immigrant Investor Program Office (IPO) restructured and hired more personnel (see the "Fraud and Security Risks" section). Pending petitions increased again between 2019 and 2020. In the third quarter of FY2020, there were 15,955 pending I-526 petitions.

Once USCIS approves the I-526, the foreign national must obtain a visa from the Department of State (DOS) to enter the United States if they

[47] EB-5 Affiliate Network, "EB-5 Program Processing Statistics," *EB5 Affiliate Network* (blog), January 25, 2020, https://eb5affiliatenetwork.com/eb-5-program-processing-statistics/.

[48] Daniel M. Kowalski, "Expert Predicts 'Surge' Then 'Decline' Due to EB-5 Investor Visa Rule Changes," *LexisNexis Immigration Law*, July 25, 2019, https://www.lexisnexis.com/legal newsroom/immigration/b/outsidenews/posts/expert-predicts-surge-then-decline-due-to-eb-5-investor-visa-rule-changes.

[49] Department of Homeland Security, U.S. Citizenship and Immigration Services, Office of Performance and Quality. Performance Reporting Tool, queried 08/2020, TRK 6358.

[50] Suzanne Lazicki, "FY2020 Q3 Processing Data," *EB-5 Updates* (blog), November 17, 2020, https://blog.lucidtext.com/2020/11/17/fy2020-q3-processing-data/.

are not currently in the country, or adjust status[51] to conditional permanent residency with USCIS if they are.[52]

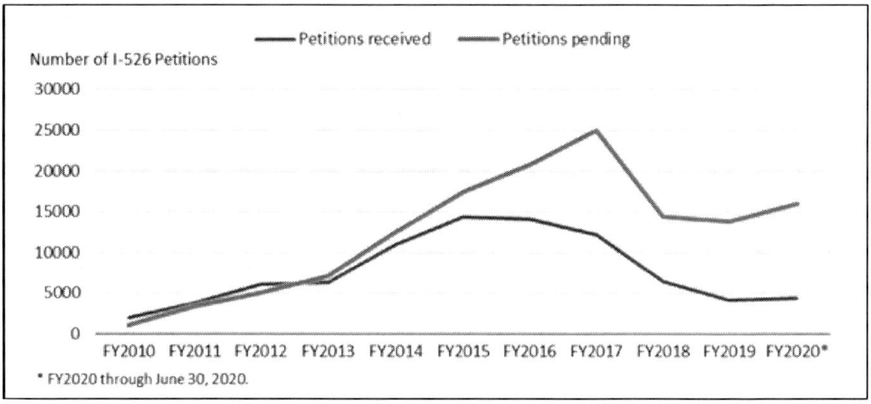

Source: CRS analysis of data from the U.S. Department of Homeland Security, U.S. Citizenship and Immigration Services, Performance Reporting Tool, queried January 2020, TRK 5607.

Note: FY2020 data through third quarter.

Figure 2. Form I-526 Petitions (Applications) Received and Pending, FY2008-FY2020.

Individuals not in the United States file Form DS-260 *Immigrant Visa Electronic Application* with DOS and individuals within the United States file Form I-485 *Application to Register Permanent Residence or Adjust Status* with USCIS. At this stage, DOS and USCIS also check that the foreign national is not inadmissible under the grounds of inadmissibility of the Immigration and Nationality Act (INA).[53]

---

[51] "Adjustment of status is the process by which an eligible individual already in the United States can get permanent resident status (a green card) without having to return to their home country to complete visa processing." U.S. Citizenship and Immigration Services, Adjustment of Status, https://uscis.gov/green-card/green-card-processes-and-procedures/adjustment-of-status.

[52] A visa must be available for the foreign national to apply for the visa or to adjust to conditional permanent residence status—immigrant visas for employment-based immigrant preference categories are numerically limited, so they are not always immediately available.

[53] The grounds of inadmissibility include criminal, national security, health, and indigence grounds as well as past violations of immigration law. INA §212(a). See also CRS Report R41104, *Immigration Visa Issuances and Grounds for Exclusion: Policy and Trends*.

Those who adjust status within the United States receive their conditional residence once the I-485 is approved. Those who receive a visa from DOS receive their conditional residence once they are admitted into the United States.

In FY2004, the number of EB-5 visas granted to new arrivals (60) and the number granted to those who adjusted their status (69) were roughly equal. This ratio has shifted as the growth in visas granted to new arrivals outpaced the number granted to those who adjusted their status, as seen in *Figure 3*. In FY2019 visas issued to new arrivals accounted for 82% of EB-5 admissions. Most EB-5 petitioners, therefore, must have their visas processed abroad through a U.S. consulate or embassy.

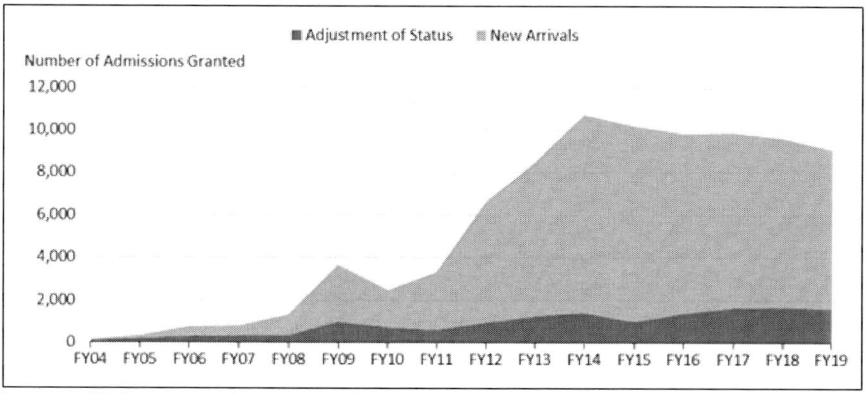

Source: CRS presentation of data from the U.S. Department of Homeland Security, Yearbook of Immigration Statistics, Table 7, multiple years.

Notes: New Arrivals refers to individuals who obtained an EB-5 visa from DOS outside the United States. Adjustment of Status refers to individuals who applied for an EB-5 visa number from within the United States and adjusted their status with USCIS.

Figure 3. EB-5 Admissions Granted to New Arrivals or through Adjustment of Status, FY2004-FY2019.

An investor can petition to remove the conditional status after approximately two years by filing Form I-829 *Petition by Investor to Remove Conditions on Permanent Resident Status*.[54] Form I-829 requires a $3,750 filing fee and $85 biometric fee.[55] If the I-829 is approved, the conditionality on the residency of the immigrant investor and his/her derivative family members is removed.[56] A 2019 DHS regulation clarified that derivative family members who were not included on the principal investor's I-829 must file their own forms to remove conditions on their permanent residence.[57] If the investor did not meet the requirements to adjust to full LPR status, the investor (and their family members who immigrated together) must depart from the United States or adjust to another immigration status. USCIS will issue a notice-to-appear (NTA)[58] to foreign nationals who do not apply to have the conditional status removed or who are denied adjustment to full LPR status.

The number of I-829 petitions received annually by USCIS grew from 391 in FY2008 to 3,756 in FY2018. As with forms I-526, there has been a substantial increase in the number of pending I- 829 petitions. At the end of the third quarter of FY2020, there were 10,332 pending I-829 petitions to remove conditions on permanent residence status.[59]

---

[54] The I-829 form instructions state that an investor can petition to remove the conditions within the 90-day period immediately preceding the second anniversary of obtaining his/her conditional permanent resident status.

[55] Under 8 CFR 103.17, "DHS may charge a fee to collect biometric information, to provide biometric collection services, to conduct required national security and criminal history background checks, to verify an individual's identity, and to store and maintain this biometric information for reuse to support other benefit requests." During a biometric services appointment, USCIS captures fingerprints, photographs, and signatures from I-829 applicants.

[56] U.S. Citizenship and Immigration Services, *EB-5 Immigrant Investor Process,* June 25, 2014, http://www.uscis.gov/working-united-states/permanent-workers/employment-based-immigration-fifth-preference-eb-5/eb-5-immigrant- investor-process.

[57] 8 C.F.R. §216.6.

[58] This document starts the removal process.

[59] Department of Homeland Security, U.S. Citizenship and Immigration Services, Office of Performance and Quality. Performance Reporting Tool, queried August 2020, TRK 6358.

EB-5 ADMISSIONS

Each year, approximately 10,000 EB-5 visas are available for investors and their derivative family members, who include spouses and unmarried children under age 21.[60] From FY2003 to FY2005, the number of EB-5 visas issued grew five-fold (from 64 to 346), and then increased by seven-fold by FY2010 (to 2,480). After being underutilized during its first 18 years, the program has grown in popularity since 2008, when U.S. financial crisis reduced the availability of commercial lending funds and made EB-5 an attractive alternative funding source.[61] Annual EB-5 admissions rose above 10,000 for the first time in FY2014 and again in FY2015, and remained just under 10,000 during FY2016, FY2017, FY2018, and FY2019 (*Figure 1*).

Because the allotment for EB-5 visas includes derivative family members, the total number of immigrants admitted through the investor visa program does not reflect the actual number of investors. On average, individual immigrant investors (principal investors) account for slightly more than one-third of all those granted EB-5 visas.[62] Between FY2010 and FY2019, each investor had approximately two relatives granted conditional LPR status along with them.

Table 2 lists the top 10 EB-5 visa receiving countries in FY2019, FY2014, and FY2009. Foreign nationals from China have received the most EB-5 visas, accounting for approximately 46% (4,327) of all EB-5 visas granted in FY2019 and 85% (9,128) in 2014.[63]

---

[60] Derivatives are counted against the numerical limit for the category.

[61] Department of Homeland Security, "EB-5 Immigrant Investor Program Modernization," 84 *Federal Register* 35762, July 24, 2019; and Testimony of Jeanne Calderon, NYU Stern School of Business Clinical Associate Professor, in U.S. Congress, House Committee on the Judiciary, *Is the Investor Visa Program an Underperforming Asset?*, hearing, 114th Cong., 1st sess., February 11, 2016, at https://docs.house.gov/meetings/JU/JU00/20160211/104454/HHRG-114-JU00- Wstate-CalderonJ-20160211.pdf.

[62] CRS calculation using data from the U.S. Department of Homeland Security Office of Immigration Statistics, *Yearbook of Immigration Statistics*; multiple years.

[63] U.S. Department of State, *Report of the Visa Office*, Table V Immigrant Visas Issued and Adjustments of Status Subject to Numerical Limitations (by Foreign State of Chargeability), Part 3; multiple years.

Table 2. EB-5 Visas Issued and Adjustments of Status by Country (Top 10 Countries: FY2019, FY2014, and FY2009)

FY2019				**FY2014**			**FY2009**		
	Country	Visas	% of Total EB-5 Visas	Country	Visas	% of Total EB-5 Visas	Country	Visas	% of Total EB-5 Visas
1	China	4,327	46%	China	9,128	85%	China	1,979	47%
2	India	760	8%	South Korea	225	2%	South Korea	903	21%
3	Vietnam	716	8%	Mexico	129	1%	Great Britain & N. Ireland	324	8%
4	South Korea	695	7%	Taiwan	126	1%	Taiwan	170	4%
5	Brazil	496	5%	Vietnam	121	1%	Canada	85	2%
6	Taiwan	432	5%	Russia	100	0.9%	Japan	84	2%
7	Venezuela	172	2%	India	96	0.9%	India	72	2%
8	Hong Kong	167	2%	Venezuela	96	0.9%	Russia	60	1%
9	Mexico	138	1%	Iran	76	0.7%	Netherlands	38	0.9%
10	South Africa	120	1%	Canada	52	0.5%	Mexico	33	0.8%

Source: U.S. Department of State, Report of the Visa Office, Table V Immigrant Visas Issued and Adjustments of Status Subject to Numerical Limitations (by Foreign State of Chargeability), Part 3; multiple years, https://travel.state.gov/content/travel/en/legal/visa-law0/visa-statistics/annual-reports.html.

Notes: Visas issued represents visas granted to individuals outside of the United States. Adjustments of status represents individuals already in the United States who adjusted their status. This table represents the sum of these two groups.

In FY2019, Indian nationals had the second largest number of EB-5 visas granted, with 8% (760), followed closely by Vietnamese nationals with 8% (716) and South Korean nationals with 7% (695).[64] No more than 7% of all employment-based visas may go to a country each year unless those allocations would otherwise go unused.[65] Currently, China and Vietnam are both oversubscribed for the EB-5 visa, meaning that their countries' demand for visas exceeds the allocation under the per-country cap.

Foreign nationals of oversubscribed countries face longer wait times. As of December 2020, DOS was processing visas for Chinese applicants whose petitions had been approved through August 2015 and for Vietnamese applicants whose petitions were approved through September 2017.[66] In January 2020, USCIS announced it would begin processing I-526 forms with priority given to petitions from countries without backlogs.[67]

ECONOMIC IMPACT

The EB-5 visa category was created as a way to increase investment and job creation in the U.S. economy. However, a lack of data has impeded comprehensive, longitudinal analyses of the program's economic impact and job creation, especially at the local level.[68] In 2013, the DHS Office of

---

[64] Ibid.

[65] For more information, see CRS Report R45447, *Permanent Employment-Based Immigration and the Per-country Ceiling*.

[66] Department of State, *Visa Bulletin for December 2020*, Washington, DC, at https://travel.state.gov/content/travel/en/legal/visa-law0/visa-bulletin/2021/visa-bulletin-for-december-2020.html.

[67] U.S. Citizenship and Immigration Services, "USCIS Adjusts Process for Managing EB-5 Visa Petition Inventory," news release, January 29, 2020, at https://www.uscis.gov/news/news-releases/uscis-adjusts-process-for-managing-eb-5- visa-petition-inventory.

[68] Audrey Singer and Camille Galdes, *Improving the EB-5 Investor Visa Program: International Financing for U.S. Regional Economic Development*, Brookings-Rockefeller, Project on State and Metropolitan Innovation, February 2014.

Inspector General (OIG) raised concerns[69] about the validity of USCIS estimates of economic impact.[70] In response to the OIG's recommendation, USCIS commissioned an economic impact study by the Department of Commerce Economics and Statistics Administration.

Published in 2017, the study examined EB-5 investor projects during FY2012 and FY2013. It identified $16.7 billion in total EB-5 capital, of which $5.8 billion was generated by approximately 11,000 EB-5 immigrant investors.[71] An estimated 174,039 jobs were generated through EB-5 related projects during this period, and this included non-EB-5 investment spending. Most investment spending and jobs were generated through regional centers.[72]

Additional studies of economic impact have been published by stakeholder groups and other organizations not affiliated with the federal government.[73] A 2019 economic impact study commissioned by two advocacy groups, the EB-5 Investment Coalition and Invest in the USA, examined projects during FY2014 and FY2015. The study identified approximately $11 billion in capital investment through the Regional Center Program, which represented 2% of foreign direct investment in the United States during that period. Two-thirds of investments were in the construction sector. Other sectors receiving these investments were hotels

---

[69] U.S. Department of Homeland Security Office of Inspector General, *United States Citizenship and Immigration Services: Employment-Based Fifth Preference (EB-5) Regional Center Program*, OIG-14-19, December 2013.

[70] USCIS reported that from FY1990 to FY2014, the EB-5 visa had generated more than $11.2 billion in investments and at least 73,730 jobs, U.S. Congress, House Committee on the Judiciary, *Is the Investor Visa an Under Performing Asset?* testimony of Rebecca Gambler, Director of Homeland Security and Justice at the U.S. Government Accountability Office, 114th Cong., 2nd sess., February 11, 2016.

[71] Non EB-5 investments included domestic and foreign sources of capital including equity from project developers, commercial loans, and investment from other project participants.

[72] David K. Henry et al., "Estimating the Investment and Job Creation Impact of the EB-5 Program" (U.S. Department of Commerce, Office of the Chief Economist, 2017), https://www.commerce.gov/news/reports/2017/01/estimating- investment-and-job-creation-impact-eb-5-program.

[73] See, for example, David Kay, "The Economic Impact and Contribution of the EB-5 Immigration Program, 2013" (Commissioned by Invest in the USA, 2015), https://iiusa.org/wp-content/uploads/2020/05/Economic-Impacts-of-the-EB-5-Immigration-Program_2013_FINAL-web.pdf. and Audrey Singer and Camille Glades, *Improving the EB-5 Investor Visa Program: International Financing for U.S. Regional Economic Development*, Brookings-Rockefeller, Project on State and Metropolitan Innovation, February 2014.

and motels; real estate; wholesale trade; architecture, engineering, and related services; and health care. Investments supported an estimated 355,200 jobs.[74]

Although these studies have identified substantial capital investments, the EB-5 program has been scrutinized for the high proportion of investments that have gone to projects in affluent, urban areas.[75] Prior to reforms applied through a 2019 federal regulation (see the "EB-5 Immigrant Investor Program Modernization" section), a broader interpretation of TEAs meant that these investments were made at the discounted rate for TEA investments.[76]

EB-5 Immigrant Investor Program Modernization

Members of Congress have introduced several legislative measures aiming to change the EB-5 program in recent years but none have become law.[77] The most significant changes to the program have come from the Executive Branch through the DHS EB-5 Immigrant Investor Program Modernization regulation.[78] The regulation, proposed in January 2017 and implemented in November 2019, made the most substantial overhaul to the EB-5 program since Congress introduced the Regional Center pilot program in 1992.

---

[74] Jeffrey B. Carr and Robert A. Chase, "Assessment of the Economic Value and Job Creation Impacts of Project Capital Investment Activity Under the EB-5 Program," Economic & Policy Resources, February 28, 2019.

[75] Eliot Brown, "How a U.S. Visa-for-Cash Plan Funds Luxury Apartment Buildings," *Wall Street Journal*, September 10, 2015, sec. US, https://www.wsj.com/articles/how-immigrants-cash-funds-luxury-towers-in-the-u-s-1441848965.

[76] Testimony of Jeanne Calderon, NYU Stern School of Business Clinical Associate Professor, in U.S. Congress, House Committee on the Judiciary, *Is the Investor Visa Program an Underperforming Asset?*, hearing, 114th Cong., 1st sess., February 11, 2016, at https://docs.house.gov/meetings/JU/JU00/20160211/104454/HHRG-114-JU00-Wstate-CalderonJ-20160211.pdf.

[77] Previous legislative attempts included, in the 113th Congress: S. 744, H.R. 2131, H.R. 3163, H.R. 4178, H.R. 4659; in the 114th Congress: H.R. 616, S. 1501, H.R. 3370, S. 2115, S. 2415, S. 2122, H.R. 5992; and in the 115th Congress, S. 727; H.R. 3471.

[78] Department of Homeland Security, "EB-5 Immigrant Investor Program Modernization," 84 *Federal Register* 35750, July 24, 2019.

The regulation applies to all petitioners who file an I-526 on or after the regulation's effective date of November 21, 2019. As mentioned previously, there were three major sets of changes under the regulation, affecting priority date retention, minimum investment amounts, and TEA designations. In addition, the regulation made technical clarifications and adjustments. (For a brief summary of the rule's major changes, (see Table 3).

The regulation has generated opposition from some Members and industry stakeholders. Senator Rand Paul introduced a joint resolution to prohibit the rule changes.[79] Major industry stakeholders and advocates submitted public comments to the proposed version of the rule requesting that it be withdrawn.[80] Some public comments submitted in response to the proposed rule expressed the view that EB-5 reforms should be made by Congress through the legislative process, rather than through federal regulation.[81] Shortly after the regulation was implemented, a Florida regional center sued DHS over it.[82] The motion for a preliminary injunction against the regulation was denied.

DHS has argued that regulatory action was necessary because Congress had failed to pass comprehensive EB-5 reform legislation and explained that it was acting with authority granted under the Immigration and Nationality Act. Some Members of Congress, on both sides of the aisle, urged implementation of the new rule after its proposal, arguing that

---

[79] S.J.Res. 55 was introduced in the 116th Congress.

[80] Letter from Robert Maples on behalf of American Immigration Lawyers Association, U.S. Chamber of Commerce, EB-5 Investment Coalition, Invest in the USA, The Real Estate Roundtable, and EB-5 Rural Alliance to Honorable John F. Kelly, Secretary of Homeland Security, February 24, 2017, https://www.regulations.gov/document?D=USCIS-2016-0006-0031.

[81] Department of Homeland Security, "EB-5 Immigrant Investor Program Modernization," 84 *Federal Register* 35757, July 24, 2019.

[82] Genevieve Douglas, "Overhaul of Immigrant Investor Program Challenged in Court (1)," *Bloomberg Law*, November 29, 2019, https://www.bloomberglaw.com/document/X35VNSMK000000?bna_news_filter=daily-labor-report&jcsearch=BNA%252000000016eb761dbcaa16ebfef7d170001#jcite.

it would "advance the national interest" and re-align the program with congressional intent.[83]

Priority Date Retention

The regulation allows petitioners to retain the priority dates of approved I-526 petitions for subsequent I-526 petitions.[84] For example, if an initial application by a petitioner is with a regional center that is terminated through no fault of the petitioner, the petitioner may still retain that priority date. DHS claims that this will provide investors with greater predictability, certainty, and flexibility, given that it expects the visa to "remain oversubscribed for the foreseeable future."[85] As of April 2020, there were more than 24,000 EB-5 petitions that had been approved and were awaiting visa availability, 98% of which were filed by petitioners from China.[86] According to DHS, several commenters on the rule expressed general support for this change.[87]

Changes to Minimum Investment Amounts

Since the EB-5 program was established in 1990, minimum investment requirements had remained the same: $1 million or $500,000 in a TEA. The regulation increased these amounts for the first time to $1.8 million or $900,000 in a TEA, maintaining the same 50% differential for TEA and

---

[83] "Grassley, Leahy Press Trump Administration on EB-5 Regulations," news release, March 11, 2019, https://www.grassley.senate.gov/news/news-releases/grassley-leahy-press-trump-administration-eb-5-regulations.

[84] 8 C.F.R. §204.6(d).

[85] Department of Homeland Security, "EB-5 Immigrant Investor Program Modernization," 84 *Federal Register* 35751, July 24, 2019.

[86] Department of Homeland Security, U.S. Citizenship and Immigration Services, Office of Performance and Quality, CLAIM3, queried April 2020, TRK 5965. https://www.uscis.gov/sites/default/files/document/data/EB_I140_I360_I526_performancedata_fy2020_Q1_Q2.pdf.

[87] See, for example, Letter from Peter D. Joseph, Invest in the USA Executive Director, to Samantha Deshommes, Acting Chief, USCIS Regulatory Coordination Division, April 11, 2017, https://www.regulations.gov/document?D= USCIS-2016-0006-0287.

non-TEA projects.[88] DHS determined these amounts to be the present-day value of the initial investment requirement amounts established by Congress, as adjusted for inflation using the unadjusted CPI-). The regulation sets a schedule for adjustment for inflation every five years, beginning from the regulation's effective date.

Opponents to the increased minimums state that they disadvantage less wealthy investors, could reduce overall investment and economic development, and make EB-5 less competitive compared with other countries' investor programs.[89]

DHS acknowledged that higher investment amounts may dissuade some investors, which could impact job creation, make it more costly for regional centers to match investors to projects, and drive interest to other countries' foreign investor visa programs. However, it argues that these increases are necessary to keep pace with inflation, will increase overall investment, and that greater funding could reduce burdens on regional centers to recruit more investors. DHS also asserts that EB-5 will remain competitive with other countries' visa programs.[90]

TEA Designations

Investors qualify for a reduced minimum investment amount for investments in NCEs that are located in rural areas or areas of high unemployment (for more information, see the "What is a targeted employment area (TEA)?" section). The regulation made a substantial change regarding high unemployment areas by removing states' authority

---

[88] 8 C.F.R. §204.6(f).

[89] See, for example, Dear Colleague Letter from Senator Rand Paul, August 20, 2019, https://www.eb5investors.com/ resources/sen-rand-paul-dear-colleague-on-eb-5.pdf; and Dillon Colucci, "New EB-5 Regulations: Winners and Losers," *EB-5 Insights*, July 24, 2019, at https://www.eb5insights.com/2019/07/24/new-eb-5-regulations-winners-and-losers/.

[90] Department of Homeland Security, "EB-5 Immigrant Investor Program Modernization," 84 *Federal Register* 35763, July 24, 2019.

to designate those areas—now only USCIS may approve TEA geographies.[91]

The regulation also specifies how determinations are made when considering groups of census tracts. The weighted average of the unemployment rate in the census tract(s) in which the NCE is principally doing business must be at least 150% of the national average. Only census tracts that are directly related to EB-5 projects may be included in these groupings. The regulation also allows cities and towns with populations of 20,000 or more that are located outside of Metropolitan Statistical Areas to qualify as high unemployment areas.

Some have argued that removing states' authority to designate TEAs creates additional burdens for investors who may have to hire economists to analyze unemployment data to submit for TEA determinations and disallows states from participating in decisions related to their own economic development.[92]

DHS stated its goal with this change was to reduce inconsistencies between states and to ensure that the investments that qualify for the lower minimum amount are actually directed toward areas with high levels of unemployment, creating jobs where they are most needed and thereby better fulfilling Congress's intent for TEAs. This change addresses previous allegations that wealthy, urban areas were being gerrymandered into TEAs. DHS estimates that 43% of NCEs with TEA designations could be impacted by the change.

Technical Adjustments and Clarifications

The regulation also makes a number of clarifications and technical adjustments. One clarification relates to derivative family members and I-

---

[91] 8 C.F.R. §204.6(i).

[92] See, for example, Dillon Colucci, "New EB-5 Regulations: Winners and Losers," EB-5 Insights (blog), July 24, 2019, https://www.eb5insights.com/2019/07/24/new-eb-5-regulations-winners-and-losers/; Suzanne Lazicki, "Targeted Employment Areas from November 21," *EB-5 Updates* (blog), November 22, 2019, https://blog.lucidtext.com/2019/11/22/targeted-employment-areas-from-november-21/.

829 petitions. If a family member is not included on the principal investor's I-829 petition because the principal investor fails or refuses to file a Form I-829, they may file their own I-829 to remove conditions on their permanent residence. The regulation also provides greater flexibility in interview locations for I-829 petitions.[93] Additional changes update regulations to reflect statutory changes and clarify key terms for the program.

Table 3. Summary of major changes under the EB-5 immigrant investor program modernization regulation

	Before November 21, 2019	On or After November 21, 2019
Minimum Investment Amounts	Investment amounts had not changed since the visa's inception: $1 million or $500,000 in a TEA	Investment amounts increased to $1.8 million or $900,000 in a TEA. The amounts will be adjusted for inflation, tied to the CPI-U, every five years.
TEA Designations	State governments could certify a TEA by identifying a particular geographic or political subdivision as an area of high unemployment	States may no longer designate geographic and political subdivisions as high unemployment areas. Only USCIS can make special designations of a high unemployment area of a census tract or contiguous census tracts in which the new commercial enterprise is principally doing business.
Priority Date Retention	Investors were unable to use the priority date on an approved I-526 for future petitions.	EB-5 petitioners will retain the priority dates of approved I-526 petitions for use in connection with any subsequent I-526 petition.

Source: CRS summary of the DHS EB-5 Immigrant Investor Program Modernization regulation.

Note: The EB-5 Immigrant Investor Program Modernization regulation applies to all petitions filed on or after November 21, 2019.

[93] 8 C.F.R. §216.6.

POLICY ISSUES

USCIS implementation of the EB-5 modernization regulation in 2019 addressed several longstanding perceived deficiencies of the EB-5 program, including concerns about TEA gerrymandering and investment amounts that had not been changed since the program's inception. Nevertheless, concerns about the program remain, particularly with regard to fraud and national security risks, data collection, and backlogs in application processing. In addition, new concerns have emerged related to the COVID-19 pandemic. The following sections review these issues and, where applicable, discuss changes USCIS has made to address them.

Fraud and Security Risks

Some Members of Congress have repeatedly expressed concerns about instances of fraud and national security concerns associated with the EB-5 visa category and the Regional Center Program and have questioned whether these issues merit reform or ending the program entirely.[94] The Government Accountability Office (GAO) found that EB-5 faces the risk of fraud in three unique respects that stem from its investment components.[95] First, immigrant investors must provide evidence that their investment funds were obtained through lawful means. It can be difficult, however, for USCIS to verify these sources.

---

[94] See, for example, U.S. Congress, Senate Committee on the Judiciary, *Citizenship for Sale: Oversight of the EB-5 Investor Visa Program*, hearing, 115th Cong., 2 sess., June 19, 2018; U.S. Congress, House Committee on the Judiciary, *The Department of Homeland Security's Proposed Regulations Reforming the Investor Visa Program*, hearing, 115th Cong., 1 sess., March 8, 2017; U.S. Congress, House Committee on the Judiciary, *Is the Investor Visa Program an Underperforming Asset?*, hearing, 114th Cong., 2 sess., February 11, 2016; and U.S. Congress, Senate Committee on the Judiciary, *The Failures and Future of the EB-5 Regional Center Program: Can it be Fixed?*, hearing, 114th Cong., 2nd sess., February 2, 2016.

[95] U.S. Government Accountability Office, *Immigrant Investor Program Additional Actions Needed to Better Assess Fraud Risks and Report Economic Benefit,* GAO-15-696, August 2015.

Second, the potential for large financial gains through the EB-5 visa may motivate regional center operators and intermediaries[96] to take advantage of foreign investors. Some intermediaries have used aggressive tactics to recruit investors abroad and some misrepresent the Regional Center Program. For example, because of these tactics, some investors mistakenly believe that regional centers are government-run even though most are administered by limited liability companies.[97] There have been cases of regional center developers and managers defrauding immigrant investors for personal gain[98] and putting at risk their immigration status.[99]

U.S. Securities and Exchange Commission (SEC) officials reported over 100 tips, complaints, and referrals on possible security fraud violations concerning the EB-5 visa from January 2013 to January 2015, and just over half were referred for further investigation.[100] Further, from February 2013 to December 2015, SEC filed 19 cases involving EB-5 offerings, of which almost half involved fraud allegations.[101] USCIS Fraud Detection and National Security (FDNS) has identified the program's susceptibility to "Ponzi schemes" and financial fraud.[102] Several EB-5

---

[96] Regional center operators and intermediaries can include the individual who created the regional center, the individual who manages or oversees the regional center, or the individual who connected or recruited the foreign investor to invest in a certain regional center.

[97] Audrey Singer and Camille Galdes, *Improving the EB-5 Investor Visa Program: International Financing for U.S. Regional Economic Development*, Brookings-Rockefeller, Project on State and Metropolitan Innovation, February 2014.

[98] Ellen Sheng, "Foreign Investors Defrauded Through U.S. EB-5 Visa Program," *Forbes*, August 1, 2016.

[99] Prepared Statement by Senator Chuck Grassley, Senate Judiciary Committee Chairman, in U.S. Congress, Senate Committee on the Judiciary, *Citizenship for Sale: Oversight of the EB-5 Investor Visa Program,* hearing, 115th Cong., 2nd sess., June 19, 2018. https://www.judiciary.senate.gov/grassley-statement-at-hearing-on-citizenship-for-sale-oversight-of-the-eb-5-investor-visa-program.

[100] U.S. Government Accountability Office (GAO), *Immigrant Investor Program Additional Actions Needed to Better Assess Fraud Risks and Report Economic Benefit,* GAO-15-696, August 2015.

[101] U.S. Congress, Senate Committee on the Judiciary, *The Failures and Future of the EB-5 Regional Center Program: Can it be Fixed?* testimony of Stephen L. Cohen, Associate Director of U.S. Securities and Exchange Commission's Division of Enforcement, 114th Cong., 2nd sess., February 2, 2016.

[102] Prepared Statement by Senator Chuck Grassley, Senate Judiciary Committee Chairman, in U.S. Congress, Senate Committee on the Judiciary, *Citizenship for Sale: Oversight of the EB-5 Investor Visa Program,* hearing, 115th Cong., 2nd sess., June 19, 2018. https://www.

investors have filed lawsuits against regional centers and NCEs alleging fraud and misappropriation of funds.[103]

Third, the EB-5 visa is susceptible to the appearance of favoritism and special access. A DHS OIG report identified the risk of internal and external influence on the EB-5 visa, listing USCIS's lack of protocols to document inquiries, decisionmaking, and responses to external parties who inquired about EB-5 activities as a key issue.[104] In March 2015, DHS OIG released a report prompted by USCIS employee complaints on the management of the EB-5 visa.[105] Subsequently, the DHS Secretary asked Congress to help increase the security and integrity of the visa. USCIS then issued a new ethics and integrity protocol for EB-5 that addresses application processing and stakeholder communication.[106]

USCIS has conducted risk assessments to identify, analyze, and establish solutions for issues surrounding fraud. In 2018, USCIS reported that it had begun conducting an annual fraud assessment in response to GAO recommendations.[107] USCIS has also reported to GAO that it conducts regular oversight work and collaborates with other enforcement agencies that may uncover fraud, such as the Federal Bureau of

---

judiciary.senate.gov/grassley-statement-at-hearing-on-citizenship-for-sale- oversight-of-the-eb-5-investor-visa-program.

[103] Gary Friedland and Jeanne Calderon, "EB-5 Securities: New Developments and Updated NYU Stern Database— 2018 Edition" (New York: NYU Stern School of Business, 2018), https://www.stern.nyu.edu/sites/default/files/assets/documents/EB-5%20Securities%20-%20New%20Developments%20and%20Updated%20NYU%20Stern%20Database%20-%202018%20Edition.pdf.

[104] U.S. Department of Homeland Security Office of Inspector General, *United States Citizenship and Immigration Services: Employment-Based Fifth Preference (EB-5) Regional Center Program*, OIG-14-19, December 2013.

[105] The report found that then-USCIS Director Alejandro Mayorkas had "communicated with stakeholders on substantive issues, outside of the normal adjudicatory process and intervened with the career USCIS staff in ways that benefited stakeholders." U.S. Department of Homeland Security Office of Inspector General, *Investigation into Employee Complaints about Management of U.S. Citizenship and Immigration Services' EB-5 Program,* March 2015.

[106] U.S. Department of Homeland Security, Ethics and Integrity: Protocols for Processing EB-5 Immigrant Investor Visa Petitions and EB-5 Regional Center Applications, Including Stakeholder Communications, April 30, 2015.

[107] Testimony of L. Francis Cissna, USCIS Director, in U.S. Congress, Senate Committee on the Judiciary, Citizenship for Sale: Oversight of the EB-5 Investor Visa Program, hearing, 115th Cong., 2nd sess., June 19, 2018, at https://www.judiciary.senate.gov/imo/media/doc/06-19-18%20Cissna%20Testimony.pdf.

Investigation (FBI), Immigration and Customs Enforcement's (ICE's) Homeland Security Investigations (HSI), and SEC. USCIS also reported a memorandum of understanding with the Financial Crimes Enforcement Network (FinCEN), a bureau of the U.S. Department of the Treasury, to investigate illicit use of investors' funds (e.g., money laundering).[108] USCIS has stated that these partnerships facilitate national security vetting and help identify "potential terrorists... potential spies, saboteurs, and technology thieves."[109]

USCIS has stated that "there are indications that the [regional center] program has been used to undermine our national security."[110] A 2017 FDNS report identified 40 cases with possible national security concerns from 2011 to 2015 and noted that additional cases may be missing due to limitations of law enforcement data systems.[111] A central concern related to fraud and national security risks is USCIS' interpretation that it lacks the authority to deny or terminate a regional center's participation in EB-5 based solely on fraud or national security concerns.[112]

USCIS may terminate a regional center's participation in the EB-5 program if the regional center fails to submit required information or it is no longer promoting economic growth.[113] USCIS can deny immigration benefits to individual immigrants who are considered to be a national security threat,[114] but the agency has interpreted the INA as not being applicable to regional centers because they are pooling funds from

---

[108] James Reiser, "A Dive Into EB-5: A Need for Complete Modernization of U.S. Investor-Based Immigration Program or EB-5 (Employment-Based Immigration: Fifth Preference)," *Touro Law Review* 35, no. 4 (2019): 37.

[109] Testimony of L. Francis Cissna, USCIS Director, in U.S. Congress, Senate Committee on the Judiciary, *Citizenship for Sale: Oversight of the EB-5 Investor Visa Program*, hearing, 115th Cong., 2nd sess., June 19, 2018, at https://www.judiciary.senate.gov/imo/media/doc/06-19-18%20Cissna%20Testimony.pdf.

[110] Ibid.

[111] Letter from Senator Charles E. Grassley to Kirstjen Nielsen, Department of Homeland Security Secretary, June 4, 2018, at https://www.judiciary.senate.gov/imo/media/doc/2018-06-04%20CEG%20to%20DHS%20(EB- 5%20vulnerabilities).pdf.

[112] Testimony of L. Francis Cissna, USCIS Director, in U.S. Congress, Senate Committee on the Judiciary, *Citizenship for Sale: Oversight of the EB-5 Investor Visa Program*, hearing, 115th Cong., 2nd sess., June 19, 2018, at https://www.judiciary.senate.gov/imo/media/doc/06-19-18%20Cissna%20Testimony.pdf.

[113] 8 C.F.R. §204.6(m)(6).

[114] INA §212(a)(3).

investors rather than seeking an immigrant benefit or visa.[115] USCIS officials have noted that this statutory limitation is a "major challenge and requires a significant amount of time to link findings [of fraud or national security concerns] to the statutory criteria," for terminating a regional center.[116]

During a 2018 Senate Judiciary Committee hearing on the EB-5 program, then-USCIS Director L. Francis Cissna made four requests to Congress for the agency to achieve greater oversight of the program and mitigate fraud and security risks: (1) authority to terminate regional centers involved with criminal activity, (2) the ability to prevent individuals with criminal records from holding positions as principals within centers, (3) authority to audit regional centers, and (4) authority to sanction regional centers through fines rather than termination alone. Director Cissna recommended that "Congress should consider allowing the [regional center] program to expire" if legislative reforms are not undertaken.[117]

Data Collection and Oversight

In a 2015 report, GAO identified limitations in USCIS' data collection for the EB-5 program. Addressing these could assist in its assessment and detection of fraud. For example, USCIS relies heavily on paper-based documentation and does not fully transfer information into its electronic databases or transfer information in a standardized manner.[118] These

---

[115] U.S. Department of Homeland Security Office of Inspector General, United States Citizenship and Immigration Services: Employment-Based Fifth Preference (EB-5) Regional Center Program, OIG-14-19, December 2013.

[116] U.S. Government Accountability Office (GAO), Immigrant Investor Program Additional Actions Needed to Better Assess Fraud Risks and Report Economic Benefit, GAO-15-696, August 2015.

[117] Testimony of L. Francis Cissna, USCIS Director, in U.S. Congress, Senate Committee on the Judiciary, Citizenship for Sale: Oversight of the EB-5 Investor Visa Program, hearing, 115th Cong., 2nd sess., June 19, 2018, at https://www.judiciary.senate.gov/imo/media/doc/06-19-18%20Cissna%20Testimony.pdf.

[118] For example, databases do not require that all information on paper forms be entered; certain input, such as an applicant's name from the I-924 form, is optional. U.S. Government Accountability Office, *Immigrant Investor Program Additional Actions Needed to Better Assess Fraud Risks and Report Economic Benefit,* GAO-15-696, August 2015.

practices can make it difficult to search for certain information, especially when attempting to identify fraud through the tracking of irregularities or trends.

In recent years, USCIS has cited improvements to its data collection processes. In 2017, USCIS published revised forms to improve its data collection and ability to vet regional centers, principals, and petitions.[119] For example, Form I-526 was expanded from 3 to 13 pages to collect more detailed information from filers, including employment history, address history, source of investment, and additional information on regional centers and NCEs.[120]

In 2015, GAO reported that USCIS, SEC, and HSI officials and members of the national industry association representing regional centers agreed that expanding site visits would increase the program's integrity. USCIS reported that FDNS staff increased project site visits through the USCIS Administrative Site Visit Verification program from 50 visits in 2016 to 232 in 2017.

Thirty-one percent of sites visited were classified as "not operating as expected" because the business had been sold, gone out of business, appeared to be deserted, or there was no evidence of construction.[121]

USCIS is required by statute to interview immigrant investors within 90 days of submitting Form I-829, but the agency also has the authority to waive that requirement.[122] Interviews can be a method to collect corroborating information on whether investors meet program requirements and whether the project may involve fraud. USCIS began a

---

[119] Testimony of L. Francis Cissna, USCIS Director, in U.S. Congress, Senate Committee on the Judiciary, *Citizenship for Sale: Oversight of the EB-5 Investor Visa Program*, hearing, 115th Cong., 2nd sess., June 19, 2018, at https://www.judiciary.senate.gov/imo/media/doc/06-19-18%20Cissna%20Testimony.pdf.

[120] Sylvia Sobczyk, "USCIS Releases New Edition of Form I-526 with New Changes and Information Requested From Investors," EB-5 Insights (blog), April 14, 2017, https://www.eb5insights.com/2017/04/14/uscis-releases-new-edition-of-form-i-526-with-new-changes-and-information-requested-from-investors/.

[121] Testimony of L. Francis Cissna, USCIS Director, in U.S. Congress, Senate Committee on the Judiciary, *Citizenship for Sale: Oversight of the EB-5 Investor Visa Program*, hearing, 115th Cong., 2nd sess., June 19, 2018, at https://www.judiciary.senate.gov/imo/media/doc/06-19-18%20Cissna%20Testimony.pdf.

[122] 8 U.S.C. §1186b(c)(1)(B) (INA interview requirement); 8 U.S.C. §1186b(d)(3) (discretionary waiver authority).

pilot program to conduct interviews via videoconference in 2016 and reported conducting 44 in 2018.[123]

In September 2020, USCIS proposed a new regulation to expand biometric data collection. The proposed regulation would authorize the collection of biometric data for criminal and national security background checks on all principals of regional centers under the EB-5 program, including U.S. citizens and LPRs.[124] USCIS asserts that this biometric collection would detect "instances of fraud, financial crimes, or other activities that would demonstrate a lack of ability to promote economic growth" and identify potential national security concerns associated with regional centers.[125] The regulation has been met with opposition from some stakeholders, including the American Immigration Lawyers Association (AILA), which argued in a comment on the regulation that, "DHS has failed to provide a reasoned analysis that necessitates such a significant and overbroad intrusion on the privacy of Regional Center applicants."[126]

As mentioned previously (see the "Economic Impact" section), data limitations also impede analyses of the EB-5 program's economic impacts. For example, with regard to job creation, USCIS only tracks that the minimum number of jobs (10) have been created through EB-5 investments, rather than the total number of jobs produced.[127] Some Members of Congress have expressed concern that USCIS does not collect or publicly release enough data about the program to show stakeholders where visas go and what types of projects get funded. In response, USCIS

---

[123] Testimony of L. Francis Cissna, USCIS Director, in U.S. Congress, Senate Committee on the Judiciary, *Citizenship for Sale: Oversight of the EB-5 Investor Visa Program*, hearing, 115th Cong., 2nd sess., June 19, 2018, at https://www.judiciary.senate.gov/imo/media/doc/06-19-18%20Cissna%20Testimony.pdf.

[124] U.S. Citizenship and Immigration Services, DHS, "Collection and Use of Biometrics by U.S. Citizenship and Immigration Services," 85 *Federal Register* 56338, September 11, 2020.

[125] Department of Homeland Security, "Collection and Use of Biometrics by U.S. Citizenship and Immigration Services," 85 *Federal Register* 56362, September 11, 2020.

[126] American Immigration Lawyers Association. "AILA Comment on the Biometrics Rule as it Relates to Regional Centers," October 13, 2020, at https://www.aila.org/infonet/comments-dhs-proposed-rule-biometrics.

[127] Audrey Singer and Camille Galdes, *Improving the EB-5 Investor Visa Program: International Financing for U.S. Regional Economic Development*, Brookings-Rockefeller, Project on State and Metropolitan Innovation, February 2014.

has stated that it does not track this information.[128] These limitations can make it difficult to evaluate the successes of the program.

Application and Petition Processing

Processing times for EB-5 applications (both for the regional center designation and the petitions for foreign national investors), and the impact of delays on investors and project developers, remain ongoing issues within the EB-5 program.[129] As of December 30, 2020, USCIS estimated processing times for investors filing Form I-526 to immigrate to the United States ranged from 35.0 months to 52.5 months. USCIS estimated Chinese (mainland born) investors' processing times at 50.0 to 75.5 months, while the range for all other foreign nationals was between 27.5 and 43.0 months. The processing time to remove conditionality from LPR status (Form I-829) ranged between 33.0 and 59.0 months. The processing time for applications for regional center designations (Form I-924) ranged between 52.5 and 56.0 months.[130]

Some investors who have experienced long wait times for EB-5 visas have filed lawsuits to rescind their investments and leave the EB-5 program.[131] EB-5 stakeholders have stated that USCIS needs to adjudicate EB-5 and regional center applications in a more predictable manner, noting

[128] Responses to Questions for the Record by L. Francis Cissna, USCIS Director, in U.S. Congress, Senate Committee on the Judiciary, *Citizenship for Sale: Oversight of the EB-5 Investor Visa Program*, hearing, 115th Cong., 2nd sess., June 19, 2018. https://www.judiciary.senate.gov/imo/media/doc/Cissna%20Responses%20to%20QFRs%20(Public).pdf.

[129] For example, see Office of the Citizenship and Immigration Services Ombudsman, *EB-5 Immigrant Investor Program Stakeholder Meeting*, Executive Summary, Washington, DC, March 5, 2013. See also Office of the Citizenship and Immigration Services Ombudsman, *Employment Creation Immigrant Visa (EB-5) Program Recommendations*, Department of Homeland Security, Washington, DC, March 18, 2009.

[130] USCIS Case Processing Times. "Processing Times," accessed December 30, 2020, at https://egov.uscis.gov/ processing-times/.

[131] Gary Friedland and Jeanne Calderon, *EB-5 Securities: New Developments and Updated NYU Stern Database—2018 Edition* (New York: NYU Stern School of Business, 2018), https://www.stern.nyu.edu/sites/default/files/assets/documents/EB-5%20Securities%20-%20New%20Developments%20and%20Updated%20NYU%20Stern%20Database%20-%202018%20Edition.pdf.

that the EB-5 program faces competition from other countries' immigrant investor programs that operate more predictably and quickly.

In testimony to Congress in 2018, USCIS stated a primary reason for processing delays in recent years was an increased number of EB-5 filings. In response to these delays, the agency added new staff to review, investigate, and adjudicate petitions.[132] In 2017, IPO announced an organizational restructuring that created a division of Adjudicators and Economists focused on I-829 filings and I-526 adjudication.[133] Full-time IPO staff increased from 184 employees at the end of 2017 to 245 in 2020.[134] By FY2018, IPO reported a 21.9% increase in I-526 completions and a backlog reduction of 36%.[135]

However, investors and stakeholders expressed concerns as adjudications (approvals and denials) of I-526 petitions dropped substantially in FY2019.[136] Despite a high number of pending I-526 petitions (14,394 at the end of FY2018), 4,673 were adjudicated in FY2019 compared with 15,122 in FY2018 and 12,243 in FY2017. IPO acknowledged to stakeholders that "increased processing times" were "the subject of much comment and understandable concern" and attributed delays in processing times to its focus on protecting integrity and

---

[132] Responses to Questions for the Record by L. Francis Cissna, USCIS Director, in U.S. Congress, Senate Committee on the Judiciary, *Citizenship for Sale: Oversight of the EB-5 Investor Visa* Program, hearing, 115th Cong., 2nd sess., June 19, 2018. https://www.judiciary.senate.gov/imo/media/doc/Cissna%20Responses%20to%20QFRs%20(Public).pdf.

[133] Immigrant Investor Program Office, *EB-5 Stakeholder Engagement,* remarks of Acting IPO Chief Julia Harrison, New York, NY, November 7, 2017. https://www.uscis.gov/sites/default/files/document/outreach-engagements/PED_EB5EngagementTalkingPoints_1107 2017.pdf.

[134] Immigrant Investor Program Office, *EB-5 Stakeholder Engagement,* remarks of IPO Chief Sarah Kendall, Washington, DC, March 13, 2020. https://www.uscis.gov/sites /default/files/document/outreach-engagements/PED_SarahKendallRemarksEB5_03132020.pdf.

[135] Immigrant Investor Program Office, *2018 AILA & IIUSA EB-5 Industry Forum,* remarks of IPO Chief Sarah Kendall, Chicago, IL, October 29, 2018. https://www.uscis.gov/sites/default/files/document/foia/2018_AILA_IIUSA_EB-5_Industry_Forum_Sarah_M._ Kendall_Remarks.pdf.

[136] Immigrant Investor Program Office, *EB-5 Stakeholder Engagement,* remarks of IPO Chief Sarah Kendall, Washington, DC, March 13, 2020, at https://www.uscis.gov/sites/default/files/document/outreach-engagements/PED_SarahKendallRemarksEB5_03132 020.pdf.

preventing abuse in the program, as well as a lapse in congressional authorization of the Regional Center Program.[137]

In January 2020, IPO announced that effective March 31, 2020, it would begin processing pending I-526 applications based on the availability of visas for a petitioner's country of origin instead of using its previous "first in, first out" approach to processing petitions in the order in which they were received. IPO stated that this new approach would better address congressional intent for visa allocation by enabling petitioners to use their annual per-country allocation without waiting in line behind petitioners from oversubscribed countries.[138]

COVID-19 and the EB-5 Program

In response to the COVID-19 pandemic, in April 2020, the Trump Administration issued a Presidential Proclamation barring the entry of most foreign nationals. However, the proclamation included some exemptions, including "any alien applying for a visa to enter the United States pursuant to the EB-5 Immigrant Investor Program."[139]

In response, four Senators sent President Trump a letter asking the Administration to "remove the exemption... until real reforms are adopted" citing fraud and characterizing the program as "effectively functioning as a pay-for-citizenship scheme in many cases."[140] Some industry stakeholders

---

[137] Immigrant Investor Program Office, *2019 IIUSA EB-5 Industry Forum*, remarks of IPO Chief Sarah Kendall, Seattle, WA, October 29, 2019. https://www.uscis.gov/sites/default/files/document/checklists/2019_IIUSA_EB-5_Industry_Forum.pdf.

[138] Ibid.

[139] The White House (President Donald J. Trump), "Proclamation Suspending Entry of Immigrants Who Present Risk to the U.S. Labor Market During the Economic Recovery Following the COVID-19 Outbreak," accessed October 15, 2020, https://www.whitehouse.gov/presidential-actions/proclamation-suspending-entry-immigrants-present-risk-u-s-labor-market-economic-recovery-following-covid-19-outbreak/.

[140] Sens. Tom Cotton, Ted Cruz, Chuck Grassley, and Josh Hawley, "Cotton, Colleagues Urge Expansion and Extension of Immigration Proclamation," press release, May 7, 2020, https://www.cotton.senate.gov/news/press-releases/cotton-colleagues-urge-expansion-and-extension-of-immigration-proclamation.

criticized the Senators' response, arguing that EB-5 contributes to the economy and generates jobs "at no cost to the taxpayer."[141]

Although EB-5 petitioners were exempted from entry bars, the pandemic interrupted consular processing of EB-5 visas abroad. DOS temporarily suspended visa services in March 2020 and announced a phased resumption of visa services in July.[142] As mentioned previously, most EB-5 petitioners are new arrivals who must go through consular processing (see the "EB-5 Admissions" section). Industry stakeholders expressed concern that because of the pause in consular processing, along with "stalled business projects," the COVID-19 pandemic put the program at risk of losing unclaimed visas to other employment categories.[143]

The pandemic's industry impacts have had direct implications for the EB-5 program. For example, there have been pandemic-related downturns in hospitality and commercial real estate construction projects, which are the targets of many EB-5 investments. There are also concerns about job creation requirements in light of the economic downturn impacting those industries.[144]

Additional concerns regarding delayed processing times have emerged related to the pandemic. In May 2020, USCIS, a fee-funded agency, predicted it would experience a budget shortfall due to declines in immigration filings and associated fees because of the pandemic.[145] USCIS cautioned about, though later rescinded, large-scale staff furloughs as a

---

[141] Invest in the USA, "IIUSA Urges Senators to Embrace the EB-5 Program to Help Save and Create American Jobs at No Cost to the U.S. Treasury," IIUSA Blog, May 11, 2020, https://iiusa.org/blog/iiusa-urges-senators-to-embrace-the-eb-5-program-to-help-save-and-create-american-jobs-at-no-cost-to-the-u-s-treasury/.

[142] U.S. Department of State, "Phased Resumption of Routine Visa Services," *U.S. Visas News*, November 12, 2020, https://travel.state.gov/content/travel/en/News/visas-news/phased-resumption-routine-visa-services.html.

[143] Genevieve Douglas, "Immigrant Investors Stalled by Virus Add to Economic Worries," *Bloomberg Law*, June 8, 2020, Daily Labor Report, https://news.bloomberglaw.com/daily-labor-report/immigrant-investors-stalled-by-virus- add-to-economic-worries.

[144] Andrew McIntyre, "3 Ways COVID-19 Is Reshaping The EB-5 Landscape," *Law360*, October 20, 2020, https://www.law360.com/articles/1320447/3-ways-covid-19-is-resha ping-the-eb-5-landscape.

[145] "Deputy Director for Policy Statement on USCIS' Fiscal Outlook | USCIS," June 25, 2020, https://www.uscis.gov/news/news-releases/deputy-director-for-policy-statement-on-uscis-fiscal-outlook.

result of the shortfall.[146] In the Continuing Appropriations Act, 2021 and Other Extensions Act (H.R. 8337), Congress addressed the budget shortfall by amending the INA to expand "premium processing" and authorized the agency to increase premium processing filing fees. Premium processing is not currently available for EB-5 petitions, but the bill requires the DHS Secretary to provide Congress a five-year plan that includes plans to "improve processing times for all immigration and naturalization benefit requests."[147]

APPENDIX. EB-5 RELATED TERMINOLOGY

Table A-1. Acronyms

ANPRM/NPRM	Advanced Notice of Proposed Rulemaking/Notice of Proposed Rulemaking
CPI-U	Consumer Price Index for All Urban Consumers
DHS	Department of Homeland Security
DOS	Department of State
EB-5	Investor Visa Program (fifth category of employment-based visas)
FBI	Federal Bureau of Investigation
FDNS	Fraud Detection and National Security (within USCIS)
FinCEN	Financial Crimes Enforcement Network
GAO	Government Accountability Office
HSI	Homeland Security Investigations
ICE	Immigration and Customs Enforcement
INA	Immigration and Nationality Act
IPO	Immigrant Investor Program Office
LPR	Lawful permanent resident
MSA	Metropolitan statistical area
NCE	New commercial enterprise
NTA	Notice to Appear – Form I-862
OIG	Office of Inspector General
SEC	Securities and Exchange Commission
TEA	Targeted Employment Area
USCIS	United States Citizenship and Immigration Services

[146] USCIS, "USCIS Averts Furlough of Nearly 70% of Workforce | USCIS," August 25, 2020, https://www.uscis.gov/news/news-releases/uscis-averts-furlough-of-nearly-70-of-work force.

[147] H.R. 8337-33 §4103.

Table A-2. Forms

DS-260	Immigrant Visa Electronic Application
I-485	Application to Register Permanent Residence or Adjust Status
I-526	Immigrant Petition by Alien Investor
I-829	Petition by Investor to Remove Conditions on Permanent Resident Status
I-924	Application For Regional Center Designation Under the Immigrant Investor Program
I-924A	Annual Certification of Regional Center

In: Visas
Editor: Brian A. Shelton
ISBN: 978-1-53619-966-6

Chapter 7

IMMIGRATION: "RECALCITRANT" COUNTRIES AND THE USE OF VISA SANCTIONS TO ENCOURAGE COOPERATION WITH ALIEN REMOVALS*

Jill H. Wilson

The ability to repatriate foreign nationals (aliens) who violate U.S. immigration law is central to the immigration enforcement system. The Immigration and Nationality Act (INA) provides broad authority to the Department of Homeland Security (DHS) and the Department of Justice (DOJ) to remove certain foreign nationals from the United States.

Any foreign national found to be inadmissible or deportable under the grounds specified in the INA may be ordered removed. Those ordered removed may include unauthorized aliens (i.e., foreign nationals who enter without inspection, enter with fraudulent documents, or enter legally but overstay their temporary visas). Lawfully present foreign nationals who

* This is an edited, reformatted and augmented version of Congressional Research Service Publication No. IF11025, updated July 10, 2020.

commit crimes or certain other acts may also be subject to removal. To effectuate a removal, the alien's country of citizenship must confirm the alien's nationality, issue travel documents, and accept his or her physical return by commercial flight or, where necessary, charter flight.

A 2001 Supreme Court ruling, Zadvydas v. Davis, generally limits the government's authority to indefinitely detain aliens who have been ordered removed. As a result, detained aliens subject to removal orders but for whom there is "no significant likelihood of removal in the reasonably foreseeable future," must be released into the United States after six months, with limited exceptions.

RECALCITRANT COUNTRIES

According to DHS's Immigration and Customs Enforcement (ICE), most countries adhere to their international obligations to accept the timely return of their citizens. Countries that systematically refuse or delay the repatriation of their citizens, however, are considered by DHS to be "recalcitrant," also called "uncooperative." Countries that demonstrate some but not full cooperation are considered "at risk of non-compliance" (ARON). ICE currently classifies 13 countries as recalcitrant/ uncooperative and 17 as ARON (Figure 1).

Countries are ranked on a scale ranging from uncooperative to cooperative, based on statistical data and analytic feedback on a range of assessment factors. These factors include a refusal to accept charter flight-based removals, the ratio of releases to removals, and average length of time between issuance of a removal order and removal. ICE also takes into account mitigating factors, such as a natural or man-made disaster or limited capacity (e.g., regarding law enforcement, inadequate records, and/or inefficient bureaucracy), to assess whether a country is intentionally uncooperative or incapable due to country conditions. Some countries disagree with ICE's assessments, maintaining that the United States has not adequately demonstrated that the persons ordered removed are indeed their nationals.

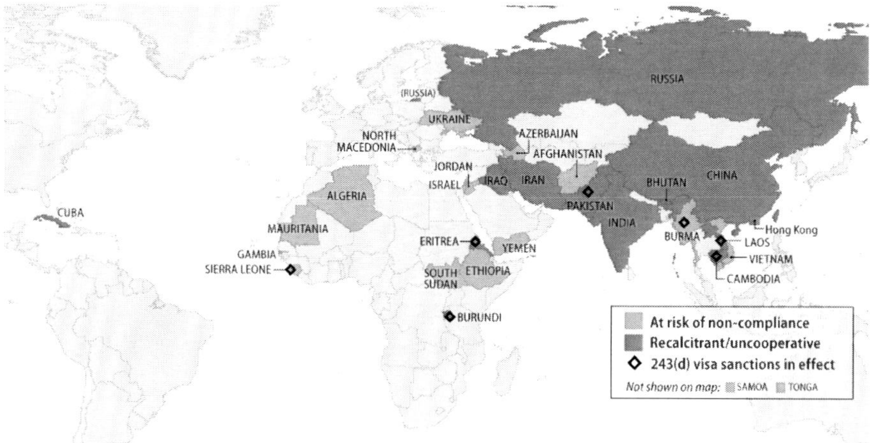

Source: Map created by CRS using data from Esri Data and Maps, 2017. Boundary representation is not necessarily authoritative. ARON/recalcitrant data provided by DHS's Immigration and Customs Enforcement (ICE), current as of June 3, 2020. Sanctions data come from publically available sources including DHS press releases, U.S. embassy websites, and the Federal Register, current as of July 10, 2020.

Figure 1. At Risk of Non-compliance (ARON), Recalcitrant, and Sanctioned Countries.

PAST USE OF VISA SANCTIONS

INA §243(d) provides that if the Secretary of Homeland Security notifies the Secretary of State that a country "denies or unreasonably delays accepting an alien who is a citizen, subject, national, or resident of that country," the Secretary of State "shall order consular officers in that foreign country to discontinue granting immigrant visas or nonimmigrant visas, or both." The Secretary of State determines which categories of visas and visa applicants will be covered by the suspension. Visa issuance resumes once the Secretary of Homeland Security notifies the Secretary of State that the country has accepted its nationals upon removal from the United States.

This provision of law was enacted in 1952, and the United States used it during the Cold War to restrict visa issuances to certain ex-Soviet bloc nationals. Between the end of the Cold War and 2016, the designation was used once, against Guyana in 2001. Citing the Supreme Court's decision in Zadvydas v. Davis, DOJ—which was then in charge of removal decisions—imposed visa sanctions to ensure removal of 113 criminally convicted Guyanese nationals then in U.S. custody whom DOJ had deemed dangerous. These sanctions followed numerous unsuccessful U.S. diplomatic attempts to effect their removal. Within two months, Guyana responded by issuing travel documents to 112 of these nationals and sanctions were lifted.

This authority was not used again until 2016, after The Gambia resisted sustained pressure to cooperate with the repatriation of its nationals. This imposition of sanctions came on the heels of a July 2016 House Committee on Oversight and Government Reform hearing in which ICE and the Department of State (DOS) discussed various measures used to persuade recalcitrant countries to cooperate (see text box). Some Members from both parties urged DHS and DOS to move beyond diplomacy and impose visa sanctions under INA §243(d) both to elicit cooperation from a country, or countries, on which sanctions are imposed and to serve as a deterrent to non-cooperation by other countries. Some Members cited the case of Jean Jacques, a Haitian who committed a murder in Connecticut in 2015 following his release from prison after a second degree murder conviction. Despite repeated attempts, DHS had been unable to repatriate Jacques due to Haiti's refusal to issue travel documents.

USE OF VISA SANCTIONS BY THE TRUMP ADMINISTRATION

Shortly after taking office, President Donald Trump issued Executive Order 13768, "Enhancing Public Safety in the Interior of the United States." Section 12 of the order, titled "Recalcitrant Countries," directs DHS and DOS to "effectively implement" the sanctions provided by INA

§243(d). It also requires the Secretary of State to "ensure that diplomatic efforts and negotiations with foreign states include as a condition precedent the acceptance by those foreign states of their nationals who are subject to removal from the United States."

In September 2017, DOS imposed visa sanctions under INA §243(d) on four countries: Cambodia, Eritrea, Guinea, and Sierra Leone. In a press release, DHS maintained that these countries had failed to establish reliable processes for issuing travel documents to their nationals ordered removed. DHS reported that it had been forced to release into the United States 2,137 Guineans and 831 Sierra Leoneans with final orders of removal, many with serious criminal convictions. DHS also reported that some 700 Eritrean nationals and 1,900 Cambodian nationals with final orders of removal—some with serious criminal convictions—were residing in the United States. Sanctions on Guinea were lifted on August 27, 2018 after the country cooperated with repatriation requests from DHS.

DHS announced sanctions for two additional countries—Burma and Laos—on July 9, 2018, citing their failure to establish reliable processes for issuing travel documents and the resulting requirement for ICE to release into the United States some of their nationals, including some convicted of serious crimes. On January 31, 2019, DHS announced 243(d) visa sanctions against Ghana, which were lifted on January 17, 2020; sanctions against Pakistan were imposed on April 5, 2019. On June 12, 2020, sanctions were imposed on Burundi. With the exception of Eritrea, Laos, and Burundi, all 243(d) sanctions apply only to tourist/business visitor (B) visas for certain government officials and, in some cases, their families and attendants. A broader set of visa categories and applicants are covered by the sanctions imposed on Eritrea, Laos, and Burundi.

Alternatives to Visa Sanctions

Visa sanctions are not the only tool available to the U.S. government to encourage cooperation with alien removals. DHS and DOS work together to identify the most effective approach in each case, beginning with diplomatic efforts. They escalate to the use of sanctions when they determine that doing so will be effective and that the benefit will outweigh the potential negative impact on foreign policy interests. Some countries sharply restrict the foreign travel of their citizens and may be unmoved by visa sanctions; others may retaliate in ways detrimental to bilateral trade, tourism, law enforcement, or other forms of cooperation. In cases in which identity documents are not readily available and the foreign country questions the nationality of individuals with removal orders, a "recalcitrant" classification or visa sanctions may impede friendly bilateral relations.

Measures to Address Recalcitrant Countries

- Issue a demarche (i.e., a formal diplomatic request)
- Hold a joint meeting with the ambassador to the United States, DOS, and ICE
- Provide notice of the U.S. government's intent to exercise visa sanctions to gain compliance
- Impose visa sanctions
- Call for inter-agency meetings to pursue withholding of aid or other funding

DHS and DOS have reported success in achieving cooperation without resorting to visa sanctions, resulting in countries being removed from the recalcitrant or ARON lists. In July 2016, there were 23 recalcitrant and 62 ARON countries; as of June 2020, those numbers had dropped to 13 recalcitrant and 17 ARON countries, a reduction that DHS and DOS attribute to pressure and diplomacy.

In: Visas
Editor: Brian A. Shelton

ISBN: 978-1-53619-966-6

Chapter 8

VISA WAIVER PROGRAM*

Abigail F. Kolker

SUMMARY

The Visa Waiver Program (VWP), originally established in 1986 as a trial program and made permanent in 2000 (P.L. 106-396), allows nationals from 39 countries, many of which are in Europe, to enter the United States as temporary visitors (nonimmigrants) for business or pleasure without first obtaining a visa. Generally, temporary visitors for business or pleasure from non- VWP countries must obtain a visa from Department of State (DOS) officers at a consular post abroad before traveling to the United States.

Some observers argue that the VWP strengthens national security because it sets standards for travel documents, requires information sharing between the member countries and the United States on criminal and security concerns, and mandates reporting of lost and stolen travel documents. VWP travelers have to present e-passports (i.e., passports with a data chip containing biometric information), which tend to be more difficult to alter than other types of passports. Nevertheless, some observers of the program have raised concerns about the possibility that terrorists will enter the United States under the VWP because those

* This is an edited, reformatted and augmented version of Congressional Research Service Publication No. RL32221, Updated June 29, 2020.

entering under the VWP undergo a biographic, rather than a biometric (i.e., fingerprint and digital photograph), security screening and do not need to interview in person with a U.S. consular official before embarking for the United States.

There is also interest in the VWP as a mechanism to promote tourism and commerce. In FY2018, there were more than 22.8 million admissions to the United States under this program, constituting nearly a third of all visitor admissions. The inclusion of countries in the VWP indicates a shared approach to national security and eases consular workloads abroad.

To qualify for the VWP, a country must offer reciprocal travel privileges to U.S. citizens; have had a nonimmigrant visa refusal rate of less than 3% for the previous year; issue their nationals machine-readable passports that incorporate biometric identifiers; issue tamper-resistant, machine-readable visa documents that incorporate biometric identifiers which are verifiable at the country's port of entry; report the loss and theft of passports; share specified information regarding nationals of the country who represent a threat to U.S. security; and not compromise the law enforcement or security interests of the United States by its inclusion in the program. Countries can be terminated from the VWP if they fail to meet any of these conditions or otherwise threaten the United States' security or immigration interests.

All foreign nationals (i.e., aliens) entering under the VWP must present passports that contain electronic data chips (e-passports). Under Department of Homeland Security (DHS) regulations, travelers who seek to enter the United States through the VWP are subject to the biometric requirements of the United States Visitor and Immigrant Status Indicator Technology (US-VISIT) program. In addition, aliens seeking to travel to the United States under the VWP must get an approval from the Electronic System for Travel Authorization (ESTA), a web-based system that checks the alien's information against relevant law enforcement and security databases, before they can board a plane to the United States.

Under statute, the Secretary of Homeland Security has the authority to waive the nonimmigrant visa refusal rate requirement, provided certain conditions are met. However, the waiver authority was suspended on July 1, 2009, because DHS had not fully implemented an air-exit system that incorporates biometric identifiers. The waiver will not be available until such a system is implemented, and it is unknown when and if a biometric exit system will be fully implemented.

Activity in the 116th Congress related to the VWP seeks to expand the number of countries by changing the criteria or by designating specific countries. Other bills would rename the VWP to "Secure Travel Partnership" to reflect one of the program's main goals of securing travel to the United States. Legislation in the 116th Congress would also address the ESTA fee paid by VWP applicants. In December 2019,

Congress authorized the continued use of the ESTA fee to partially fund Brand USA, a national tourism promotion program, through September 30, 2027. Congress also raised the ESTA fee from $14 to $21 (Division I, Title 8 of P.L. 116-94). The effective date of the new ESTA fee has not yet been announced.

INTRODUCTION

The Visa Waiver Program (VWP) allows nationals from certain countries to enter the United States as temporary visitors for business or pleasure without first obtaining a visa from a U.S. consulate abroad. Temporary visitors for business or pleasure from non-VWP countries[1] must obtain a visa from Department of State (DOS) officers at a consular post abroad before coming to the United States.

Two main goals of the VWP are increasing tourism and strengthening national security. While there tends to be agreement that the VWP benefits the U.S. economy by facilitating legitimate travel, there is disagreement on the VWP's impact on national security.[2] Proponents of the program say the VWP strengthens U.S. national security because it sets standards for travel documents, requires information sharing between member countries and the United States on criminal and security concerns, and mandates reporting of lost and stolen travel documents.[3] Critics of the program argue the VWP creates a security loophole because VWP travelers do not undergo the in-person screening generally required to receive a visa.[4]

---

[1] The two exceptions are Canada and Bermuda; they do not participate in the VWP, but their citizens do not need to obtain a nonimmigrant visa except in specified circumstances. For more information, see U.S. State Department, Bureau of Consular Affairs, *Citizens of Canada and Bermuda*, at https://travel.state.gov/content/travel/en/us-visas/tourism-visit/citizens-of-canada-and-bermuda.html.

[2] See CRS Report R46300, *Adding Countries to the Visa Waiver Program: Effects on National Security and Tourism*.

[3] For an example of this argument, see Riley Walter, *The Visa Waiver Program Is Still Great For America*, The Heritage Foundation, Issue Brief #4273, March 14, 2017, at https://www.heritage.org/sites/default/files/2017-03/ IB4664.pdf.

[4] For an example of this argument, see Federation for American Immigration Reform (FAIR), *The Visa Waiver Program: Suspend It or Eliminate It*, December 2015, at https://www.fairus.org/issue/legal-immigration/visa-waiver-program-suspend-it-or-eliminate-it.

CURRENT POLICY

In general, temporary foreign visitors for business or pleasure from most countries must obtain a B nonimmigrant visa[5] from DOS officers at a consular post abroad before coming to the United States.[6] Personal interviews are generally required, and consular officers use the Consular Consolidated Database (CCD) to screen visa applicants. The CCD indicates the outcome of any prior visa application of the alien and facilitates the flagging of issues that may make the alien ineligible for a visa under the grounds of inadmissibility of the Immigration and Nationality Act (INA), which include criminal, terrorist, and public health grounds. Consular officers are required to check the background of all aliens in the "lookout" databases, including the Consular Lookout and Support System (CLASS) and TIPOFF databases.

Eligible nationals from participating VWP countries must use the web-based Electronic System for Travel Authorization (ESTA)[7] to get an approved electronic travel authorization before embarking to the United States. ESTA authorization is generally valid for two years. VWP travelers are admitted into the United States for stays up to 90 days. The VWP constitutes one of a few exceptions under the Immigration and Nationality Act (INA) in which foreign nationals are admitted into the United States

---

[5] *Nonimmigrants* are foreign nationals lawfully admitted to the United States for a specific purpose and limited period of time. Nonimmigrants are often referred to by the letter that denotes their subparagraph in the Immigration and Nationality Act (INA §101(a)(15)), such as H-2A agricultural workers, F-1 foreign students, or J-1 cultural exchange visitors. B nonimmigrant visas are issued to short -term visitors for business or pleasure. For more information, see CRS Report R45040, *Immigration: Nonimmigrant (Temporary) Admissions to the United States*.

[6] To obtain a nonimmigrant visa, a foreign national must submit an application and undergo a background check and usually an interview. For more information on temporary admissions, see CRS Report R45040, Immigration: Nonimmigrant (Temporary) Admissions to the United States.

[7] ESTA became operational for all VWP countries on January 12, 2009; for more information, see "Electronic System for Travel Authorization," below.

without a valid visa. As of June 2020, there were 39 countries participating in the VWP.[8]

The large-scale terrorist attacks in Paris in November 2015 and in Belgium in March 2016, which were perpetrated mainly by French and Belgian citizens, increased the focus on potential security risks posed by the VWP. Prior to the December 2015 enactment of the Visa Waiver Improvement and Terrorist Travel Prevention Act (P.L. 114-113), all nationals from a VWP country were eligible to travel under the program—provided they received an ESTA approval. P.L. 114-113[9] changed eligibility for the VWP by prohibiting people who were present in certain countries since March 1, 2011, with limited exceptions, from traveling under the VWP. The specified countries include

- Iraq and Syria,
- any country designated by the Secretary of State as having repeatedly provided support for acts of international terrorism under any provision of law,[10] or
- any other country or area of concern[11] deemed appropriate by the Secretary of Homeland Security.[12]

---

[8] Poland was designated a VWP country on November 8, 2019. See Department of Homeland Security, "Designation of Poland for the Visa Waiver Program," 84 *Federal Register* 60316, November 8, 2019.

[9] For more details about P.L. 114-113, see *Appendix*.

[10] Examples of acts that use the term "repeatedly provided support for acts of international terrorism," include §6(j) of the Export Administration Act of 1979 (50 U.S.C. 2405), §40 of the Arms Export Control Act (22 U.S.C. 2780), and §620A of the Foreign Assistance Act of 1961 (22 U.S.C. 2371). Currently, these countries are Iran, Sudan, and Syria.

[11] The criteria to make the determination would include whether the presence of a foreign national in that area or country increases the likelihood that the foreign national is a credible threat to U.S. national security, whether a foreign terrorist organization has a significant presence in the area or country, and whether the country or area is a safe haven for terrorists. DHS has designated the Democratic People's Republic of Korea, Libya, Somalia, and Yemen as "countries or areas of concern."

[12] The Secretary of Homeland Security administers the VWP program. Section 402 of the Homeland Security Act of 2002 (HSA; P.L. 107-296), signed into law on November 25, 2002, states: The Secretary [of Homeland Security], acting through the Under Secretary for Border and Transportation Security, shall be responsible for the following: ... (4) Establishing and administering rules ... governing the granting of visas or other forms of permission, including parole, to enter the United States to individuals

Currently, the prohibition affects those who were present in any of the following countries: Democratic People's Republic of Korea, Iran, Iraq, Libya, Somalia, Sudan, Syria, and Yemen. The statutory exceptions from this restriction apply to foreign nationals who were in one of the specified countries in order to perform military service in the armed forces of a VWP country, or to perform official duties as an employee of the VWP country. In addition, DHS can grant waivers on a case-by-case basis.[13] The following are general categories of travelers to these countries who may be eligible for a waiver: (1) individuals who traveled on behalf of international organizations, regional organizations, and sub-national governments on official duty; (2) individuals who traveled on behalf of a humanitarian non-governmental organization (NGO) on official duty; (3) individuals who traveled as journalists for reporting purposes; (4) individuals who traveled to Iran for legitimate business-related purposes following the conclusion of the Joint Comprehensive Plan of Action (July 14, 2015);[14] and (5) individuals who have travel to Iraq for legitimate business-related purposes.[15]

In addition, anyone who is a dual national of a VWP country and the Democratic People's Republic of Korea, Iran, Iraq, Sudan, or Syria is ineligible to travel under the VWP. As with the prohibition against those who were present in certain countries, the Secretary of Homeland Security has the authority to waive the prohibition on certain dual nationals if the

who are not a citizen or an alien [sic] lawfully admitted for permanent residence in the United States.

[13] 8 U.S.C. §1187(a)(12)(C).

[14] On July 14, 2015, Iran and the six powers that have negotiated with Iran about its nuclear program since 2006 (the United States, the United Kingdom, France, Russia, China, and Germany) finalized a Joint Comprehensive Plan of Action (JCPOA). The JCPOA is intended to ensure that Iran's nuclear program can be used for purely peaceful purposes, in exchange for a broad lifting of U.S., European Union (EU), and United Nations (U.N.) sanctions on Iran. On May 8, 2018, President Trump announced that the United States would no longer participate in the JCPOA. On January 5, 2020, Iran declared it would no longer abide by the limitations of the deal. For more on the JCPOA, see CRS Report R43333, *Iran Nuclear Agreement and U.S. Exit*.

[15] There is no separate application for a waiver. A foreign national's eligibility for a waiver is determined during the ESTA application process. U.S. Customs and Border Protection, *Visa Waiver Program Improvement and Terrorist Travel Prevention Act Frequently Asked Questions*, at https://www.cbp.gov/travel/international-visitors/visa-waiver-program/visa-waiver-program-improvement-and-terrorist-travel-prevention-act-faq, accessed November 13, 2019.

Secretary determines that the waiver would be in the law enforcement or national security interests of the United States. As of the date of this chapter, DHS has not released any guidance on waivers for dual nationals.[16] DHS reports on these waivers to Congress annually, but these reports are not available to the public.

Visa Waiver Program Countries (as of June 2020)

Andorra, Australia, Austria, Belgium, Brunei, Chile, Czech Republic, Denmark, Estonia, Finland, France, Germany, Greece, Hungary, Iceland, Ireland, Italy, Japan, Latvia, Liechtenstein, Lithuania, Luxembourg, Malta, Monaco, the Netherlands, New Zealand, Norway, Poland, Portugal, San Marino, Singapore, Slovakia, Slovenia, South Korea, Spain, Sweden, Switzerland, Taiwan, and the United Kingdom.

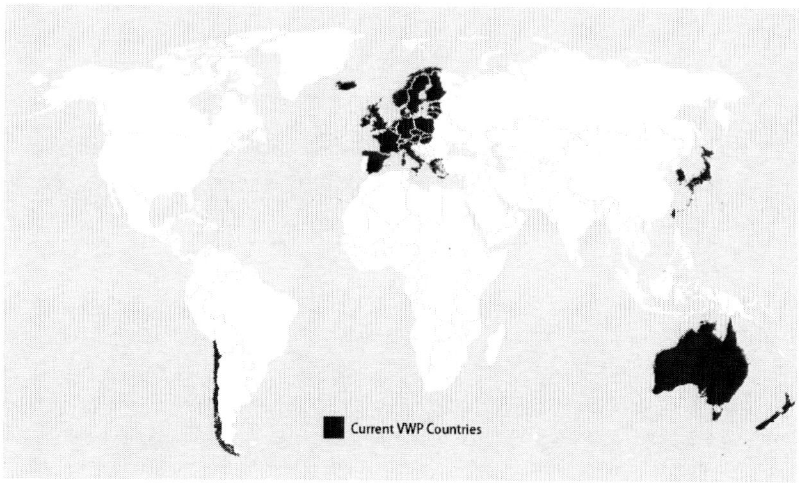

Although the VWP allows certain nationals from participating countries to enter the United States without a visa, it has important restrictions. Aliens entering with a B visa may petition to extend their length of stay in the

[16] For a discussion of some of the issues surrounding implementing the dual national provision, see Nahal Toosi, "Obama Aides Vexed by Visa Crackdown," *Politico*, April 12, 2016, Europe Edition, athttp://www.politico.eu/article/ obama-aides-vexed-by-visa-crackdown/http://www.politico.eu/article/obama-aides-vexed-by-visa-crackdown/.

United States or may petition to change to another nonimmigrant or immigrant status.[17] Aliens entering through the VWP are not permitted to extend their stays except for emergency reasons and then for only 30 days.[18] Additionally, with some limited exceptions, aliens entering through the VWP are not permitted to adjust their immigration status. An alien entering through the VWP who violates the terms of admission becomes deportable without any judicial recourse or review (except in asylum cases).[19]

VWP Qualifying Criteria

To qualify for the VWP, a country must

- offer reciprocal privileges to United States citizens;
- have had a nonimmigrant visa refusal rate[20] of less than 3% for the previous year or a lower average percentage over the previous two fiscal years;
- issue electronic, machine-readable passports that contain a biometric identifier (i.e., e-passports);[21]

---

[17] Noncitizens entering on B visas may be admitted for six months, and may apply to extend their stay for another six months.

[18] This provision was amended by P.L. 106-406 to provide exceptions for nonimmigrants who enter under the VWP and require medical treatment.

[19] To receive asylum, a foreign national must demonstrate a well-founded fear of persecution in his or her home country based on one of five grounds—race, religion, nationality, membership in a particular social group, or political opinion—and meet other requirements. For more on asylum, see CRS Report R45539, *Immigration: U.S. Asylum Policy*.

[20] This rate represents the proportion of individuals whose applications for tourist or business visas have been rejected by U.S. consular officials in their home countries.

[21] Prior to the enactment of P.L. 114-113 only passports issued after October 26, 2006, had to be machine-readable and contain a biometric identifier. In August 2015, the Secretary of Homeland Security announced that to increase security of the VWP all travelers under the program would have to use an e-passport, but the requirement had not been put into effect before the enactment of P.L. 114-113. Department of Homeland Security, "Statement by Secretary Jeh C. Johnson on Intention to Implement Security Enhancements to the Visa Waiver Program," press release, August 6, 2015, at https://www.dhs.gov/news/2015/08/06/statement-secretary-jeh-c-johnson-intention-

- issue tamper-resistant, machine-readable visa documents that incorporate biometric identifiers, which are verifiable at the country's port of entry;
- certify that it has in place mechanisms to validate machine-readable passports and e-passports at each port of entry;[22]
- enter into an agreement with the United States to report or make available through the International Criminal Police Organization (INTERPOL)[23] information about the theft or loss of passports no later than 24 hours after a theft or loss is reported to the VWP country;[24]
- certify, to the maximum extent allowed under the laws of the country, that it is screening each foreign national who is admitted to or departs from that country, using relevant INTERPOL databases and notices, or other means designated by the Secretary of Homeland Security (this requirement applies only to countries that have an international airport);[25]
- accept the repatriation of any citizen, former citizen, or national against whom a final order of removal from the United States is issued no later than three weeks after the order is issued;

---

implement-security- enhancements-visa; and telephone conversation with DHS Office of Legislative Affairs, November 3, 2015.

[22] This requirement was added by P.L. 114-113, and does not apply to travel between countries within the Schengen Area, which comprises 22 European Union (EU) member states, plus 4 non-EU countries. Within the Schengen Area, internal border controls have been largely eliminated, and individuals may travel without passport checks among participating countries. See European Commission, *Migration and Home Affairs: Schengen Area*, at http://ec.europa.eu/dgs/home-affairs/what-we-do/policies/borders-and-visas/schengen/index_en.htm.

[23] Although statute discusses sharing information on lost and stolen passports, the INTERPOL database includes other types of travel documents such as identity documents and visas. INTERPOL is the world's largest international police organization, with 194 member countries. For more information on INTERPOL see, https://www.interpol.int/Who-we- are/What-is-INT ERPOL.

[24] P.L. 114-113 added the requirement that the reporting occur within 24 hours of the country being notified about the lost/stolen passport.

[25] This screening requirement was added by P.L. 114-113, and does not apply to those traveling between countries within the Schengen Area.

- enter into and fully implement[26] an agreement with the United States to share information regarding whether a national of that country traveling to the United States represents a threat to U.S. security or welfare; and
- be determined, by the Secretary of Homeland Security, in consultation with the Secretary of State, not to compromise the law enforcement or security interests of the United States by its inclusion in the program.

The Secretary of Homeland Security, in consultation with the Secretary of State, can suspend a country's participation in the program based on a determination that the country presents a high risk to U.S. national security.[27] In addition, countries can be immediately terminated from the VWP if an emergency occurs in the country that the Secretary of Homeland Security in consultation with the Secretary of State determines threatens the law enforcement or security interest of the United States.[28] For example, because of Argentina's economic collapse in December 2001,[29] and the increase in the number of Argentine nationals attempting to use the VWP to enter the United States and remain illegally past the 90-day period of admission,[30] Argentina was removed from the VWP in

[26] The requirement to implement the agreement was added by the Visa Waiver Improvement and Terrorist Travel Prevention Act of 2015 (P.L. 114-113), enacted on December 18, 2015.

[27] The criteria to determine whether a country poses a "high risk" to national security include the number of nationals determined to be ineligible to t ravel to the United States under the VWP during the previous year; the number of nationals who were identified in U.S. government terrorism databases during the previous year, the estimated number of nationals who traveled to Iraq or Syria since March 1, 2011, to engage in terrorism; the country's capacity to combat passport fraud; the level of cooperation with U.S. counter-terrorism efforts; the adequacy of the country's border and immigration controls; and any other criteria determined by the Secretary of Homeland Security.

[28] An emergency is defined as (1) the overthrow of a democratically elected government; (2) war; (3) a severe breakdown in law and order in the country; (4) a severe economic collapse; and (5) any other extraordinary event in the program country where that country's participation could threaten the law enforcement or security interests of the United States. INA §217(c)(5)(B).

[29] Beginning in December 2001, Argentina experienced a serious economic crisis, including defaulting on loans by foreign creditors, devaluation of its currency, and increased levels of unemployment and poverty.

[30] In addition, many Argentine nationals were trying to use the VWP to obtain entry to the United States solely for the purpose of proceeding to the Canadian border and pursuing

February 2002.[31] Likewise, Uruguay joined in 1999, but it was removed from the program in April 2003 because a recession led to an increasing number of Uruguayan citizens entering the United States under the VWP to live and work illegally.[32] No country has been removed from the VWP since 2003.

Additionally, there is a probationary status for VWP countries that do not maintain a low disqualification rate.[33] VWP countries are placed on probation when they have a disqualification rate of 2% to 3.5%. Probationary countries with a disqualification rate less than 2% over a period prescribed in regulations (but not to exceed three years)[34] are removed from probationary status and may remain VWP countries.[35] Countries may also be placed on probation if an issue arises and more time is necessary to determine whether the continued participation of the country in the VWP is in the security interest of the United States. For example, in April 2003, Belgium was placed on provisional status because of concerns about the integrity of nonmachine-readable Belgian passports

an asylum claim in Canada. According to Citizenship and Immigration Canada, between 1999 and 2001, more than 2,500 Argentines filed refugee claims in Canada after transiting the United States under the VWP. *Federal Register*, February 21, 2002, vol. 67, no. 35, p. 7944.

[31] While the number of Argentine nonimmigrant travelers to the United States declined between 1998 and 2000, the number of Argentines denied admission at the port of entry and the number of interior apprehensions increased. The Department of Justice (DOJ) in consultation with DOS determined that Argentina's participation in the VWP was inconsistent with the United States' interest in enforcing its immigration laws. (The Department of Homeland Security did not exist in February 2002, and authority for the VWP resided with the Attorney General in the DOJ.) *Federal Register,* February 21, 2002, vol. 67, no. 35, pp. 7943 -7945.

[32] Between 2000 and 2003, Uruguay experienced a recession causing its citizens to enter under the VWP to live and work illegally in the United States. In 2002, Uruguayan nationals were two to three times more likely than all nonimmigrants on average to have been denied admission at the port of entry. Uruguayan air arrivals had an apparent overstay rate more than twice the rate of the average apparent overstay rate for all air arrival nonimmigrants. *Federal Register*, March 7, 2003, vol. 68, no. 45, pp. 10954-10957.

[33] *Disqualification rate* is defined as the percentage of nationals from a country who either violated the terms of the nonimmigrant visa, who were excluded from admission to the United States at a port of entry, or who withdrew their application for admission at a U.S. port of entry (8 U.S.C. §1187(f)(4)).

[34] 8 U.S.C. §1187(h)(3)(C).

[35] The Illegal Immigration Reform and Immigrant Responsibility Act of 1996 (P.L. 104-208).

and the reporting of lost or stolen passports.[36] DHS completed another country review of Belgium in 2005 and removed the country from probationary status. Belgium was the last country to have been placed on probation.

Nonimmigrant Visa Refusal Rate Waiver

Section 711 of the Implementing Recommendations of the 9/11 Commission Act of 2007 (P.L. 110-53)[37] allows the Secretary of Homeland Security, in consultation with the Secretary of State, to waive the nonimmigrant visa refusal rate requirement for admission to the VWP after the Secretary of Homeland Security certifies to Congress that

- an air exit system is in place that can verify the departure of not less than 97% of foreign nationals who exit through U.S. airports,[38] and
- the electronic travel authorization system is operational.[39]

---

[36] Department of Justice, Immigration and Naturalization Service, "Attorney General's Evaluations of the Designations of Belgium, Italy, Portugal, and Uruguay as Participants Under the Visa Waiver Program," 68 Federal Register, 10954-10957, March 7, 2003, at https://www.govinfo.gov/content/pkg/FR-2003-03-07/pdf/03-5244.pdf.

[37] P.L. 110-53 (H.R. 1), signed into law on August 3, 2007. For more details on the changes to the VWP in this act, see *Appendix,* "Legislative History."

[38] There was disagreement between some critics and DHS regarding what needed to be verified. Some contended that congressional intent was to have a functional entry-exit system that would be able to match arrival and departure records and know which aliens failed to depart from the United States rather than just matching the entry records with the records of those who were known to have departed from the United States. For example, see S. 203 introduced in the 111th Congress, which attempted to clarify the language in this provision. U.S. Congress, Senate Committee on Judiciary, Subcommittee on Terrorism, Technology and Homeland Security, *The Visa Waiver Program: Mitigating Risks to Ensure Safety to All Americans*, 110th Cong., 2nd sess., September 24, 2008.

[39] DHS determined that the law permitted it to utilize the waiver when ESTA was functional but before it was mandatory for all VWP travelers. Critics did not agree with this interpretation and thought that ESTA should have been mandatory for all VWP travelers before new countries were designated into the program. When the new countries entered the program, their citizens were required to use ESTA before travelling to the United States. U.S. Government Accountability Office, *Visa Waiver Program: Actions Are Needed to Improve Management of the Expansion Process, and to Assess and Mitigate Program Risks,* GAO-08-967, September 2008.

To participate in the program, a country that receives a visa refusal rate waiver also must

- meet all the other requirements of the program;
- be determined by the Secretary of Homeland Security to have a totality of security risk mitigation measures that provide assurances that the country's participation in the program would not compromise U.S. law enforcement and security interests, or the enforcement of U.S. immigration laws;
- have had a sustained reduction in visa refusal rates, and have existing conditions for the rates to continue to decline;
- have cooperated with the United States on counterterrorism initiatives and information sharing before the date of its designation, and be expected to continue such cooperation; and
- have had, during the previous fiscal year, a nonimmigrant visa refusal rate of less than 10%, or an overstay rate that did not exceed the maximum overstay rate established by the Secretaries of DHS and DOS for countries receiving waivers of the nonimmigrant visa refusal rate to participate in the program.

P.L. 110-53 also specified that in determining whether to waive the nonimmigrant visa refusal rate requirement, the Secretary of Homeland Security, in consultation with the Secretary of State, may take into consideration other factors affecting U.S. security, such as the country's airport security standards and whether the country has an effective air marshal program.

The nonimmigrant visa refusal rate waiver became available in October 2008 and was suspended on July 1, 2009. Under P.L. 110-53, the Secretary of Homeland Security's authority to waive the nonimmigrant visa refusal rate was suspended on July 1, 2009, and is to remain suspended until the air exit system is able to match an alien's biometric information with relevant watch lists and manifest information.[40] U.S. Customs and Border Protection (CBP) is implementing biometric air exit systems across the country; their goal is to deploy biometric exit at 20 airports by 2022, which would capture 97% of all commercial air travelers departing the United States.[41]

Electronic System for Travel Authorization

P.L. 110-53 mandated that the Secretary of Homeland Security, in consultation with the Secretary of State, develop and implement an electronic travel authorization system through which each alien electronically provides, in advance of travel, the biographical information necessary to determine whether the alien is eligible to travel to the United States and enter under the VWP. The system as implemented is known as the Electronic System for Travel Authorization (ESTA) and became fully operational for all VWP visitors traveling to the United States on January 12, 2009.[42] There is a $14 fee for travelers who use ESTA.[43] In 2019,

---

[40] Section 110 IIRIRA, as amended, requires DHS to implement an automatic, biometric entry -exit system that covers all noncitizen travelers into and out of the United States and that identifies visa overstayers. For more information, see "Debate over Biometric Exit Capacity," below.

[41] Department of Homeland Security, Transportation Security Administration and U.S. Customs and Border Protection: Deployment of Biometric Technologies, Report to Congress, August 30, 2019, p. 5, at https://www.tsa.gov/ sites/default/files/biometricsreport.pdf.

[42] Entrants under the VWP from countries that receive a waiver of the nonimmigrant visa refusal rate (Czech Republic, Estonia, Hungary, Latvia, Lithuania, Malta, Slovakia, and South Korea) had to use the system starting on the date of their formal admission to the program. For all the countries except Malta, that date was November 17, 2008. Malta was formally designated into the VWP on December 30, 2008. Department of Homeland Security, "Electronic System for Travel Authorization (ESTA) Advisory Statement," November 6, 2008. Department of Homeland Security, "Electronic System for Travel Authorization: Mandatory Compliance Required for Travel Under the Visa Waiver Program," 73 *Federal Register* 67354, November 13, 2008.

[43] The fee was instituted on September 8, 2010. The $14 fee includes $4 to cover the costs of administering ESTA and $10 for the travel promotion fee established by Congress in the Travel Promotion Act of 2009 (§9 of P.L. 111-145) and extended until September 30, 2020, by Title VI of P.L. 113-235. (Department of Homeland Security, Customs and Border Protection, "DHS, CBP Announce Interim Final Rule For ESTA Fee," press release, August 6, 2010).

Congress approved raising the ESTA fee from $14 to $21, but the effective date of the new fee has not yet been announced.[44]

ESTA screens applicants' biographical information against a number of security databases, including the Terrorist Screening Database, TECS (not an acronym, but a system used by CBP officers to screen arriving travelers to the United States),[45] the Automated Targeting System, and INTERPOL's Lost and Stolen Passport database. ESTA alerts the alien whether he or she has been approved to travel;[46] if not approved, the alien may still travel to the US but must obtain the relevant visa. The information required by ESTA includes

- biographical information including name, birth date, country of citizenship, other citizenships (i.e., dual citizenship), previous citizenships, country of residence, telephone number, other names/aliases, parents' names, national identification number (if applicable), employment information (if applicable), city of birth;[47]
- passport information including number, issuing country, issuance date, and expiration date; and
- travel information including departure city, flight number, U.S. contact information, and address while in the United States.[48]

---

[44] P.L. 116-94, Division I, Title VIII reduces the amount available for travel promotion to $7 per traveler. Of the remainder, $4 will continue to go to CBP to cover the costs of administering ESTA, and $10 will be directed to the U.S. Treasury for the general fund. Title VIII of P.L. 116-94 further extended it until September 30, 2027.

[45] TECS, managed by DHS, is an updated version of the Treasury Enforcement Communications System.

[46] In most cases, the determination process is almost instantaneous. Under statute, ESTA determinations are not reviewable by the courts.

[47] In November 2014, DHS added new questions to ESTA in response to security concerns. Department of Homeland Security, Customs and Border Protection, *ESTA - New questions to the ESTA application*, CBP INFO Center, Washington, DC, November 3, 2014, at https://help.cbp.gov/app/answers/detail/a_id/1756/~/esta—new-questions-to-the-esta-application. Although the administration was already asking the questions, P.L. 114-113 statutorily added the requirement that nationals be queried about multiple and previous citizenships.

[48] Much of the information is the same that is required on the nonimmigrant visa waiver arrival/departure form (Form I- 94W). According to DHS, when developing ESTA, the department had to balance the need for biographic information with the requirement that the participating countries did not view applying for an approval under ESTA as equivalent to applying for a visa. If countries had interpreted applying for an

Eligibility to travel, which is determined by ESTA, is valid for two years or until the person's passport expires (whichever comes first)[49] and multiple entries. Throughout this period, the ESTA system continually vets approved individuals' information against the aforementioned databases.

The Secretary of Homeland Security has the authority to shorten or revoke the determination of eligibility at any time.[50] Notably, a determination under ESTA that an alien is eligible to travel to the United States does not constitute a determination that the alien is admissible. Admissibility determinations are made by CBP inspectors at the ports of entry (the same is true for all visa holders).

Arrival and Departure Inspections

Unlike other nonimmigrants, those entering under the VWP do not have to get a visa and thus, are not inspected by U.S. governmental officials until they arrive at a U.S. port of entry. Nonetheless, in addition to getting authorization through ESTA, prior to the alien's arrival, an electronic passenger manifest is sent from the airline or commercial vessel to CBP officials, as is done for all airline and commercial vessels departing from a foreign country destined for a U.S. port of entry. This manifest is checked against security databases.

Since October 1, 2002, passenger arrival and departure information on individuals entering and leaving the United States under the VWP has been electronically collected from airlines and cruise lines, through CBP's Advanced Passenger Information System (APIS) system.[51] APIS collects

---

authorization under ESTA as having the same burden as applying for a visa, these countries might have required that U.S. citizens traveling to their countries obtain a visa.

[49] Under statute, the maximum period of time is set in regulation by the Secretary of Homeland Security but cannot exceed three years.

[50] The provision giving the Secretary of Homeland Security the authority to shorten an ESTA validity period was enacted as part of P.L. 114-113.

[51] APIS is required pre-departure (i.e., before securing the doors) for all air carrier flights to and from the United States. For inbound cruise ships the data must be received 96 hours before arrival at a U.S. port, and for cruise ships leaving the United States, the data must be transmitted 60 minutes before departure. For private aircraft, a passenger and

carrier information (e.g., flight number, airport of departure, and other information), as well as travelers' personal information, including complete name, date of birth, passport number, country of citizenship, and country of residence.[52] APIS sends the data to the DHS's Arrival and Departure Information System (ADIS) for matching arrivals and departures and reporting purposes. If the carrier fails to submit the information, an alien may not enter under the VWP.

At U.S. ports of entry, CBP officers observe and question foreign nationals, examine passports, and conduct checks against a computerized system to determine whether the applicant is admissible to the United States. Primary inspection consists of a brief interview with a CBP officer, a check of the traveler's documents, and a query of the Interagency Border Inspection System (IBIS)[53] and entry of certain biographic and biometric the information on the travelers into the United States Visitor and Immigrant Status Indicator Technology (US-VISIT) system. The US-VISIT system uses biographical (e.g., passport information) and biometric identification (finger scans and digital photographs) to check identity.[54] Officers at the border collect the following information on aliens entering under the VWP: name, date of birth, nationality, gender, passport number, country of issuance, a digital photograph, and prints for both index finders.

---

crew manifest listing all persons traveling on the aircraft must be sent electronically using the online eAPIS system at least one hour prior to departure for an inbound or outbound international flight.

[52] The transmission, retention policies, data security, and redress procedures pertaining to APIS data (and other Passenger Name Record data) received by CBP is to comport with the US/EU Passenger Name Record Agreement. For more information, see CRS Report RS22030, *U.S.-EU Cooperation Against Terrorism.*

[53] ADIS feeds information to the Interagency Border Inspection System (IBIS). IBIS is a database of suspect individuals, businesses, vehicles, aircraft, and vessels that is used during inspections at the border. IBIS interfaces with the FBI's National Crime Information Center (NCIC), the Treasury Enforcement and Communications System (TECS II), National Automated Immigration Lookout System (NAILS), Non-immigrant Information System (NIIS), CLASS and TIPOFF terrorist databases. Because of the numerous systems and databases that interface with IBIS, the system is able to obtain such information as an alien's criminal history and whether an alien is wanted by law enforcement. Department of Homeland Security, Customs and Border Protection, *IBIS- General Information*, Washington, DC, July, 31, 2013.

[54] For more information on US-VISIT, see CRS Report R43356, *Border Security: Immigration Inspections at Ports of Entry*.

Primary inspections are typically quick; however, if the CBP officer is suspicious that the traveler may be inadmissible under the INA or in violation of other U.S. laws, the traveler is referred to a secondary inspection. Those travelers sent to secondary inspections are questioned extensively, travel documents are further examined, and additional databases are queried.[55]

Additionally, the Implementing Recommendations of the 9/11 Commission Act (P.L. 110-53) required that the Secretary of Homeland Security, no later than one year after enactment (i.e., by August 3, 2008), establish an exit system that records the departure of every alien who entered under the VWP and left the United States by air. The exit system is required to match the alien's biometric information against relevant watch lists and immigration information, and compare such biographical information against manifest information collected by airlines to confirm that the alien left the United States.

In April 2008, DHS published a Notice of Proposed Rulemaking in the Federal Register that would have created biometric exit procedures at airports and seaports for international visitors.[56] DHS was expected to publish the final rule for this system by October 15, 2008.[57] However, in legislation that became law on September 30, 2008,[58] Congress required DHS to complete and report on at least two studies testing biometric exit procedures at airports.[59] After piloting various biometric programs, CBP, in partnership with the Transportation Security Administration (TSA), is currently deploying the Traveler Verification Service (TVS). TVS is a private-public partnership[60] that uses facial recognition technology to

---

[55] For more information on the screening process, see CRS Report R43356, *Border Security: Immigration Inspections at Ports of Entry*.

[56] Department of Homeland Security, "Collection of Alien Biometric Data Upon Exit From the United States at Air and Sea Ports of Departure," 73 *Federal Register* 22065, April 24, 2008.

[57] CRS analyst conversation with Department of Homeland Security Congressional Affairs, September 22, 2008.

[58] P.L. 110-329.

[59] One pilot tested DHS's recommended solution that carriers collect biometrics from passengers; the other pilot tested CBP officers collecting passenger biometrics at the boarding gate.

[60] Private partners include airports and airlines.

verify travelers' identities. DHS in January 2020 reported TVS capturing roughly 60%[61] of in-scope travelers.[62] CBP's goal is to deploy TVS at 20 airports by 2022, which would capture 97%[63] of all commercial air travelers departing the United States.[64]

Another step in implementing an exit system occurred in December 2011, when DHS announced an agreement with Canada to share entry records so that an entry into Canada along the land border would be counted as an exit in U.S. records.[65] This is part of the joint Beyond the Border initiative,[66] which is currently in Phase III of implementation.[67]

Trends in Use of the VWP

Arrivals of international visitors to the United States have generally increased in most years over the past decade. International visitors to the United States increased from 32.9 million in 2007 to 73.8 million in 2018.[68] The growth during this time has mostly been consistent except for a decrease in 2009 caused by the Great Recession. Visitor admissions will

---

[61] Based on CRS discussion with CBP officials on January 30, 2020.

[62] In-scope travelers include non-U.S. citizens aged 14-79.

[63] This would fulfill the final requirement needed to reinstate the nonimmigrant visa refusal rate waiver.

[64] Department of Homeland Security, *Transportation Security Administration and U.S. Customs and Border Protection: Deployment of Biometric Technologies,* Report to Congress, August 30, 2019, p. 5, at https://www.tsa.gov/sites/default/files/biometrics report.pdf.

[65] Testimony of David F. Heyman, U.S. Congress, House Committee on the Judiciary, Subcommittee on Immigration Policy and Enforcement, *Next Steps for the Visa Waiver Program,* 112th Cong., 1st sess., December 7, 2011. For more on this agreement, see CRS Report R43356, *Border Security: Immigration Inspections at Ports of Entry.*

[66] The White House, " Declaration by President Obama and Prime Minister Harper of Canada - Beyond the Border, press release, February 4, 2011, at https://obamawhite house.archives.gov/the-press-office/2011/02/04/declaration-president-obama-and-prime-minister-harper-canada-beyond-bord.

[67] For more information, see Department of Homeland Security, " U.S. and Canada Continue Commitment to Securing our Borders, Begin Phase III of the Entry/Exit Project Under the Beyond the Border Initiative," press release, July 11, 2019, at https://www.dhs.gov/news/2019/07/11/us-and-canada-continue-commitment-securing-our-borders-begin-phase-iii-entryexit.

[68] Department of Homeland Security, *Yearbook of Immigration Statistics*, multiple years; Table 25.

likely fall sharply in 2020 due to the decline in international travel associated with the Coronavirus Disease 2019 (COVID-19) pandemic.

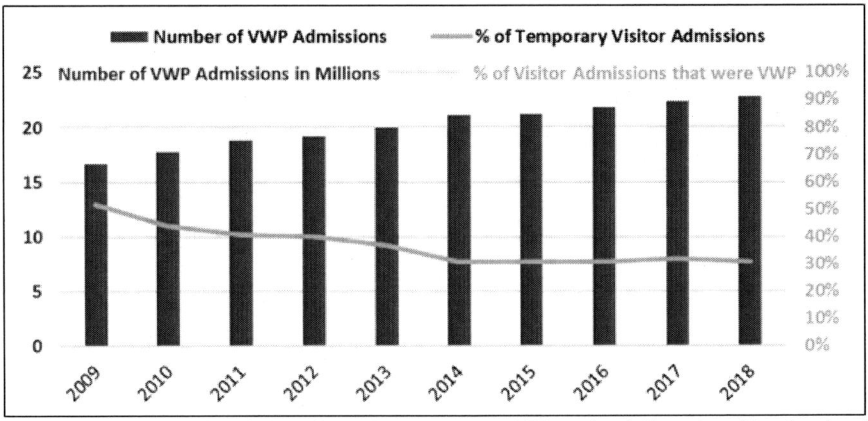

Source: CRS analysis of data from Department of Homeland Security, Yearbook of Immigration Statistics, multiple years; Table 25.

Note: Number of countries participating in the VWP at the end of the fiscal year: FY2009, 35; FY2010-FY2012, 36; FY2013, 37; FY2014-FY2018, 38. Visitor admissions count those who entered with B visas, those who entered under the Guam Visa Waiver Program, and those who entered under the VWP.

Figure 1. Number of Visa Waiver Program (VWP) Admissions, FY2009-FY2018, and Percentage of Visitor Admissions That Were VWP.

Figure 1 shows the number of admissions under the VWP and VWP admissions as a percentage of all temporary visitor admissions.[69] Since FY2009, the number of admissions under the VWP has steadily increased. In FY2018, there were 22.8 million admissions under the VWP, the largest number ever under the program. However, from FY2009 to FY2016, the proportion of total visitor admissions represented by VWP admissions declined.[70] In FY2018, VWP admissions constituted 31% of all temporary

[69] Temporary visitors include aliens who entered with B visas, those who entered under the Guam Visa Waiver Program, and those who entered under the VWP.

[70] Visitor admissions from large, non-VWP countries have increased during this period, thereby reducing the proportion of VWP visitor admissions to the United States. For example, in 2018, Brazil, China, and India were among the top 10 overseas countries by visitor volume and accounted for 6.5 million visitors to the United States that year. (NTTO, *Non-Resident Arrivals to the United States: Overseas, Canada, Mexico, and*

visitor admissions to the United States, the smallest percentage in more than 20 years.

POLICY ISSUES

The VWP is supported by the U.S. travel and tourism industry and the business community. The travel and tourism industry views the VWP as a tool to facilitate and encourage foreign visitors for business and pleasure, which results in increased economic growth generated by foreign tourism and commerce for the United States.[71]

The Department of State also supports the VWP. DOS argues that by waiving the visa requirement for high-volume/low-risk countries, consular workloads are significantly reduced, allowing for streamlined operations, cost savings, and concentration of resources on greater-risk nations in the visa process.[72] The travel industry argues that DOS would have to hire many more consular officers to meet the demand for B visas from VWP countries absent the program.[73]

While there tends to be agreement that the VWP benefits the U.S. economy by facilitating legitimate travel, there is disagreement on the VWP's impact on national security, with some arguing that the VWP presents a significant security risk and others arguing that it enhances national security.

International, Trend Line Data — Country of Residence, November 2019, at https://travel.trade.gov/view/m-2017-I-001/index.asp).

[71] For more information, see CRS Report R46300, Adding Countries to the Visa Waiver Program: Effects on National Security and Tourism.

[72] U.S. Congress, Senate Committee on Homeland Security and Governmental Affairs, *The Visa Waiver Program: Implications for U.S. National Security*, Testimony of Edward J Ramotowski, Deputy Assistant Secretary for Visa Services, U.S. Department of State, 114th Cong., 1st sess., March 12, 2015.

[73] For example, in his testimony before the House Immigration and Claims Subcommittee on February 28, 2002, William S. Norman, President and Chief Executive Officer of the Travel Industry Association of America, stated that it would take hundreds of new consular staff and tens of millions of dollars to issue visas to visitors currently entering under the VWP. Since Mr. Norman testified, the number of people entering under the VWP has increased by more than 5 million entrants per year.

Security

There has been significant debate about whether the VWP increases or decreases national security. As discussed, travelers under the VWP do not undergo the in-person screening generally required to receive a B nonimmigrant visa. Moreover, ESTA is a biographical system and cannot be used to run checks against databases that use biometrics as identifiers, such as DHS's Automated Biometric Identification System (IDENT) and FBI's Next Generation Identification (NGI).[74] While VWP travelers are not checked against these systems before boarding a plane or ship, they are checked against these systems through US-VISIT when they are at a U.S. port of entry.[75] In addition, some contend that the relaxed documentary requirements of the VWP increase immigration fraud and decrease security.[76]

Others argue that the VWP enhances security by setting standards for travel documents and information sharing.[77] For example, all travelers entering under the VWP must present e- passports, which tend to be more difficult to alter than other types of passports.[78] Unlike ESTA

---

[74] IDENT is the primary DHS-wide system for the biometric identification and verification of individuals encountered in DHS mission-related processes. NGI is a DHS-wide system for the storage and processing of biometric and limited biographic information. For more information on IDENT, see Department of Homeland Security, *Privacy Impact Assessment for the Automated Biometric Identification System (IDENT)*, July 31, 2006, p. 2, at http://www.dhs.gov/ xlibrary/assets/privacy/privacy_pia_usvisit_ ident_final.pdf. For more information on NGI, see Federal Bureau of Investigation, *Next Generation Identification (NGI),* at https://www.fbi.gov/services/cjis/fingerprints-and-other- biometrics/ngi.

[75] CRS Report R43356, Border Security: Immigration Inspections at Ports of Entry.

[76] For an example of this argument, see "Congressman Claims Allowing Poland Visa-Free Travel to the US Would Pose Security Threat," workpermit.com, June 20, 2012, at http://www.workpermit.com/news/2012-06-20/us/congressman-claims-allowing-poland-visa-free-travel-to-us-would-pose-security-threat.htm.

[77] For an example of this argument, see Heritage Foundation, *The Visa Waiver Program: A Security Partnership*, Fact Sheet #66, Washington, DC, June 25, 2010.

[78] There is not a specific requirement to present an e-passport when entering under the VWP. Any passports issued after October 26, 2006, and used by VWP travelers to enter the United States are required to have integrated chips with information from the data page (i.e., e-passports). Most passports are valid for 10 years, and thus, it is likely that by October 2016, all VWP entrants had e-passports.

authorization, many B visas are valid for 10 years[79] and are not continuously vetted.[80]

Another concern about the national security implications of the program centers on DHS's ability to conduct reviews of the current VWP countries. In 2002, Congress mandated that DHS evaluate each VWP country every two years to make sure that their continued participation was in the security, law enforcement, and immigration interests of the United States.[81] In a review of the Visa Waiver Program Office's (VWPO's) administration of the VWP, the DHS's Office of the Inspector General found that as of July 2012, there were 11 (out of 36) reports that exceeded the congressionally mandated two-year reporting cycle.[82] A Government Accountability Office (GAO) report found that as of October 31, 2015, approximately 25% of the most recent reports were submitted or remained outstanding at least five months past the statutory deadline. Since then, DHS has made progress in meeting the mandated two-year reporting cycle, but some gaps remain.[83]

---

[79] The length of validity of a visa is mostly dependent on reciprocity with the United States (i.e., that visas from that country for U.S. citizens are valid for the same period of time). For a full list of reciprocity schedules, see Department of State, *U.S. Visa: Reciprocity and Civil Documents by Country*, at https://travel.state.gov/content/travel/en/us-visas/Visa-Reciprocity-and-Civil-Documents-by-Country.html.

[80] CBP screens travelers on nonimmigrant visitor visas at ports of entry each time they enter the United States.

[81] P.L. 107-53, §711.

[82] VWPO cited a number of reasons for the reporting delays, including inadequate staffing of the office to manage the workload, and not receiving intelligence assessments in a timely manner. However, VWPO officials stated that "these delays have not posed any undue risks or threats to U.S. security interests, since any issues within a VWP country that might affect its continued compliance with VWP requirements are continuously monitored." Department of Homeland Security, Office of the Inspector General, *The Visa Waiver Program*, OIG-13-07, Washington, DC, November 2, 2012, p. 12, http://www.oig.dhs.gov/assets/Mgmt/2013/OIG_13-07_Nov12.pdf.

[83] According to GAO, In 2018, DHS completed a strategic review of the reporting process to better distribute the workload and adding staff in the Visa Waiver P rogram Office. As of October 2019, DHS reported taking several steps that should address prior delays in meeting the report deadlines, such as refining their request for information and modifying the report clearance process. To fully address this recommendation, DHS needs to demonstrate these steps have addressed the delays by issuing a report to Congress on each VWP country within the last two years. GAO will continue to monitor DHS efforts. U.S. Government Accountability Office (GAO), "Recommendations for Executive Action." in *Visa Waiver Program: DHS Should Take Steps to Ensure Timeliness of Information Needed to Protect U.S. National Security*, GAO-16-498, for the May 5, 2016, at https://www.gao.gov/products/GAO-16-498.

Debate over Biometric Exit Capacity

As discussed, the Secretary of Homeland Security's authority to waive the nonimmigrant visa refusal rate has been suspended until the air exit system is able to match an alien's biometric information with relevant watch lists and manifest information.[84] Some contend that the current biographic system provides suitable data for most security and immigration enforcement activities, and that the cost of implementing a biometric exit system would not justify the small increase in additional security.[85] However, others express concerns about the general security of the program and argue that until more security measures are in place, such as a biometric exit capacity, more countries should not be designated into the program.[86]

Information Sharing

According to GAO, all VWP countries provide data on lost and stolen passports (LASP) to the United States.[87] However, concerns have been raised about information sharing on LASP, specifically whether countries are reporting data in a timely manner.[88] The mechanisms to obtain data on LASP have differed over time (e.g., reporting to the U.S. Embassy, access

---

[84] The suspension can be lifted once the biometric exit system captures 97% of in -scope travelers (P.L. 110-53; Section 110 IIRIRA, as amended). Currently, the system captures 60% of in-scope travelers. (Based on CRS discussion with CBP officials on January 30, 2020.)

[85] Testimony of James Jay Carafano, U.S. Congress, House Committee on the Judiciary, Subcommittee on Immigration Policy and Enforcement, *Next Steps for the Visa Waiver Program*, 112th Cong., 1st sess., December 7, 2011.

[86] Statement of Chairman Elton Gallegly, U.S. Congress, House Committee on the Judiciary, Subcommittee on Immigration Policy and Enforcement, *Next Steps for the Visa Waiver Program*, 112th Cong., 1st sess., December 7, 2011.

[87] U.S. Government Accountability Office, Visa Waiver Program: Additional Actions Needed to Address Risks and Strengthen Overstay Enforcement, GAO-12-287T, December 7, 2011; U.S. Government Accountability Office, Visa Waiver Program: DHS Should Take Steps to Ensure Timeliness of Information Needed to Protect U.S. National Security, GAO-16-498, May 2016, p. 11.

[88] VWP passports are supposedly highly valued since the bearer does not need a visa to enter the United States. For example, see U.S. Government Accountability Office, *Visa Waiver Program: Additional Actions Needed to Address Risks and Strengthen Overstay Enforcement*, GAO-12-287T, December 7, 2011. See also, Giulia Paravicini, " EU's Passport Fraud 'Epidemic'," *Politico*, January 28, 2016, Europe Edition, at http://www.politico.eu/article/europes-fake-forged-stolen-passport-epidemic-visa-free-travel-rights/.

to a common database) and by country (e.g., MOUs, Diplomatic Notes).[89] While DHS receives a few countries' LASP data via direct links to those countries' databases, most data on LASP come from the International Criminal Police Organization's (INTERPOL's) Stolen and Lost Travel Documents (SLTD) database[90]—DHS's preferred method of data sharing. Notably, ESTA screens passport information using the INTERPOL database. CBP also accesses LASP data via INTERPOL, but it is unclear if this information is checked during primary inspection.[91] P.L. 114-113 amended the provision mandating that the reporting of lost or stolen passports be done no later than 24 hours after a theft or loss was reported to the VWP country.

As discussed, all VWP countries are also required to enter into information-sharing agreements with the United States on whether the citizens or nationals of that country travelling to the United States represent a security or criminal threat to the United States. All VWP countries have entered into the required arrangements for the sharing of information on known and suspected terrorists pursuant to Homeland Security Presidential Directive 6 (HSPD-6),[92] and have also signed Preventing and Combating Serious Crime (PCSC) Agreements or equivalent agreements with the United States for the sharing of information on potential serious criminals and terrorists. DHS, DOJ, and DOS worked with VWP countries to fully implement HSPD-6 arrangements and PCSC Agreements.[93] P.L. 114-113

---

[89] In the past, before access to and the content of the INTERPOL database were reliable, DHS required countries to submit LASP data to the U.S. embassies in those countries.

[90] The United States began providing information on LASP to the U.S. National Central Bureau of the International Criminal Police Organization (INTERPOL) in May 2004. The INTERPOL Stolen and Lost Travel Document (SLTD) database is available to law enforcement and immigration authorities worldwide. INTERPOL, *Border Management*, at https://www.interpol.int/How-we-work/Border-management.

[91] U.S. Government Accountability Office, Visa Waiver Program: Actions Are Needed to Improve Management of the Expansion Process, and to Assess and Mitigate Program Risks, GAO-08-1142T, September 24, 2008, p.5.

[92] U.S. President (George W. Bush), "Homeland Security Presidential Directive/HSPD–6—Directive on Integration and Use of Screening Information To Protect Against Terrorism," Weekly Compilation of Presidential Documents, September 16, 2003, p. 1174. For a discussion of HSPD-6, see CRS Report R42336, Terrorist Watch List Screening and Background Checks for Firearms.

[93] E-mail from Department of Homeland Security, Office of Legislative Affairs, November 16, 2015.

requires that the HSPD-6 arrangements and PCSC Agreements not only be signed but be fully implemented before a country can be designated into the VWP. A GAO report released in May 2016 found that, as of that date, more than one third of VWP countries had not shared terrorist identity information through the HSPD-6 agreements, and a similar percentage of VWP countries had not shared criminal history information through the PCSC agreements.[94] No countries were removed from the program, but

> DHS has reported progress towards implementing the required agreements and, in cases where agreements are not fully implemented, time frames and steps for bringing VWP countries into compliance with the information-sharing requirements. As a result, information sharing under the required agreements has improved.[95]

Terrorism, Foreign Fighters, and the VWP

Since 9/11, significant national security concerns about the VWP came from fears that terrorists could enter the United States under the VWP. In recent years, U.S. concerns have focused on citizens from VWP countries who are aligned with the Islamic State terrorist group (also known as ISIS or ISIL). Many perpetrators of recent terrorist attacks were European citizens who trained and/or fought with the Islamic State in the Syria-Iraq region.[96]

For example, several of the perpetrators of the November 2015 attacks in Paris were citizens of France.[97] In addition, the alleged mastermind, Abdelhamid Abaaoud, was a national of Belgium.[98]

---

[94] U.S. Government Accountability Office, Visa Waiver Program: DHS Should Take Steps to Ensure Timeliness of Information Needed to Protect U.S. National Security, GAO-16-498, May 2016.

[95] U.S. Government Accountability Office, "Recommendations for Executive Action," in Visa Waiver Program: DHS Should Take Steps to Ensure Timeliness of Information Needed to Protect U.S. National Security, GAO-16-498, May 5, 2016, at https://www.gao.gov/products/GAO-16-498.

[96] For more information, see CRS In Focus IF10561, Terrorism in Europe.

[97] BBC News, "Paris attacks: Who were the attackers?" April 27, 2016, at ews/world-europe-34832512.

[98] Lonnie Shekhtman, "Abdelhamid Abaaoud: Mastermind of the Paris attacks?,"Christian Science Monitor, November 16, 2015, at http://www.csmonitor.com/World/ Europe/2015/ 1116/Abdelhamid-Abaaoud-Mastermind-of- the-Paris-attacks-video.

Most of the perpetrators of these attacks had trained and/or fought with the Islamic State in Syria and/or Iraq.[99] These terrorists may have been able to travel to the United States under the VWP, if ESTA did not find any derogatory information about them in U.S. biographic databases. Once citizens of VWP countries arrive in the United States, a CBP officer is to decide on their admissibility and check their information in biometric and biographic databases. Without having specific classified information, it is unknown whether or not these individuals would have been eligible to travel under the VWP and/or been admitted into the U.S. at a port of entry.

In addition, if the assumption is made that these terrorists would have been eligible to travel under the VWP, it is unknown whether or not the requirement to get a visa would have changed their eligibility to travel to the United States. As discussed, individuals who are not eligible to travel under the VWP (either individuals from non-VWP countries or those who do not receive an ESTA authorization) must get a visa before traveling to the United States. Unlike those traveling under the VWP, those who apply for a visa undergo an interview with a consular officer, and provide fingerprints and a digital photograph to be used to run checks against databases that use biometrics (e.g., IDENT, NGI).

Authorities also remain concerned that terrorists could exploit refugee and migrant flows into Europe, especially given press reports that two of the terrorists involved in the November 2015 attacks in Paris may have entered Greece by posing as refugees with fake or stolen Syrian passports before making their way to Paris.[100] For a foreign national to travel under the VWP he or she must possess a passport from a VWP country. Thus, unless refugees or migrants who settle in VWP countries receive citizenship or

---

[99] For more information, see CRS In Focus IF10561, *Terrorism in Europe*.

[100] Alison Smale and Kimberly Bradley, "Refugees Across Europe Fear Repercussions From Paris Attacks," *New York Times,* November 18, 2015, at http://www. nytimes. com/2015/11/19/world/europe/refugees-paris-attacks.html?hp&action=click&pgtype= Homepage&clickSource=story-heading&module=b-lede-package-region&region=top-news& WT.nav=top-news; and " At least two Paris attackers 'traveled through Greece,'" *France 24,* November 21, 2015, at https://www.france24.com/en/20151121-least-two-paris-attackers-travelled-through-greece-refugees-syria-migrants.

nationality[101] from those countries and are issued passports from the VWP country, they are ineligible to travel to the United States under the VWP.[102]

Adding Countries to the VWP

While some view the VWP as a security risk, others contend that the inclusion of countries in the VWP increases U.S. national security by setting standards for travel documents and information sharing.[103] In addition, supporters of the VWP argue that increasing membership in the VWP could be used as an incentive to get additional countries to share intelligence information with the United States.[104] Since 2010, DHS has designated four new countries—Chile, Greece, Poland, and Taiwan—into the program.

Most recently, on November 8, 2019, DHS designated Poland into the VWP.[105] Poland had been working with DHS for more than a decade to meet the VWP criteria.[106] Prior to Poland's inclusion in the VWP, the Polish government had been outspoken in expressing frustration over the failure to include the country in the VWP.[107] Reportedly, President Barack Obama said

---

[101] A national is a citizen or subject of a particular nation and is someone who would be eligible for a passport from that nation.

[102] INA §217(a)(2). The situation regarding the position of many countries in regard to acceptance of Syrian refugees is fluid and, as such, it is unclear whether any of these refugees would ever be eligible for citizenship in these countries.

[103] For an example of this argument, see Testimony of Hillary Batjer Johnson, Deputy Coordinator for Homeland Security, Screening, and Designations Bureau of Counterterrorism, in U.S. Department of State, U.S. Congress, House Committee on Oversight and Government Reform, Subcommittees on National Security and Government Operations, *The President's Waiver of Restrictions on the Visa Waiver Program,* hearings, 114th Cong., 2nd sess., February 10, 2016, H.Hrg. 114-104 (Washington, DC: GPO, 2017).

[104] For examples of this argument, see James Jay Carafano, *With a Little Help from Our Friends: Enhancing Security by Expanding the Visa Waiver Program*, Heritage Foundation, Executive Memorandum no. 991, February 3, 2006; and Jena Baker McNeill, *Time to Decouple Visa Waiver Program from Biometric Exit*, Heritage Foundation, Web Memorandum no. 2867, April 15, 2010.

[105] Department of Homeland Security, "Designation of Poland for the Visa Waiver Program," 84 *Federal Register* 60316, November 8, 2019.

[106] For more information, see CRS Report R45784, *Poland: Background and U.S. Relations*.

[107] For examples, see " Polish President to Remind Obama of Visa Promise," Polskie Radio, September 9, 2012, at http://www.thenews.pl/1/10/Artykul/113122,Polish-president-to-

in 2010 that he was going to make it a priority to get Poland into the VWP.[108] President Donald Trump, in public remarks before a September 2018 meeting with Poland's President Andrezej Duda, said in reference to Poland's designation into the VWP that his administration was "looking at that very strongly."[109]

In FY2019, Poland met the requirement of having a nonimmigrant visitor visa refusal rate below 3%.[110] On October 4, 2019, President Trump announced that DOS had formally nominated Poland for the VWP, [111] and the following month, DHS announced Poland's designation into the program.[112] As of November 11, 2019, Polish nationals, like other visitors from VWP countries, are able to apply online for ESTA, which authorizes travel to the United States without a visa.

According to DHS, from November 11, 2019, through January 2020, approximately 40,000 Polish ESTA applications were approved.[113]

Other countries have expressed a desire to be included in the VWP because of the possible economic benefits (e.g., increasing commerce and tourism), the benefits to their populace of easier and cheaper travel to the

---

remind-Obama-of-visa-promise; and Nowy Dziennik Wuem, translated by Aleksangra Slabisz from Polish, " Polish Students Appeal to White House on Visa Waiver," *Voices of NY*, October 10, 2012.

[108] For examples, see " Polish President to Remind Obama of Visa Promise," Polskie Radio, September 9, 2012, at http://www.thenews.pl/1/10/Artykul/113122,Polish-president-to-remind-Obama-of-visa-promise; and Nowy Dziennik Wuem, translated by Aleksangra Slabisz from Polish, " Polish Students Appeal to White House on Visa Waiver," *Voices of NY*, October 10, 2012.

[109] The White House, "Remarks by President Trump and President Duda of the Republic of Poland Before Bilateral Meeting," September 18, 2018, at https://www.whitehouse.gov/briefings-statements/remarks-president-trump-president-duda-republic-poland-bilateral-meeting/.

[110] Department of State, "Adjusted Refusal Rate—B-Visas Only by Nationality Fiscal Year 2019," at https://travel.state.gov/content/dam/visas/Statistics/Non-Immigrant-Statistics/RefusalRates/FY19.pdf; also, see full list of criteria in the section, "VWP Qualifying Criteria."

[111] The White House, "Statement from the Press Secretary Regarding the Nomination of Poland for Entry into the Visa Waiver Program," press release, October 4, 2019, at https://www.whitehouse.gov/briefings-statements/statement-press-secretary-regarding-nomination-poland-entry-visa-waiver-program/.

[112] Department of Homeland Security, "Acting Secretary McAleenan Announces Designation of Poland into the Visa Waiver Program," press release, November 6, 2019, at https://www.dhs.gov/news/2019/11/06/acting-secretary-mcaleenan-announces-designation-poland-visa-waiver-program.

[113] Based on CRS discussion with DHS representatives about the VWP, January 30, 2020.

United States (i.e., since their citizens do not have to apply for and pay for a visa), and because membership in the program is often perceived as evidence of close ties with the United States.[114]

EU and Reciprocity

Of the European Union's 27 member states, 4 are not VWP countries (Bulgaria, Croatia, Cyprus, and Romania). A visa is required for citizens from non-VWP EU countries wishing to travel to the United States, whereas, under EU law, no EU country requires visas of U.S. citizens for stays up to 90 days.[115] The EU contends that "visa reciprocity is a fundamental principle of the European Union's common visa policy" and has long urged the United States to admit all EU member states to the VWP.[116] The lack of short-term, visa-free privileges for all EU member states has been a point of contention between the United States and the EU for many years.

In January 2014, a revised EU visa reciprocity mechanism entered into force, aimed at injecting greater momentum into EU efforts to achieve full visa reciprocity with countries, such as the United States, whose citizens can travel to the EU for short-term business or tourism without a visa. The EU considered suspending its visa waiver for U.S. nationals in 2017 but

---

[114] In 2005, the George W. Bush Administration began providing countries interested in joining the VWP with "road maps" to aid the countries in meeting the program's criteria. Some of the countries complained that since the "road maps" did not contain milestones or time tables, it was difficult to measure the amount of progress made toward fulfilling the criteria for VWP membership. There were 13 "road map" countries: Bulgaria, Cyprus, Czech Republic, Estonia, Greece, Hungary, South Korea, Latvia, Lithuania, Malta, Poland, Romania, and Slovakia. Eight of these countries have been admitted to the VWP. For a discussion of the current "road map," or "aspiring" VWP countries, see CRS Report R46300, *Adding Countries to the Visa Waiver Program: Effects on National Security and Tourism.*

[115] For a discussion of EU visa policy, see European Commission, *Visa Policy*, at https://ec.europa.eu/home-affairs/what-we-do/policies/borders-and-visas/visa-policy_en.

[116] European Commission, "Visa non-reciprocity: Commission takes stock of progress and developments," press release, December 18, 2018, at https://ec.europa.eu/commission/presscorner/detail/en/IP_18_6821.

decided not to do so.[117] The United States remains the only country on the EU's visa-free list that does not fully reciprocate.[118]

Overstays

Some maintain that the nonimmigrant visa refusal rate is "not sufficiently probative" of a country's eligibility because it is based on decisions made by consular officers rather than on the behavior of nonimmigrants.[119] When the program was conceived, planners expected that the number of nonimmigrants who overstay the terms of their entry under this program would be a better standard for future program participation, but it was not used at the time because of the lack of reliable data on overstays. Using biographic departure information from passenger manifests, DHS has calculated overstay rates for all VWP countries (as well as other countries). Nonetheless, this method of measuring overstays has limitations because persons entering by air or sea but exiting at a land port of entry may be mischaracterized as overstays.[120]

---

[117] European Commission, "Visa Reciprocity: Commission responds to Parliament," press release, May 1, 2017, at https://ec.europa.eu/commission/presscorner/detail/en/IP_17_1148. However, in 2018, the European Union (EU) announced that before travel, visitors to the Schengen Area from all visa-free countries would need to complete an online application similar to the U.S. EST A system, and they will be required to pay a fee of €7 to use the European Travel Information and Authorization System (ETIAS). ETIAS will apply to people traveling to all 26 countries currently in the Schengen Area (the majority of which are EU member states) and EU countries Croatia, Cyprus, Bulgaria, and Romania, which are expected to join the Schengen Area in the future. ETIAS is expected to be operational in early 2021. An approved ETIAS will be valid for three years or the date of passport expiration (whichever happens first), and it can be used for stays for up to 90 days.

[118] For more background, see CRS Report RS22030, *U.S.-EU Cooperation Against Terrorism*.

[119] U.S. Congress, House Committee on the Judiciary, *Visa Waiver Permanent Program Act*, report together with additional views to accompany H.R. 3767, 106th Cong., 2nd sess., H.Rept. 106-564 (Washington, DC: GPO, 2000), p. 32.

[120] For example, a 2019 GAO report says there are "existing limitations in collecting departure data in the land environment." See GAO, *Department of Homeland Security: Review of the Fiscal Year 2017 Entry/Exit Overstay Report*, GAO-19-298R, February 22, 2019, p. 3, at https://www.gao.gov/products/GAO-19-298R.

In January 2016, DHS released its first report on overstay rates.[121] In a subsequent report on FY2018 overstays, all the VWP countries had overstay rates of less than 0.5%. In contrast, the worldwide overstay rate for non-VWP countries in FY2018 was 2%.[122]

Although the refusal rate was seen as an alternative to the overstay rate when the program was conceived, people are denied visas for reasons other than being unable to prove that they will not remain illegally in the United States (i.e., they are intending immigrants).[123] During the visa application process, consular officers[124] must confirm that an alien is not ineligible for a visa under any of the grounds of inadmissibility of the INA, such as having a criminal history, engaging in terrorist activity, or having previously violated U.S. immigration law.[125] Although most B visa denials are because the alien cannot prove that he or she is not an intending immigrant, there are other reasons a person could be denied a visa that are captured as part of a country's visa refusal rate.

LEGISLATION IN THE 116TH CONGRESS

The Further Consolidated Appropriations Act of 2020 (P.L. 116-94) extended the authority for Brand USA, a public-private travel promotion

---

[121] See, Department of Homeland Security, *Entry/Exit Overstay Report, Fiscal Year 2015*, January 19, 2016, at http://www.dhs.gov/publication/entryexit-overstay-report. An annual report on overstays was originally mandated by Congress in 1998 (P.L. 105-173, codified at 8 U.S.C. §1376), and Congress required the report again in P.L. 114-113.

[122] Department of Homeland Security, *Fiscal Year 2018 Entry/Exit Overstay Report,* at https://www.dhs.gov/sites/default/files/publications/19_0417_fy18-entry-and-exit-overstay-report.pdf.

[123] INA §214(b) generally presumes that all aliens seeking admission to the United States are coming to live permanently; as a result, aliens seeking to qualify for a B visa (and most other nonimmigrant visas) must demonstrate that they are not coming to reside permanently in the United States. CRS Report R45040, Immigration: Nonimmigrant (Temporary) Admissions to the United States.

[124] Determinations of inadmissibility are also made by CBP officers at ports of entry.

[125] The so-called grounds of inadmissibility under INA §212(a) include health-related grounds; criminal history; security and terrorist concerns; public charge (e.g., indigence); seeking to work without proper labor certification; illegal entrants and immigration law violations; ineligibility for citizenship; and aliens who are illegally present or have previously been removed.

entity, to receive fees from the VWP through the end of September 2027 and raises the ESTA fee, as described above in "Electronic System for Travel Authorization (ESTA)." The private sector still must provide at least $100 million per year in in-kind contributions and cash to the Brand USA program in order for it to receive these federal funds. The effective date of the new ESTA fee has not yet been announced.

Multiple proposals introduced in the 116th Congress aim to give DHS greater flexibility to designate countries that do not meet the criteria discussed above into the VWP. Representative Mike Quigley introduced the Jobs Originated through Launching Travel (JOLT) Act (H.R. 2187), which would reinstate DHS's authority to grant a waiver for the nonimmigrant visitor visa refusal rate. The bill would also change the name of the VWP to "Secure Travel Partnership."[126] H.R. 1996, also introduced by Representative Quigley, would solely rename the VWP to "Secure Travel Partnership." Representative Dan Lipinski introduced the Allied Nations Travel Modernization Act (H.R. 2946), which would allow countries to be designated into the VWP if, instead of a low nonimmigrant visitor visa refusal rate, they have a low visa overstay rate and agree to spend 2% of their gross domestic product on defense;[127] according to Representative Lipinski, the bill was drafted "to create an alternative pathway into the program for NATO nations like Poland."[128] As noted above, Poland was designated into the VWP on November 6, 2019. Both bills were referred to the Subcommittee on Immigration and Citizenship.

One proposal in the 116th Congress seeks to deter VWP overstays. Senator John Cornyn introduced the Humanitarian Upgrades to Manage and

---

[126] Unrelated to the VWP, H.R. 2187 would also allow Canadians over age 50 entering on tourist visas who own or have rented property in the United States to be admitted for up to 240 days. Currently, the maximum duration of stay on a tourist visa is 180 days. Additionally, H.R. 2187 includes sections related to visa processing, such as developing a secure remote videoconferencing program for visa interviews.

[127] For more information, see North Atlantic Treaty Organization, "Wales Summit Declaration," press release, September 5, 2014, at https://www.nato.int/cps/en/natohq/official_texts_112964.htm?selectedLocale=en.

[128] Congressman Dan Lipinski, " Lipinski Praises Step Forward Towards Admitting Poland to the Visa Waiver Program as Polish President Visits U.S.," press release, June 13, 2019, at https://lipinski.house.gov/press-releases/lipinski-praises-step-forward-towards-admitting-poland-to-the-visa-waiver-program-as-polish-president-visits-us/.

Assist our Nation's Enforcement (HUMANE) Act of 2019 (S. 1303). Among other provisions, the bill endeavors to reduce VWP overstays by amending the INA's terms and conditions of admission for VWP travelers, the VWP waiver of rights, and the detention and repatriation of visa waiver violators. This bill was referred to the Committee on the Judiciary.

Another proposal would address the spending of funds generated from ESTA fees. Senator Mike Enzi introduced the Responsibly Enhancing America's Landscapes Act (S. 2783), which would establish the National Park Service Legacy Restoration Fund to help with the backlog of maintenance projects in national parks. This fund would be paid for by a $16 ESTA fee along with a $25 nonimmigrant visitor visa fee and a $5 park entrance fee. This bill was referred to the Committee on the Judiciary.

APPENDIX. LEGISLATIVE HISTORY AND SELECTED ADMINISTRATIVE ACTION

Visa Waiver Pilot Program

The Visa Waiver Program was established initially as a temporary program (Visa Waiver Pilot Program) by the Immigration Reform and Control Act of 1986 (P.L. 99-603). To become a program country under the pilot program, a country must have offered reciprocal privileges to U.S. citizens and have had an average nonimmigrant visa refusal rate of 2% or less for the previous two years with neither year's refusal rate exceeding 2.5%. Participation in the pilot program was originally limited to up to eight countries.[129] Since the establishment of the pilot program, Congress has periodically passed legislation to extend the program's authorization, expand the number of countries allowed to participate in the program, and modify the qualifying criteria. Between 1986 and 1997, Congress passed five bills that were subsequently signed into law that made changes to the Visa Waiver Pilot Program:

[129] 8 U.S.C. §1187, amendments.

- the Immigration Technical Corrections Act of 1988 (P.L. 100-525);
- the Immigration Act of 1990 (P.L. 101-649), which inserted further qualifying criteria and reporting requirements for the program and removed the limit on the number of countries that could participate in the program;
- the Miscellaneous and Technical Immigration and Naturalization Amendments of 1991 (P.L. 102-232);
- the Immigration and Nationality Technical Corrections Act of 1994 (P.L. 103- 416), which created a probationary status to allow countries whose nonimmigrant visa refusal rates were higher than 2% but less than 3.5% to enter the program on a probationary basis if other qualifying criteria are met; and
- the Illegal Immigrant Reform and Immigrant Responsibility Act of 1996 (P.L. 104-208), which created a new type of probationary status for countries in the program that failed to meet certain criteria, and removed the probationary status that had allowed countries with nonimmigrant visa refusal rates higher than 2% but less than 3.5% to enter the program.

The pilot visa waiver program was scheduled to expire on September 30, 1997, but short-term extensions were included in the Continuing Resolutions passed in the 105th Congress.[130] The Departments of Commerce, Justice, and State, the Judiciary and Related Agencies Appropriations Act, 1998 (P.L. 105-119) contained an extension of the program through April 30, 1998. In 1998, Congress passed legislation (P.L. 105-173) that not only extended the program through April 30, 2000, but made other changes to the standard by which countries are selected

[130] An extension of the pilot program was included in the first Continuing Resolution (P.L. 105-56 §117) for FY1998. The five subsequent Continuing Resolutions—P.L. 105-64, P.L. 105-68, P.L. 105-69, P.L. 105-71, and P.L. 105-84— simply extended the expiration date of the provisions in the first Continuing Resolution for FY1998 (P.L. 105-56).

(designated) to participate in the VWP.[131] By 1999, program participation had grown to include 29 countries.[132]

Visa Waiver Permanent Program Act

On October 30, 2000, the Visa Waiver Permanent Program Act was signed into law (P.L. 106- 396). The statutory authority for the Visa Waiver Pilot Program had expired on April 30, 2000, but in the interim, the Commissioner of the former Immigration and Naturalization Service (INS)[133] exercised the Attorney General's parole authority to extend the program temporarily.[134] Besides making this program's authorization permanent, the Visa Waiver Permanent Program Act included provisions designed to strengthen documentary and reporting requirements. P.L. 106-396 included provisions that

- mandated that by October 1, 2007, all entrants under the VWP must have machine-readable passports;
- required that all VWP applicants be checked against lookout systems;

[131] Originally, to qualify for the Visa Waiver Pilot Program countries needed to have had an average nonimmigrant visa refusal rate of no more than 2% over the past two fiscal years with neither year going above 2.5%. P.L. 105-173 added the criteria that a country could have a nonimmigrant visa refusal rate of less than 3% for the previous year and qualify for the program.

[132] The 29 countries were: Andorra, Argentina, Australia, Austria, Belgium, Brunei, Denmark, Finland, France, Germany, Iceland, Ireland, Italy, Japan, Liechtenstein, Luxembourg, Monaco, the Netherlands, New Zealand, Norway, Portugal, San Marino, Singapore, Slovenia, Spain, Sweden, Switzerland, the United Kingdom, and Uruguay. Argentina was removed from the VWP in February 2002, and Uruguay was removed in April 2003. From April 2003 until November 2008, the VWP included 27 countries. As of March 2020, there are 39 countries participating in the VWP.

[133] The Homeland Security Act of 2002 (P.L. 107-296) abolished the Immigration and Naturalization Service (INS) and effective March 1, 2003, transferred most of its functions to three bureaus in the new Department of Homeland Security (DHS): Citizenship and Immigration Services (USCIS); Immigration and Customs Enforcement (ICE); and, Customs and Border Protection (CBP).

[134] Parole is a temporary authorization to enter the United States and is normally granted when the alien's entry is determined to be in the public interest (INA §212(d)(5)(A)).

- required ongoing evaluations of participating countries (not less than once every five years);
- required the collection of VWP arrival/departure data at air and sea ports of entry; and
- required that the calculation of visa refusal rates for determining country eligibility shall not include any refusals based on race, sex, or disability.[135]

At the time, many maintained that P.L. 106-396 balanced the competing concerns of facilitating travel and tightening immigration controls.

USA PATRIOT Act of 2001

The USA PATRIOT Act (P.L. 107-56), signed into law on October 26, 2001, shortened the time frame for all entrants under the VWP to have machine-readable passports to October 1, 2003, but allowed the Secretary of State to waive this requirement until October 1, 2007, if the VWP country could show that it was making progress toward issuing machine-readable passports. In addition, the USA PATRIOT Act directed the Secretary of State to ascertain, each year until 2007, that VWP countries had established programs to develop tamper-resistant passports.

On September 24, 2003, the Secretary of State extended the deadline for visitors from 21 VWP countries to present a machine-readable passport at the ports of entry until October 26, 2004.[136]

---

[135] Many of these requirements were included to address shortcomings in the program, as identified by the Inspectors General of both the Departments of Justice and State.

[136] The 21 countries granted a postponement were: Australia, Austria, Denmark, Finland, France, Germ any, Iceland, Ireland, Italy, Japan, Monaco, the Netherlands, New Zealand, Norway, Portugal, San Marino, Singapore, Spain, Sweden, Switzerland, and the United Kingdom. On November 11, 2003, Luxembourg was granted an extension of the deadline. Five VWP countries (Andorra, Brunei, Liechtenstein, Luxembourg, and Slovenia) were eligible to receive and extension but did not request one because "all of their citizens already have machine-readable passports." Belgium was not eligible to receive an extension, as DOJ had already required their citizens to present machine-readable passports as of May 15, 2003 (see footnote 36). U.S. Department of State,

Enhanced Border Security and Visa Entry Reform Act of 2002

The Enhanced Border Security and Visa Entry Reform Act of 2002 (Border Security Act),[137] signed into law on May 14, 2002, required all VWP countries to certify that they report in a timely manner the theft of blank passports, and required, prior to admission to the United States, that all aliens, including those who enter under the VWP, are checked against a lookout system. The act also mandated that by October 26, 2004, the government of each VWP country needed to certify that it has established a program to issue to its nationals machine-readable passports that are tamper-resistant and incorporate a biometric identifier.[138] The act specified that any person applying for admission to the United States under the VWP must have a tamper-resistant, machine-readable passport with a biometric identifier unless the passport was issued prior to October 26, 2004. The USAPATRIOT Act established the deadline for all foreign nationals entering under the VWP to have machine-readable, tamper-resistant passports, and the new requirement of biometrics in the passports did not change the deadline in the USA PATRIOT Act for the presentation of machine-readable, tamper-resistant passports. The biometric passport requirement deadline was extended to October 26, 2005, by P.L. 108-299.[139] Thus, as of October 27, 2005 (the day after the new deadline), all entrants under the VWP were required to present machine-readable, tamper-resistant passports (as required by the USA PATRIOT Act, and P.L. 108-299), but only passports issued after October 26, 2005, were required to have a biometric identifier.

Although Congress extended the deadline for VWP countries to certify that they had a program to issue machine-readable passports with biometric identifiers, most VWP countries would have been unable to meet the new,

---

"Machine-Readable Passports for Visa Waiver Program Travel Postponed," press release, September 23, 2003, at https://2001-2009.state.gov/r/pa/prs/ps/2003/24407.htm.

[137] P.L. 107-173. The original bill, H.R. 3525, was sponsored by Representative F. James Sensenbrenner.

[138] The act tasked the International Civil Aviation Organization (ICAO) with developing the biometric standard.

[139] Signed into law on August 9, 2004.

October 26, 2005, deadline, especially if the biometric requirement could only have been fulfilled by countries who had electronic data chips in their passports (e-passports). In addition, there was resistance in Congress to grant another extension of the biometric deadline.[140] As a result, the U.S. government clarified that a digitized photograph printed on a data page in the passport would count as a biometric for the October 26, 2005, requirement. Only France and Italy were unable to meet the new deadline, but have since come into compliance. In addition, any passports used by VWP travelers issued after October 26, 2006, requires integrated chips with information from the data page (e-passports).

The Intelligence Reform and Terrorism Prevention Act of 2004

P.L. 108-458,[141] the Intelligence Reform and Terrorism Prevention Act of 2004, added the requirement that by October 26, 2006, as a condition of being in the VWP, each VWP country must certify that it is developing a program to issue tamper-resistant, machine-readable visa documents that incorporate biometric identifiers which are verifiable at the country's port of entry.

Implementing the 9/11 Commission Recommendations Act of 2007

Signed into law on August 3, 2007, Section 711 of P.L. 110-53 (H.R. 1) required the Secretary of Homeland Security, no later than one year after enactment, to establish an exit system that records the departure of every alien who entered under the VWP and left the United States by air. The exit system is required to match the alien's biometric information

---

[140] For example, see letter from Rep. F. James Sensenbrenner, Jr., to Luc Frieden, President of the European Counsel of Ministers, and Franco Frattini, Vice-President of the European Commission, April 7, 2005.

[141] The original bill, H.R. 2845, was sponsored by Senator Susan M. Collins and signed into law on December 17, 2004.

against relevant watch lists and immigration information, and compare such biographical information against manifest information collected by airlines to confirm that the alien left the United States.[142]

P.L. 110-53 also allows the Secretary of Homeland Security, in consultation with the Secretary of State, to waive the nonimmigrant visa refusal rate requirement for admission to the VWP on the date on which the Secretary of Homeland Security certifies to Congress that an air exit system is in place that can verify the departure of not less than 97% of foreign nationals who exit through U.S. airports. In addition, the Secretary of Homeland Security also had to certify to Congress that the electronic travel authorization system (discussed below) was operational, prior to being able to waive the nonimmigrant visa refusal rate requirement.

When P.L. 110-53 took effect, the Secretary of Homeland Security could waive the nonimmigrant refusal rate even if the air exit system did not yet incorporate biometric identifiers. However, if after June 30, 2009, the air exit system was unable to match an alien's biometric information with relevant watch lists and manifest information, the Secretary of Homeland Security's authority to waive the nonimmigrant visa refusal rate would be suspended until the air exit system had the specified biometric capacity.

For admission to the VWP, a country who receives a refusal rate waiver also has to

- meet all the security requirements of the program;
- be determined by the Secretary of Homeland Security to have a totality of security risk mitigation measures that provide assurances that the country's participation in the program would not compromise U.S. law enforcement and security interests, or the enforcement of U.S. immigration laws;

---

[142] This exit system is not necessarily the same as the exit system required for the nonimmigrant visa refusal rate waiver authority. DHS appears to have incorporated this requirement as part of the exit portion of automated entry and exit data system known as US-VISIT.

- have had a sustained reduction in visa refusal rates and have existing conditions for the rates to continue to decline;
- have cooperated with the United States on counterterrorism initiatives and information sharing before the date of its designation and be expected to continue such cooperation; and
- have, during the previous fiscal year, a nonimmigrant visa refusal rate of not more than 10%, or an overstay rate that did not exceed the maximum overstay rate established by the Secretaries of Homeland Security and State for countries receiving waivers of the nonimmigrant visa refusal rate to participate in the VWP the program.

P.L. 110-53 also specified that in determining whether to waive the nonimmigrant visa refusal rate requirement, the Secretary of Homeland Security, in consultation with the Secretary of State, may take into consideration other factors affecting U.S. security, such as the country's airport security and passport standards, whether the country has an effective air marshal program, and the estimated overstay rate for nationals from the country.

In addition, P.L. 110-53 made several changes to the criteria to qualify as a VWP country, which were intended to enhance the security of the program. As previously mentioned, the act mandated that the Secretary of Homeland Security, in consultation with the Secretary of State, develop and implement an electronic travel authorization system,[143] through which each alien electronically provides, in advance of travel, the biographical information necessary to determine whether the alien is eligible to travel to the United States and enter under the VWP. Aliens using the system are charged a fee that is required to be set at a level so that the cost of creating and administering the system is covered by those fees.

Furthermore, under P.L. 110-53, to participate in the VWP, countries are required to enter into an agreement with the United States to report or make available through INTERPOL information about the theft or loss of

---

[143] The system as implemented is known as the Electronic System for Travel Authorization (ESTA).

passports. The agreements must specify strict time limits for the reporting of this information. In addition, to be part of the VWP, countries have to accept the repatriation of any citizen, former citizen, or national against whom a final order of removal is issued no later than three weeks after the order is issued. Also, the countries are required to enter into an agreement with the United States to share information regarding whether a national of that country traveling to the United States represents a threat to U.S. security or welfare. The act requires the Secretary of Homeland Security to provide technical assistance to VWP countries to assist the countries in fulfilling the requirements of the program.

In addition, P.L. 110-53 requires the Director of National Intelligence to conduct intelligence assessments of countries. For new VWP countries, the reviews must occur prior to their designation into the VWP. For existing VWP countries, the reviews should be done in conjunction with the biannual country reviews.

The act also requires the Director of National Intelligence to immediately inform the Secretary of Homeland Security of any current and credible threat of imminent danger to the United States or its citizens that originates from a VWP country. Upon receiving such notification, the Secretary of Homeland Security, in consultation with the Secretary of State, may suspend a country from the VWP without any prior notice. Once the country's participation in the VWP no longer poses a security threat, the Secretary of Homeland Security shall reinstate the country in the VWP.

Obama Administration Initiated VWP Security Enhancements

In August and November 2015, the Obama Administration announced a series of changes to the VWP to enhance security. Some of the Administration's changes were codified by the Visa Waiver Program Improvement and Terrorist Travel Prevention Act (P.L. 114-113). See below for a full discussion of the legislation.

In August 2015, the then-Secretary of Homeland Security Jeh C. Johnson announced an intention to implement new security measures in the VWP.[144] Most significant among them were

- requiring e-passports of all VWP travelers coming to the United States,
- requiring VWP countries to use the INTERPOL Stolen and Lost Travel Document (SLTD) database to screen travelers crossing a VWP country's borders, and
- negotiating for the expanded use of U.S. air marshals on flights from VWP countries to the United States.

In November 2015, the Obama Administration announced more changes to the VWP meant to enhance national security. These changes included

- modifying ESTA to capture information regarding any past travel to countries constituting a terrorist safe haven;
- accelerating the review process for VWP countries;
- requiring, within 60 days, that DHS report to the President on possible pilot programs designed to assess the collection and use of biometrics (fingerprints, photographs, or both) and on any countries that are deficient in key areas of cooperation, along with recommended options to engender compliance;
- requiring, within 60 days, that the Federal Bureau of Investigation (FBI) provide an evaluation to the President on the terrorism information sharing that occurs between the United States and VWP countries and identify options to mitigate any deficiencies;
- offering assistance to countries to better facilitate terrorism information sharing, specifically to include the use of biometrics[145]

[144] Department of Homeland Security, "Statement by Secretary Jeh C. Johnson on Intention to Implement Security Enhancements to the Visa Waiver Program," press release, August 6, 2015, https://www.dhs.gov/news/2015/08/06/statement-secretary-jeh-c-johnson-intention-implement-security-enhancements-visa.

and deploying "Foreign Fighter Surge Teams" to work with countries to counter terrorist travel; and

- expanding and promoting the use of the Global Entry program (a trusted traveler program),[146] which includes biometric checks within VWP countries.

The Visa Waiver Program Improvement and Terrorist Travel Prevention Act of 2015

The Visa Waiver Program Improvement and Terrorist Travel Prevention Act (H.R. 158) was passed by the House on December 8, 2015, and enacted as part of the Consolidated Appropriations Act of 2016 (P.L. 114-113) on December 18, 2015.

P.L. 114-113 requires, as of April 1, 2016, that all foreign nationals traveling under the VWP present an electronic passport (e-passport) that is fraud resistant and incorporates biographic and biometric information (as determined by the Secretary of Homeland Security). No later than October 1, 2016, each VWP country had to certify that it had in place mechanisms to validate machine-readable passports and e-passports at each port of entry. This requirement does not apply to travel between countries within the Schengen Area.[147]

---

[145] One proposed example of this assistance includes having DHS and the FBI's Terrorist Screening Center (TSC) assist interested VWP countries in screening refugees or asylum seekers, utilizing the terrorism information already provided to VWP countries, and by piloting programs to conduct "near real time" biometric checks. The TSC maintains the U.S. government's consolidated Terrorist Screening Database often referred to as the Terrorist Watchlist. Federal Bureau of Investigation, *About the Terrorist Screening Center*, https://www.fbi.gov/about-us/nsb/tsc/about-the-terrorist-screening-center.

[146] As of July 11, 2019, the Global Entry program is available to citizens of Argentina, Australia, Canada, Colombia, Germany, India, Mexico, New Zealand, Panama, Republic of Korea (South Korea), Singapore, Switzerland, and Taiwan (see CBP, *Global Entry: International Arrangements*, at https://www.cbp.gov/travel/trusted-traveler-programs/ global-entry/international-arrangements). For a discussion of the Global Entry program, see CRS Report R43356, *Border Security: Immigration Inspections at Ports of Entry*.

[147] The Schengen Area enables citizens of the European Union (EU), as well as many non - EU nationals, to cross select international borders in Europe without being subject to

The act also prohibited people who were present in certain countries on or after March 1, 2011, from traveling under the VWP. The specified countries include

- Iraq and Syria;
- any country designated by the Secretary of State as having repeatedly provided support for acts of international terrorism under any provision of law,[148] or
- any other country or area of concern[149] deemed appropriate by the Secretary of Homeland Security.

In addition, anyone who is a dual national of a VWP country and one of these specified countries is ineligible to travel under the VWP. Importantly, the VWP only applies to foreign nationals coming to the United States; it does not impact U.S. citizens, even those with dual nationality. In other words, dual U.S.-Iranian, U.S.-Iraqi, U.S.-Sudanese, or U.S.-Syrian citizens still do not need a visa to travel to the United States. If the Secretary of Homeland Security determines that the foreign national was in one of the specified countries in order to perform military service in the armed forces of a VWP country or to perform official duties as an employee of the VWP country, the prohibition on traveling under the VWP does not apply. Similarly, P.L. 114-113 gives the Secretary of Homeland Security the authority to waive the prohibition on travel under

---

border checks. See European Commission, *Migration and Home Affairs: Schengen Area*, November 13, 2015, http://ec.europa.eu/dgs/home-affairs/what-we-do/policies/borders-and-visas/schengen/index_en.htm.

[148] Examples of acts that use the term "repeatedly provided support for acts of international terrorism," include §6(j) of the Export Administration Act of 1979 (50 U.S.C. 2405), §40 of the Arms Export Control Act (22 U.S.C. 2780), and §620A of the Foreign Assistance Act of 1961 (22 U.S.C. 2371). Currently, these countries are Iran, Sudan, and Syria.

[149] The Secretary of Homeland Security, in consultation with the Director of National Intelligence, is required to make this determination within 60 days of enactment. The criteria to make the determination would include whether the presence of a foreign national in that area or country increases the likelihood that the foreign national is a credible threat to U.S. national security, whether a foreign terrorist organization has a significant presence in the area or country, and whether the country or area is a safe haven for terrorists.

the VWP if the Secretary determines that the waiver would be in the law enforcement or national security interests of the United States. The Secretary of Homeland Security is required to submit an annual report to Congress on each instance where the waiver authority was exercised.

Likewise, P.L. 114-113 amended the lost or stolen passports reporting requirement to require countries to report lost or stolen passports to the United States or make the information available through INTERPOL no later than 24 hours after a theft or loss is reported to the VWP country. The act also required, no later than September 13, 2016,[150] that each program country with an international airport certify, to the maximum extend allowed under the laws of the country, that it is screening each foreign national who is admitted to or departs from that country, using relevant INTERPOL databases and notices or other means designated by the Secretary of Homeland Security. Consequently, a country that fails to screen foreign nationals arriving in or departing from that country will be terminated from the VWP. This screening requirement does not apply to those traveling between countries within the Schengen Area.

P.L. 114-113 also specifies that the HSPD-6 arrangements and PCSC Agreements (discussed in "Information Sharing") not only have to be signed before a country can be designated as a VWP country but have to be fully implemented. If the Secretary of Homeland Security and the Secretary of State jointly determine that the VWP country is not sharing information regarding whether a citizen of that country traveling to the United States represents a threat to the security or welfare of the United States or U.S. citizens, the country will be terminated from the program. The country will be redesignated as a program country as soon as it fulfills the information- sharing requirements.

The act also requires that DHS report biennially to Congress on the national security threat posed by each program country.[151] The Secretary of Homeland Security, in consultation with the Director of National Intelligence and the Secretary of State, is also required to annually evaluate

---

[150] This is 270 days after the enactment of P.L. 114-113.

[151] The first of such reports would be due 90 days after the bill is enacted.

program countries based on specified criteria[152] and to identify any country for which nationals of that country present a "high risk" to U.S. national security.[153] The Secretary of Homeland Security, in consultation with the Secretary of State, can suspend a program country based on a determination that the country presents a high risk to U.S. national security.

P.L. 114-113 allows the Secretary of Homeland Security to shorten the validity period of any ESTA determination, in addition to revoking the determination. The Secretary of Homeland Security is also required to collect information, through ESTA, on an applicant's previous or multiple citizenships and to research opportunities to incorporate into ESTA technology to detect and prevent fraud or deception.

The act also requires DHS to report annually on the number of individuals (identified by citizenship) who were denied eligibility to travel under ESTA or whose eligibility to travel was revoked because they were determined to represent a security threat to the United States.[154] Additionally, DHS was required to report within 30 days from December 18, 2015, on ways to strengthen the ability of ESTA to prevent terrorists and instruments of terrorism from entering the United States.

The act requires DHS, in consultation with the Department of State, to provide assistance, in a risk-based manner, to non-VWP countries to assist the countries in submitting information on lost or stolen travel documents to INTERPOL and issuing and validating e-passports at ports of entry. The act also contained Sense of Congress language that the International Civil Aviation Organization (ICAO)[155] is expected to establish standards for e-

---

[152] The criteria include the number of nationals determined to be ineligible to travel to the United States under the VWP during the previous year; the number of nationals who were identified in U.S. government terrorism databases during the previous year, the estimated number of nationals who traveled to Iraq or Syria since March 1, 2011, to engage in terrorism; the country's capacity to combat passport fraud; the level of cooperation with U.S. counter-terrorism efforts; the adequacy of the country's border and immigration controls; and any other criteria determined by the Secretary of Homeland Security.

[153] The first report would be due 60 days after enactment.

[154] The first report would be due 30 days after enactment.

[155] The International Civil Aviation Organization (ICAO) is a United Nations specialized agency established to manage the administration and governance of the Convention on International Civil Aviation. The ICAO works with Convention Member States and

passports and obligate the 191 member countries to utilize e-passports as soon as possible.

industry groups to reach consensus on international civil aviation standards and practices. International Civil Aviation Organization, *About ICAO*, at https://www.icao.int/about-icao/Pages/ default.aspx.

In: Visas
Editor: Brian A. Shelton
ISBN: 978-1-53619-966-6

Chapter 9

ADDING COUNTRIES TO THE VISA WAIVER PROGRAM: EFFECTS ON NATIONAL SECURITY AND TOURISM*

Abigail F. Kolker and Michaela D. Platzer

SUMMARY

The Visa Waiver Program (VWP), which allows citizens of certain countries to visit the United States for up to three months without a visa, has two explicit missions: to enhance national security and to boost the U.S. travel and tourism sectors. On November 8, 2019, the United States designated Poland into the VWP, bringing the number of participating countries to 39. A concern for Congress is whether the VWP exposes the United States to security threats, despite implementation of strict security requirements over recent years. At the same time, because of longstanding congressional interest in promoting the U.S. travel and tourism sectors, many lawmakers support adding more countries to the VWP.

* This is an edited, reformatted and augmented version of Congressional Research Service Publication No. R46300, dated April 1, 2020.

A key goal of the VWP is to improve standards for aviation security, travel documents, and law enforcement in countries around the world. To qualify for the VWP, countries must issue electronic passports, report information on all lost and stolen passports to the United States through the International Criminal Police Organization (INTERPOL), and share information on travelers who may pose a terrorist or criminal threat. Every VWP traveler must obtain preclearance to board a flight to the United States through the Electronic System for Travel Authorization (ESTA). Supporters of the VWP see admission into the program as an incentive for foreign countries to increase their security infrastructure and information sharing with the United States. A competing view is that despite security improvements following the 2015 terrorist attacks in Europe, such as screening of passengers entering under the VWP based on past travel to a country known as a terrorist sanctuary, the program remains a national security vulnerability.

Another objective of the VWP is to facilitate and encourage foreign business and leisure travel from high-volume and low- risk countries to the United States. In FY2018, 22.8 million nonimmigrant visitors—constituting nearly one-third of all visitor admissions to the United States—arrived through the VWP. Figures from U.S. Travel, the industry group representing travel and tourism organizations, show that nationals from VWP countries generated an estimated $190 billion in economic activity and supported close to 1 million jobs in the United States in 2017. In addition, the U.S. government's National Travel and Tourism Office (NTTO) reports that a record 80 million international travelers visited the United States in 2018, with the number falling slightly in 2019. The number of foreign visitor arrivals in 2019 indicated that the United States would likely fall short of the goal set by the federal government's travel and tourism strategy of attracting 100 million visitors annually by the end of 2021. The COVID-19 pandemic has sharply reduced foreign tourism in 2020 as countries have discouraged international travel and required arriving passengers to quarantine themselves for extended periods, probably putting the 2021 goal out of reach. Nonetheless, advocates for the U.S. travel and tourism industries argue that adding more countries to the VWP would further promote tourism, trade, and commerce by increasing the number of overseas visitors traveling to the United States.

Activity in the 116th Congress related to the VWP seeks to expand the number of countries by changing the qualification criteria or designating specific countries. Other bills would rename the VWP to "Secure Travel Partnership" to reflect one of its main goals of securing U.S. borders. Legislation in the 116th Congress also addresses the ESTA fee paid by VWP applicants. In December 2019, Congress authorized the continued use of the ESTA fee to partially fund Brand USA, a national tourism promotion program, through September 30, 2027. Congress also raised the ESTA fee from $14 to $21 (Division I, Title 8 of P.L. 116-94). The effective date of the new ESTA fee has not yet been announced.

INTRODUCTION

The U.S. government's Visa Waiver Program (VWP) allows eligible nationals[1] from 39 countries to enter the United States for stays of fewer than 90 days for tourism or business purposes without applying for a visa from a U.S. embassy or consulate (see Figure 1). Originally established in 1986 as a pilot program, the VWP was made permanent in 2000.[2] VWP countries now account for the largest group of visitors to the United States other than travelers from neighboring Canada and Mexico. In FY2018, 22.8 million VWP visitors were admitted to the United States, the largest number of people ever to enter under the program in a single year, up almost 30% from 17.6 million in FY2008.[3]

Countries that want to join the VWP must meet strict criteria, including signing on to information-sharing agreements, issuing tamper-proof travel documents, and upholding security standards at their borders. Travelers from VWP countries are not automatically guaranteed admission into the United States. Every VWP traveler must obtain preclearance to board a flight or ship to the United States through the Electronic System for Travel Authorization (ESTA). This web-based application checks the traveler's information against relevant law enforcement and security databases and determines eligibility for travel under the VWP. In addition, as with all international travelers, Customs and Border Protection (CBP) officers may deny entry to a VWP traveler upon arrival.

This chapter offers an overview of the VWP. It discusses the potential effects on national security and considers the likely economic effects on

---

[1] In this chapter, the term *nationals* refers to a person who is a citizen or a person owing permanent allegiance to a state.

[2] P.L. 106-396.

[3] U.S. Department of Homeland Security (DHS), Yearbook of Immigration Statistics 2018, Table 25, Nonimmigrant Admissions by Class of Admission: Fiscal Years 2008 to 2018, https://www.dhs.gov/immigration-statistics/ nonimmigrant.

the U.S. travel and tourism industries if more countries were to be added to the program. The report also reviews legislative proposals in the 116th Congress related to the expansion and implementation of the VWP, and legislation targeting U.S. travel promotion—namely the Brand USA program, which is partially funded by ESTA.

VISA WAIVER PROGRAM DESIGNATION

The Department of Homeland Security (DHS), in consultation with the Department of State (DOS), has the authority to designate participants into the VWP. The Secretary of State must formally make the nomination; DHS then conducts a final review and certifies that the aspiring participant meets all the requirements. To be eligible, a country[4] must comply with an extensive list of conditions specified in several different laws. It must

- offer reciprocal privileges to U.S. citizens;[5]
- have had a nonimmigrant visitor visa refusal rate of less than 3% for the previous year or a lower average percentage over the previous two fiscal years;[6]
- issue electronic, machine-readable passports[7] that contain a biometric identifier (known as e-passports);[8]
- certify that it issues tamper-resistant, machine-readable visa documents that incorporate biometric identifiers, which are verifiable at the country's port of entry;[9]

---

[4] Throughout this chapter, the term *country* is used. However, the VWP can and does include areas the United States does not formally consider countries, such as Taiwan.

[5] P.L. 99-603.

[6] Originally, to qualify for the Visa Waiver Pilot Program countries needed to have had an average nonimmigrant refusal rate of no more than 2% over the past two fiscal years with neither year going above 2.5% (P.L. 99-603). However, P.L. 105-173 added the criterion that a country could have a nonimmigrant refusal rate of less than 3% for the previous year to qualify for the program.

[7] P.L. 106-396, P.L. 107-56.

[8] P.L. 107-173, P.L. 114-113.

[9] P.L. 108-458.

- certify that it has in place mechanisms to validate machine-readable passports and e-passports at each port of entry;[10]
- enter into an agreement with the United States to report or make available through INTERPOL information about the theft or loss of passports no later than 24 hours after a theft or loss is reported to the VWP country;[11]
- certify, to the maximum extent allowed under its laws, that it is screening each foreign national who is admitted or departs, using relevant INTERPOL databases and notices, or other means designated by the Secretary of Homeland Security (this requirement only applies to countries that have an international airport);[12]
- accept the repatriation of any citizen, former citizen, or national against whom a final order of removal from the United States is issued no later than three weeks after the order is issued;[13]
- enter into and fully implement an agreement with the United States to share information regarding whether a national traveling to the United States represents a threat to U.S. security or welfare;[14] and
- be determined, by the Secretary of Homeland Security, in consultation with the Secretary of State, not to compromise the law enforcement or security interests of the United States by its inclusion in the program.[15]
- As of March 2020, 31 European countries, 7 Asia-Pacific countries, and 1 country in South America are in the program (see *Figure 1).*

---

[10] P.L. 114-113.

[11] P.L. 110-53, P.L. 114-113. The International Criminal Police Organization (INTERPOL) is an inter-governmental organization that enables its 194 member countries to share information on crime and criminals.

[12] P.L. 114-113.

[13] P.L. 110-53.

[14] P.L. 110-53.

[15] P.L. 114-113.

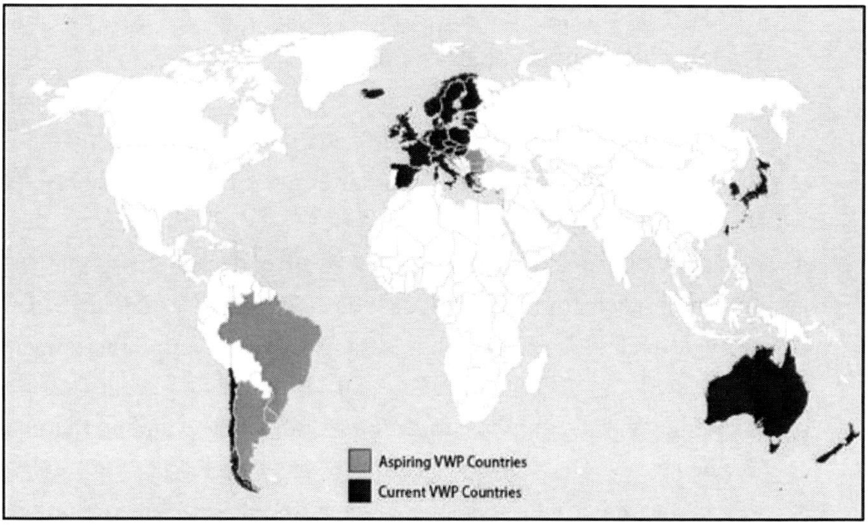

Source: Congressional Research Service (CRS), compiled from information from U.S. Travel and from CRS Report RL32221, Visa Waiver Program.

Figure 1. Current and Selected Aspiring VWP Countries.

Nonimmigrant Visitor Visa Refusal Rate Versus Overstay Rate

One of the VWP criteria—the nonimmigrant, or temporary, visitor visa refusal rate—has been the subject of scrutiny by Congress. This rate represents the proportion of individuals whose applications for tourist or business visas have been rejected by U.S. consular officials in their home countries. When the VWP was conceived, some legislators argued that the number of nonimmigrants who overstay the terms of their entry under the VWP would be a better standard for future program participation, as the nonimmigrant visitor visa refusal rate is not based on the actual behavior of nonimmigrants.[16] However, DHS is not able to calculate overstay rates

[16] U.S. Congress, House Committee on the Judiciary, *Visa Waiver Permanent Program Act,* report together with additional views to accompany H.R. 3767, 106th Cong., 2nd sess., H.Rept. 106-564 (Washington, DC: GPO, 2000), p. 32. Importantly, although the refusal rate was seen as a proxy for the overstay rate when the program was conceived, people are denied visas for reasons other than being unable to prove that they will not remain illegally in the United States (i.e., they are *intending immigrants*). During the visa application process, consular officers must confirm that an alien is not ineligible for a visa under any of

accurately; because it relies on information from passenger manifests, persons entering by air or sea but exiting at a land port of entry may be mischaracterized as overstays.[17]

Advocates of expanding the VWP contend that the 3% nonimmigrant visitor visa refusal rate criterion, which has been a significant barrier to entry into the VWP, should be replaced with the overstay rate, or the refusal rate threshold should be raised and used in conjunction with the overstay rate.[18]

Some advocates have called for the return of the nonimmigrant visitor visa refusal rate waiver, which was available from October 2008 to July 2009.[19] The waiver allowed DHS to admit into the VWP countries that had met all of the security requirements if they had a low overstay rate and a declining nonimmigrant visitor visa refusal rate that was below 10% in the previous fiscal year.[20] Due to this waiver, eight countries that otherwise would not have qualified for the VWP were added in 2008.[21] For current aspiring VWP countries, a complicating factor is that the Secretary of Homeland Security's authority to waive the nonimmigrant visitor visa

---

the so-called *grounds for inadmissibility* of the Immigration and Nationality Act (INA), such as having a criminal history, engaging in terrorist activity, or having previously violated U.S. immigration law. Although most visitor visa denials are because the alien cannot prove that they are not an intending immigrant, there are other reasons a person could be denied a visa that are captured as part of a country's visa refusal rate.

[17] For example, a 2019 Government Accountability Office (GAO) report says there are "existing limitations in collecting departure data in the land environment." See GAO, *Department of Homeland Security: Review of the Fiscal Year 2017 Entry/Exit Overstay Report*, GAO-19-298R, February 22, 2019, p. 3, at https://www.gao.gov/products/ GAO-19-298R.

[18] Testimony of Steven Bucci, Director of the Douglas and Sarah Allison Center for Foreign and National Security Policy at the Heritage Foundation, in U.S. Congress, House Committee on Homeland Security, Subcommittee on Border and Maritime Security, *Combatting Terrorist Travel: Does the Visa Waiver Program Keep Our Nation Safe?*, hearings, 114th Cong., 1st sess., March 17, 2015, H.Hrg, 114-8 (Washington, DC: GPO, 2015).

[19] The waiver is authorized in P.L. 110-53 but is suspended until the United States fully implements a biometric air exit system. For more information, see CRS Report RL32221, *Visa Waiver Program*.

[20] A low overstay rate is defined in statute (P.L. 110-53, §711) as an overstay rate that does not meet the maximum overstay rate established by the Secretary of Homeland Security and the Secretary of State for countries receiving waivers of the nonimmigrant visitor visa refusal rate to participate in the VWP. A declining nonimmigrant visitor visa refusal rate is defined as a sustained reduction in visa refusal rates and an expectation of continued decline.

[21] These were the Czech Republic, Estonia, Hungary, Latvia, Lithuania, Malta, Slovakia, and South Korea.

refusal rate is suspended[22] until the airline passenger exit system is able to match an alien's biometric information with relevant watch lists and manifest information.[23]

In FY2018, all the VWP countries had DHS-estimated overstay rates of less than 0.5% (Poland, which had not yet been admitted to the VWP, had a DHS-estimated overstay rate of less than 1%).[24] The worldwide DHS-estimated overstay rate for non-VWP countries in FY2018 was 2%. Figure 2 shows the most recently available nonimmigrant visitor visa refusal rates and the DHS- estimated overstay rates for selected aspiring VWP countries. All of these countries (except Brazil) had a nonimmigrant visitor visa refusal rate of less than 10% in FY2019, and all of them had a DHS-estimated overstay rate of less than 2% in FY2018.

ADDING COUNTRIES TO VWP

Since the establishment of the VWP, the number of participating countries has been increased several times and two countries have been removed. The United Kingdom was the first country to be admitted, in July 1988, followed by Japan in December of the same year (see Figure 3). Six countries were added in 1989. An additional 13 countries were admitted in 1991, and another eight countries joined from 1993 to 1999. There was a gap until 2008, when another eight countries were admitted.[25] In the past 10 years, Chile, Greece, Taiwan, and, most recently, Poland have been added. Adding countries to the VWP is done through bilateral negotiations,

[22] The suspension of the waiver is required by P.L. 110-53, Section 711.

[23] As mandated by various statutes (e.g., P.L. 108-458 and P.L. 110-53) and Executive Order 13780, Customs and Border Protection (CBP) has been developing a biometric exit system for years, aiming to implement it in 20 international airports by 2022, which would cover 97% of commercial air travelers departing the United States; see DHS, *Transportation Security Administration and U.S. Customs and Border Protection: Deployment of Biometric Technologies*, Report to Congress, August 30, 2019, p. 5.

[24] For a discussion of the methodology used to calculate overstay rates, see DHS, FY2018 Entry/Exit Overstay Report, at https://www.dhs.gov/sites/default/files/publications/19_0417_fy18-entry-and-exit-overstay-report.pdf.

[25] These countries received a waiver for the nonimmigrant visa refusal rate; see the section on "Nonimmigrant Visitor Visa Refusal Rate Versus Overstay Rate."

and membership is often perceived as evidence of close ties with the United States. Argentina and Uruguay are the only two countries that have been removed from the program, in 2002 and 2003, respectively.

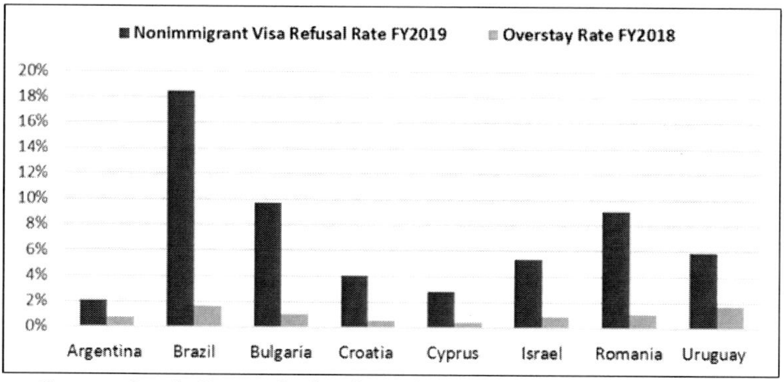

Source: Congressional Research Service (CRS), with data compiled from DOS, Adjusted Refusal Rate – B-Visas Only by Nationality Fiscal Year 2019; and DHS, FY2018 Entry/Exit Overstay Report.

Notes: Data are from the most recent year for which statistics are available.

Figure 2. Nonimmigrant Visitor Visa Refusal Rate Versus Overstay Rate for Selected Aspiring VWPCountries.

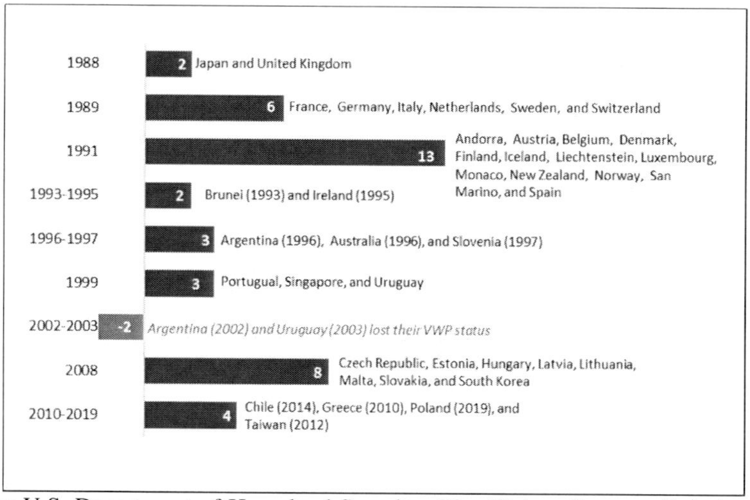

Source: U.S. Department of Homeland Security, Visa Waiver Program Requirements, http://www.dhs.gov/visa- waiver-program-requirements.

Figure 3.VWP Participants. (1988-2019)

Poland: The Latest VWP Addition

On November 8, 2019, DHS designated Poland into the VWP. Poland had been working with DHS for more than a decade to meet the program's criteria.

The Polish government had been outspoken in expressing frustration over the failure to include the country in the VWP. Reportedly, President Barack Obama said in December 2010 that he was going to make it a priority to get Poland into the program. President Donald Trump, in public remarks before a September 2018 meeting with Poland's President Andrzej Duda, said in reference to Poland's designation into the VWP that his administration was "looking at that very strongly."

In FY2019, Poland met the requirement of having a nonimmigrant visitor visa refusal rate below 3%. On October 4, 2019, President Trump announced that the Department of State had formally nominated Poland for the VWP, and the following month DHS announced Poland's designation into the program. As of November 11, 2019, Polish nationals, like other visitors from VWP countries, are able to apply online for ESTA, which authorizes travel to the United States without a visa. According to DHS, from November 11, 2019, through January 2020, approximately 40,000 Polish ESTA applications were approved.

Aspiring VWP Countries

Since 2010, DHS has admitted four countries into the VWP (Figure 3). Many other countries would like to join the program to make it easier for their nationals to travel to the United States. In 2005, the George W. Bush Administration began providing countries interested in joining the VWP with road maps to aid them in meeting the program's criteria. The original 13 aspiring countries were Bulgaria, Cyprus, Czech Republic, Estonia, Greece, Hungary, South Korea, Latvia, Lithuania, Malta, Poland, Romania, and Slovakia. Of these, 10 have since been admitted. This chapter examines a selected list of aspiring VWP countries: Argentina, Brazil, Bulgaria, Croatia, Cyprus, Israel, Romania, and Uruguay (see Figure 1).[26]

Four currently aspiring countries—Bulgaria, Croatia, Cyprus, and Romania—are in the European Union (EU). They are the only EU countries not in the VWP. U.S. citizens are permitted to travel to all the EU member states for short-term business or tourism purposes without a visa, whereas citizens of the four EU countries outside the VWP need a visa to travel to the United States.[27] The European Commission has pointed out that the United States is the only country on the EU's visa- free list that does not fully reciprocate, adding that "visa reciprocity is a fundamental principle of the European Union's common visa policy."[28] The European Union considered suspending its visa waiver for U.S. nationals in 2017, but decided not to do so.[29]

Israel has also been vocal about wanting to enter the VWP, but it has faced challenges meeting certain criteria. For instance, Israel's Biometric Database Law prohibits sharing fingerprint data with foreign authorities, though reportedly the United States and Israel came to an agreement to share data for those with a criminal background.[30] Another hurdle for Israel is that to become a VWP member, foreign countries must treat all

---

[26] While the Bush Administration specified these 13 "road map," or aspiring, VWP countries, no subsequent administration has publicly released a list of aspiring VWP countries. CRS updated this list by identifying additional aspiring VWP countries based on multiple sources, such as think tank publications, travel industry sources, and news reports.

[27] In 2018, the European Union (EU) announced that before travel, visitors from all visa-free countries will need to complete an online application similar to the U.S. ESTA system, and they will be required to pay a fee of €7 to use the European Travel Information and Authorization System (ETIAS). ETIAS will apply to people traveling to Europe's Schengen Zone, an area comprising 26 countries, the majority of which are EU member states, including France, Germany, and Spain. The United Kingdom will not be part of this new European visa system. ETIAS is expected to be operational in early 2021. An approved ETIAS will be valid for three years or the date of passport expiration (whichever happens first), and it can be used for stays for up to 90 days.

[28] European Commission, "Visa non-reciprocity: Commission takes stock of progress and developments," press release, December 18, 2018, at https://ec.europa.eu/commission/presscorner/detail/en/IP_18_6821.

[29] European Commission, "Visa Reciprocity: Commission responds to Parliament," press release, May 1, 2017, at https://ec.europa.eu/commission/presscorner/detail/en/IP_17_1148.

[30] Stuart Winer, "Israel nearing long-sought visa waiver deal with US—ministers," *Times of Israel*, November 13, 2017, at https://www.timesofisrael.com/israel-nearing-long-sought-visa-waiver-deal-with-us-ministers/.

American visa applicants equally; however, Israel has been accused of discriminating against Arab Americans.[31] Moreover, Israel has yet to meet the 3% nonimmigrant visitor visa refusal rate criterion; its rate was 5.33% in FY2019.[32]

Brazil is often included in reports about aspiring VWP countries.[33] It has recently made changes to its visa policy for U.S. citizens. In June 2019, Brazil introduced visa-free entry for U.S. citizens and citizens of three other countries, reportedly to stimulate tourism.[34]

Countries Removed from the VWP

A country can be terminated from the program if the Secretary of Homeland Security, in consultation with the Secretary of State, determines that a country's participation in the VWP undermines U.S. law enforcement, including immigration enforcement.

Argentina and Uruguay are former members of the VWP. Argentina joined in 1996, but the United States removed it in 2002 after poor economic conditions in the country led to an increase in the number of Argentine nationals entering the United States without visas and remaining illegally past the 90-day period of admission.[35] Uruguay joined in 1999,

---

[31] Ran Dagoni, "U.S. State Dep't: Israel Won't Get Visa Waiver So Fast," *Globes,* November 15, 2017, at https://en.globes.co.il/en/article-us-state-dept-israel-wont-get-visa-waiver-so-fast-1001211881.

[32] DOS, *Adjusted Refusal Rate – B-Visas Only by Nationality Fiscal Year 2019,* at https://travel.state.gov/content/dam/visas/Statistics/Non-Immigrant-Statistics/RefusalRates/FY19.pdf.

[33] For example, see Ruth Ellen Wasem, "The U.S. Visa Waiver Program: Facilitating Travel and Enhancing Security," *Chatham House,* October 25, 2017, at https://www.chathamhouse.org/sites/default/files/publications/research/2017-10-25-us-visa-waiver-wasem.pdf; U.S. Travel, *Brazil: International Inbound Travel Market Profile*, November 20, 2019, p. 3, at https://www.ustravel.org/research/brazil-international-inbound-travel-market-profile-2018.

[34] Michele Herrmann, "Brazil Waives Entry Visa Requirements for U.S. Citizens," *Forbes,* March 21, 2019, at https://www.forbes.com/sites/micheleherrmann/2019/03/21/brazil-waives-entry-visa-requirements/#5c7380833470.

[35] In addition, many Argentine nationals were trying to use the VWP to obtain entry to the United States solely for the purpose of proceeding to the Canadian border and pursuing an asylum claim in Canada. According to Citizenship and Immigration Canada, between 1999 and 2001 more than 2,500 Argentines filed refugee claims in Canada after transiting the United States under the VWP. 67 *Federal Register* 7944, February 21, 2002.

but it was removed in 2003 because a recession led to an increasing number of Uruguayan citizens entering the United States under the VWP to live and work illegally.[36]

NATIONAL SECURITY

National security is a key goal of the VWP. Over the years, Congress has continued to add security criteria for VWP participation.[37] One of the VWP's most significant security additions was ESTA, which was put in place in 2009 and is administered by DHS. In addition, several laws require VWP partner countries to share information with the United States and to set standards for travel documentation. Nevertheless, debate remains as to whether the VWP sufficiently vets individual travelers prior to arrival at a U.S. port of entry.

Electronic System for Travel Authorization (ESTA)

Before traveling to the United States, a VWP traveler must submit biographical information through DHS's ESTA. This web-based application checks the traveler's information against relevant law enforcement and security databases and determines eligibility for travel under the VWP. ESTA alerts the foreign national whether he or she has been approved to travel. If not approved, the individual must obtain a visa prior to coming to the United States.[38] This normally involves making an appointment for an interview with a U.S. consular official, a process that could delay the individual's departure for the United States.

---

[36] In 2002, Uruguayan nationals were two to three times more likely than all nonimmigrants, on average, to have been denied admission at the border. Uruguayan air arrivals had an apparent overstay rate more than twice that of the average apparent overstay rate for all air-arrival nonimmigrants. 68 *Federal Register* 10954, March 7, 2003.

[37] For the full legislative history of the VWP, see CRS Report RL32221, *Visa Waiver Program*.

[38] In most cases, the ESTA decision is almost instantaneous. Under statute, ESTA determinations are not reviewable by the courts.

ESTA became fully operational for all VWP visitors traveling to the United States by airplane or cruise ship on January 12, 2009.[39] Prior to the implementation of ESTA, the first time a foreign national traveling under the VWP to the United States was screened was after checking in for a flight to the United States at a foreign airport. Under the current system, at the time a foreign national submits an ESTA application (at least 72 hours before travel), he or she is screened against a number of security databases, including the Terrorist Screening Database; TECS (not an acronym), a system used by U.S. Customs and Border Protection officers to screen arriving travelers to the United States;[40] the Automated Targeting System; and INTERPOL's Lost and Stolen Passport database. *Appendix B* offers an explanation of these systems and databases.

An ESTA authorization is generally valid for multiple entries over a period of two years. Throughout this period, the ESTA system continually vets approved individuals' information against these databases. DHS can immediately revoke an ESTA approval if new derogatory information is discovered.[41] In addition, the validity period can be shortened at any time for any reason.[42] ESTA only screens against biographical security databases; VWP travelers do not submit biometric information (e.g., fingerprints and photographs) until they reach a U.S. port of entry, at which point their biometrics are run through multiple security databases.

---

[39] VWP countries that received a waiver of the nonimmigrant refusal rate (i.e., Czech Republic, Estonia, Hungary, Latvia, Lithuania, Malta, Slovakia, and South Korea) had to use ESTA starting on the date of their formal admission to the program. For all these countries (except Malta, which was admitted at the end of 2008) that date was November 17, 2008. DHS, "Electronic System for Travel Authorization (ESTA) Advisory Statement," November 6, 2008; and DHS, "Electronic System for Travel Authorization: Mandatory Compliance Required for Travel Under the Visa Waiver Program," 73 Federal Register 67354, November 13, 2008.

[40] TECS, managed by DHS, is an updated version of the Treasury Enforcement Communications System.

[41] Testimony of Hillary Batjer Johnson, Deputy Coordinator for Homeland Security, Screening, and Designations Bureau of Counterterrorism, U.S. Department of State, in U.S. Congress, House Committee on Oversight and Government Reform, Subcommittees on National Security and Government Operations, *The President's Waiver of Restrictions on the Visa Waiver Program,* hearings, 114th Cong., 2nd sess., February 10, 2016, H.Hrg. 114-104 (Washington, DC: GPO, 2017).

[42] P.L. 114-113, Title II, Section 207 gave the Secretary of Homeland Security the authority to issue a shortened ESTA validity period.

Notably, a determination under ESTA that a foreign national is eligible to travel to the United States does not constitute a determination that the individual is admissible. The foreign national may still be deemed inadmissible and denied entry by CBP inspectors upon arrival at a U.S. port of entry.[43]

Travelers who use ESTA pay a $14 fee, which was instituted in September 2010.[44] The fee includes $4 to cover the costs of administering ESTA and $10 for the travel promotion fee established by Congress in the Travel Promotion Act of 2009.[45] In December 2019, the Further Consolidated Appropriations Act of 2020 directed that the ESTA fee be raised to $21 (see section on "The VWP and U.S. Travel Promotion Efforts").[46] This fee increase has not been put into effect.

Security Debate

Although there tends to be agreement that the VWP benefits the U.S. economy by facilitating tourism (see section on "U.S. Travel and Tourism Economy"), disagreement exists about VWP's effect on national security. The VWP contains provisions that affect national security at two levels: country-to-country security agreements and individual traveler security screening.

Country-to-Country Security Agreements

To participate in the VWP, countries must agree to share extensive information with the United States about lost passports, known and suspected terrorists, and serious criminals.[47] Since 2015, the Secretary of

---

[43] A foreign national will be denied entry if he or she is found to be inadmissible under any of the Immigration Nationality Act's (INA's) grounds of inadmissibility (8 U.S.C. §1182).

[44] DHS, Customs and Border Protection, "DHS, CBP Announce Interim Final Rule for ESTA Fee," press release, August 6, 2010.

[45] The ESTA fee was established in P.L. 111-145, Section 9 and later extended by P.L. 113-235, Title 6.

[46] P.L. 116-94, Division I, Title 8.

[47] For example, VWP countries must provide data on lost and stolen passports (LASP) through INTERPOL, share information on known and suspected terrorists pursuant to Homeland Security Presidential Directive 6 (HSPD-6), and have signed the Preventing and Combating

Homeland Security had been authorized to immediately suspend a country's participation in the VWP if the country fails to provide information related to security threats.[48]

The VWP also sets standards for participating foreign countries' passports, visas, and border security. As previously mentioned, VWP countries must issue biometric e-passports and tamper- resistant, machine-readable visa documents. Furthermore, since December 2017, DHS requires VWP countries to use U.S. counterterrorism information to screen travelers crossing their borders and to implement certain aviation security measures.[49]

Moreover, foreign countries' participation in the VWP allows the United States to monitor their border operations. Since 2002, DHS is statutorily obligated to assess and report on VWP countries' compliance with VWP criteria every two years.[50] Thus, to remain in the program participating countries are subject to regular audits of their security operations, which include "rigorous and thorough inspection of airports, seaports, land borders, and passport production/issuance facilities as well as continuous monitoring."[51] According to DHS, "no other program enables the U.S. Government to conduct such broad and consequential assessments of foreign partners' border security operations."[52]

The possibility of joining the VWP is an incentive for aspiring VWP countries to share such information and improve their border security.

Serious Crime (PCSC) Agreements, which require them to share information on potential serious criminals and terrorists with the United States.

[48] P.L. 114-113, Title II.

[49] DHS, "Secretary Kirstjen Nielsen Announces Targeted Security Enhancements to the Visa Waiver Program," press release, December 15, 2017, at https://www.dhs.gov/news/2017/12/15/secretary-kirstjen-nielsen-announces-targeted-security-enhancements-visa-waiver.

[50] P.L. 107-52, §711. According to a 2016 GAO report, DHS needs to improve the timeliness of these biannual reports; GAO, *Visa Waiver Program: DHS Should Take Steps to Ensure Timeliness of Information Needed to Protect U.S. National Security,* GAO-16-498, May 2016.

[51] Testimony of Hillary Batjer Johnson, Deputy Coordinator for Homeland Security, Screening, and Designations Bureau of Counterterrorism, in U.S. Department of State, U.S. Congress, House Committee on Oversight and Government Reform, Subcommittees on National Security and Government Operations, *The President's Waiver of Restrictions on the Visa Waiver Program,* hearings, 114th Cong., 2nd sess., February 10, 2016, H.Hrg. 114-104 (Washington, DC: GPO, 2017), p, 27.

[52] Ibid.

According to DHS, "many countries not in the VWP complete program requirements in the hope of joining the program."[53] For participating countries that wish to remain in the VWP program, DHS contends that "VWP requirements provide our allies with the impetus to implement security measures that can sometimes be politically challenging for them, like amending legislation and updating their data privacy frameworks."[54]

Individual VWP Traveler Screening

The vetting of VWP travelers contains some features absent from the traditional screening required to receive a nonimmigrant visitor visa for business and tourist travel. As previously mentioned, ESTA screens the data of those authorized for VWP travel on a daily basis throughout ESTA's two-year validity period; new derogatory information could result in a denial of ESTA authorization.[55] In contrast, many nonimmigrant visitor visas are valid for 10 years and are not continuously vetted.[56] Moreover, travelers entering under the VWP must present e-passports, which tend to be more difficult to alter than other types of passports.

VWP travelers do not undergo the same screening required of travelers from most countries to receive a nonimmigrant visitor visa, which typically includes a personal interview with a U.S. consular officer.[57] As such, VWP travelers' first face-to-face encounter with U.S. officials could be at a port of entry.[58] Additionally, ESTA is a name-based system and cannot be used to run checks against databases that use biometrics, such as the Automated

---

[53] Ibid., p. 19.

[54] Ibid., p. 27.

[55] Testimony of Gil Kerlikowske, Commissioner, U.S. Customs and Border Protection, in U.S. Congress, House Committee on Oversight and Government Reform, Subcommittees on National Security and Government Operations, *The President's Waiver of Restrictions on the Visa Waiver Program,* hearings, 114th Cong., 2nd sess., February 10, 2016, H.Hrg. 114-104 (Washington, DC: GPO, 2017).

[56] Although nonimmigrant visitor visas are not continuously vetted, CBP screens individuals traveling on them at ports of entry each time they enter the United States.

[57] Federation for American Immigration Reform (FAIR), "The Visa Waiver Program: Suspend It or Eliminate It," December 2015, at https://www.fairus.org/issue/legal-immigration/visa-waiver-program-suspend-it-or-eliminate-it.

[58] VWP travelers may have previously applied for a visa to the United States and undergone an interview with a U.S. consular officer.

Biometric Identification System and Next Generation Identification.[59] However, when VWP travelers enter the United States, CBP takes their fingerprints and photographs and checks them against these biometric systems.[60] Finally, visitor visa applicants are required to submit social media identifiers, but this is optional for VWP travelers.[61]

Another concern, following a number of high-profile terrorist attacks in Europe in recent years perpetrated mainly by European citizens, has been the possible threat posed by nationals from VWP countries who are aligned with the Islamic State. A focus had been on radicalized citizens of VWP countries who could have fought in the Middle East for the Islamic State or other terrorist groups. Conceivably, these individuals may have been able to travel to the United States under the VWP if there was no derogatory information about them in U.S. biographic databases. In response, Congress passed the Visa Waiver Program Improvement and Terrorist Travel Prevention Act, enacted as part of the FY2016 Consolidated Appropriations Act.[62] This makes citizens of VWP countries ineligible for admission to the United States under the VWP if they are dual nationals of the Democratic People's Republic of Korea, Iran, Iraq, Sudan, or Syria or had been present in any of those countries, or in Libya, Somalia, or Yemen, at any time on or after March 1, 2011 (with limited exceptions). These individuals can still apply for a visa to travel to the United States.

Another point of contention is whether the VWP threatens the United States' immigration enforcement interests.[63] As of December 2017, VWP

---

[59] See *Appendix B* for more details about these systems.

[60] CRS Report R43356, Border Security: Immigration Inspections at Ports of Entry.

[61] DHS is considering a proposal to require VWP travelers to submit social media identifiers on their ESTA applications; see DHS, "Agency Information Collection Activities: Generic Clearance for the Collection of Social Media Information on Immigration and Foreign Travel Forms," 84 Federal Register 46557, September 4, 2019. Some stakeholders are concerned that this could have a "chilling effect" on U.S. tourism; see Rosie Spinks, "Social Media Requirement for Visa Waivers May Have chilling Effect on U.S. Tourism," Skift, September 16, 2019, at https://skift.com/2019/09/16/social-media-requirement-for-visa-waivers-may-have-chilling-effect-on-u-s-tourism/.

[62] P.L. 114-113.

[63] Although some stakeholders fear that foreign nationals could utilize the VWP to enter the United States and remain past the 90-day period of admission, current VWP countries have a relatively low overstay rate (an average of 0.5%).

countries that have an overstay rate of over 2% must initiate a public information campaign to educate their citizens about the conditions for admission to the United States.[64] If this does not reduce overstay violations, a country could be removed from the program, as occurred with Argentina and Uruguay in 2002 and 2003, respectively.[65]

U.S. TRAVEL AND TOURISM ECONOMY

A principal objective of the VWP is to boost the U.S. travel and tourism sectors by encouraging travel from high-volume and low-risk countries to the United States. The number of international visitors arriving in the United States totaled 79.3 million in 2019, down slightly from a record high of 79.7 million in 2018. Because of the sharp decline in international travel in the wake of the COVID-19 pandemic, many international flights have been cancelled and visitor volume is likely to fall sharply in 2020.[66]

In 2018, the travel and tourism sectors accounted for 2.9% of U.S. gross domestic product, a larger share than many other industries, including agriculture, mining, or utilities,[67] and they directly and indirectly employed 9.2 million workers.[68]

Every dollar international visitors spend in the United States counts as an export. Collectively, foreign visitors spent about $256 billion in 2018 on

---

[64] DHS, "Secretary Kirstjen Nielsen Announces Targeted Security Enhancements to the Visa Waiver Program," press release, December 15, 2017, at https://www.dhs.gov/news/2017/12/15/secretary-kirstjen-nielsen-announces-targeted-security-enhancements-visa-waiver.

[65] A country can be terminated from the program if the Secretary of Homeland Security, in consultation with the Secretary of State, determines that a country's participation in the VWP threatens U.S. law enforcement, including immigration enforcement.

[66] National Travel and Tourism Office (NTTO), *Non-Resident Arrivals to the United States: Overseas, Canada, Mexico, and International, Trend Line Data—Country of Residence*, March 2020, at https://travel.trade.gov/view/m- 2017-I-001/index.asp.

[67] Connor Franks and Sarah Osborne, *U.S. Travel and Tourism Satellite Account for 1998-2018*, U.S. Bureau of Economic Analysis (BEA), Survey of Current Business, November 2019, p. 5.

[68] Of those jobs, 5.9 million were direct tourism jobs and 3.3 million were indirect tourism jobs. U.S. Bureau of Economic Analysis (BEA), Tourism Satellite Accounts Data Sheets, Tourism Satellite Accounts 2018, at https://www.bea.gov/tourism-satellite-accounts-data-sheets.

domestic passenger fares aboard U.S. airlines and on travel-related goods and services, which makes tourism the United States' single-largest services sector export.[69] Every year since 1989, the U.S. travel and tourism industries have posted a trade surplus, which in 2018 was $69.6 billion. Travel- and tourism-related exports accounted for 31% of all U.S. services exports and 10% of total exports in 2018.[70]

Each overseas visitor spends, on average, about $4,200 per trip in the United States on travel activities such as shopping, lodging, dining, and sightseeing.[71] According to the Bureau of Economic Analysis (BEA), international travelers account for a disproportionate amount of all travel and tourism spending in the United States. One reason for this is that international visitors have relatively longer stays than domestic visitors, spending, on average, 18 nights in the United States.[72]

Travelers from VWP countries are among the highest in spending and visitor volume (see *Table 1*). However, an increasing number of overseas visitors come from non-VWP countries, notably China, Venezuela, Brazil, and India. Combined, these four non-VWP countries accounted for nearly 6.7 million visitors to the United States in 2019, down 4% from a year earlier.[73] Travelers from these countries spent more than $5,000 on average per trip during their visits to the United States, with visitors from China leading in country-level travel spending. Spending in the United States by visitors from large source markets has risen substantially in recent years, up 45% from China and 78% from India since 2013.[74]

---

[69] Travel exports cover travel for all purposes, including education and health-related spending. U.S. Bureau of Economic Analysis (BEA), *U.S. International Trade in Services*, October 15, 2019.

[70] National Travel and Tourism Office (NTTO), *Fast Facts: United States Travel and Tourism Industry, 2018*, October 2019.

[71] U.S. Travel, Top 20 Travel Export Markets (2018), October 26, 2019.

[72] U.S. Travel, U.S. Travel Answer Sheet: Facts About a Leading American Industry That's More than Just Fun, 2019.

[73] The number of overseas visitors, excluding travelers from Canada and Mexico, to the United States was down 3% in 2019 from 2018. Because of travel restrictions due to the global pandemic (COVID-19), overseas visitation to the United States is likely to decline significantly in 2020.

[74] U.S. Bureau of Economic Analysis (BEA), *U.S. International Trade in Services*, October 15, 2019.

Table 1. Travel spending and volume of visitors in the United States by selected countries (Ranked by average travel spending, 2018)

Country	Travel Spending (in $ millions)	Volume of Visitors to the United States	Average Travel Spending
China	$19,520	2,992,000	$6,524
Australia (VWP Member)	$8,352	1,362,000	$6,132
Venezuela	$2,827	502,000	$5,631
Brazil	$11,501	2,209,000	$5,206
India	$7,162	1,378,000	$5,197
Switzerland (VWP Member)	$2,388	463,000	$5,158
Argentina	$4,795	994,000	$4,824
Japan (VWP Member)	$15,062	3,493,000	$4,312
Germany (VWP Member)	$7,873	2,062,000	$3,818
Italy (VWP Member)	$4,073	1,073,000	$3,796

Source: Calculated by the Congressional Research Service (CRS) using data from the U.S. Department of Commerce's Bureau of Economic Analysis (BEA) and the National Travel and Tourism Office (NTTO).

Notes: Countries selected from top 20 markets by number of visitors. Travel spending covers travel spending, excluding travel for education and medical purposes, and passenger fares. Average travel spending is calculated by adding travel spending and passenger fares and dividing by the number of visitors to the United States.

Global Competitiveness of the U.S. Travel and Tourism Sectors

Although the number of foreign visitors to the United States has continued to rise, the U.S. share of total global tourism arrivals declined from 6.4% in 2015 to 5.7% in 2017, the most recent year for which statistics are available.[75] One reason for this declining market share is that it is now much easier for travelers to visit many parts of the world, including Asia and Africa, compared to a few years ago.[76]

In 2012, the Obama Administration established a Task Force on Travel and Competitiveness, which set a goal of welcoming 100 million international visitors in 2021.[77] Among other things, the task force recommended expediting visa processing for tourists from certain emerging economies, such as China and Brazil, and adding countries to the VWP in order to encourage tourism. Before the advent of the global pandemic (COVID-19) in 2020, the U.S. government had forecasted that the volume of tourist arrivals would not meet the task force's goal, with the number of total international visitors to the United States expected to reach close to 82.9 million in 2021.[78] It is too early to know what the repercussions of shutting down a significant share of overseas travel to the United States may mean for the U.S. travel and tourism industries. Current indications suggest that the stated goal in overseas travelers to the United States is beyond reach by 2021 as potential visitors modify their travel plans.

---

[75] The World Bank, *Travel and Tourism Number of Arrivals and Receipts*, at https://data.worldbank.org/indicator/ST.INT.ARVL and https://data.worldbank.org/indicator/ST.INT.RCPT.CD.

[76] World Economic Forum, *The Travel & Tourism Competiveness Report 2019*, September 4, 2019, p. 8, at https://www.weforum.org/reports/the-travel-tourism-competitiveness-report-2019.

[77] The White House (Obama Administration), Executive Order 13597, "Establishing Visa and Foreign Visitor Processing Goals and the Task Force on Travel and Competitiveness," 77 *Federal Register* 3373, January 24, 2012. Also see *National Travel & Tourism Strategy: Task Force on Travel & Competitiveness*, 2012.

[78] The National Travel and Tourism Office's (NTTO's) prediction rests on several assumptions, which did not include the effects of the coronavirus that started in January 2020. One is an annual rate of growth in overseas visitors of 2.7% or more, and another is a yearly increase in visitors from countries such as China and India of at least 4%. The only decrease NTTO anticipates among international visitors over the next four years is a drop from Venezuela to around 380,000 travelers by 2024 from more than 500,000 in 2018. NTTO, *International Visitors to the U.S. and Projections, 2000-2024*, October 2019, at https://travel.trade.gov/view/f-2000-99-001/index.html.

Economic Impact of Visitors from VWP Countries

Table 2. Top 20 VWP Participants by Number ofVisitors (FY2013 and FY2018, ranked by FY2018 admissions)

Country	Year Admitted to VWP	VWP Admissions FY2013	VWP Admissions FY2018	% Change FY2013 to FY2018
United Kingdom	1988	4,163,297	4,635,480	11%
Japan	1988	4,035,039	3,509,759	-13%
South Korea	2008	1,212,739	2,290,705	89%
Germany	1989	2,173,849	2,130,453	-2%
France	1989	1,804,035	2,022,153	12%
Australia	1996	1,351,238	1,412,605	5%
Italy	1989	1,108,013	1,315,270	19%
Spain	1991	838,935	1,080,300	29%
Netherlands	1989	730,997	812,905	11%
Ireland	1995	442,533	576,099	30%
Sweden	1989	512,299	529,534	3%
Taiwan	2012	228,515	442,622	94%
Switzerland	1989	437,567	403,095	-8%
New Zealand	1991	269,654	345,102	28%
Denmark	1991	299,941	338,063	13%
Belgium	1991	293,217	303,669	4%
Norway	1991	292,812	276,912	-5%
Austria	1991	218,779	206,643	-6%
Portugal	1999	160,183	205,780	28%
Finland	1991	148,524	150,440	1%

Source: Department of Homeland Security, Yearbook of Immigration Statistics, Table 28, "Nonimmigrant Admissions (I-94 Only) by Selected Category of Admission and Region and Country of Citizenship," multiple years.

Determining whether the VWP has directly led to increased travel to the United States is not straightforward because many factors affect international travel, including general economic conditions, currency exchange rates, and even the nature of bilateral relations. Nevertheless, the VWP could be a factor that has encouraged more visits to the United State because it arguably reduces uncertainty, inconvenience, and costs associated with a visa application.[79]

Of the 37 nations in the VWP as of 2012, all but 10 recorded an increase in the volume of tourists and business visitors to the United States from FY2013 to FY2018. Three-fourths of the top 20 countries by number of VWP visitors recorded double-digit growth rates in VWP admissions over this period, including Taiwan, South Korea, Spain, and New Zealand, although the annual change for VWP countries has been uneven. Germany, Austria, Switzerland, and Japan are among the 20 VWP countries that posted drops in U.S. VWP admissions between FY2013 and FY2018 (see Table 2).

Economic Impact of Adding New Countries to the VWP

U.S. Travel, an advocacy group for the travel industry, has produced several analyses of the effects of adding countries to the VWP. All of the organization's reports conclude that adding new countries to the program would yield positive results. For example, in a 2014 report U.S. Travel estimated that if Brazil, Bulgaria, Croatia, Israel, Poland, Romania, and Uruguay were included in the program, annual visitation from those countries would increase by more than 500,000, adding $5.3 billion per year to the U.S. economy and supporting 31,600 additional jobs in the United States.[80] Likewise, an economic analysis of U.S. Department of Commerce data on travel and tourism from 1980 to 2013 found that the VWP had a "meaningful impact driving increases in U.S. tourist

---

[79] A barrier for non-VWP travelers on nonimmigrant visitor visas is that they must arrange for an in-person appointment at an embassy or consulate and pay a non-refundable $160 visa application fee before they can visit the United States, and, moreover, visa approvals are not guaranteed.

[80] U.S. Travel, "Visa Waiver Works: Expanding the U.S. Visa Waiver Program Brightens the American Economy and Safeguards Security: Republic of Korea Case Study," March 2014, p. 5.

volumes."[81] In a 2019 report, U.S. Travel predicted that over the first three years of Poland's participation in the VWP, travel spending by Polish visitors to the United States would increase by $312 million, the number of Polish arrivals would rise by 97,000, and visitors from Poland would support 4,200 American jobs.[82]

Visitors from the four non-VWP EU countries (Bulgaria, Croatia, Cyprus, and Romania), who currently enter the United States on nonimmigrant visitor visas, accounted for approximately 1% of total EU visitor spending in the United States in 2018 (approximately $580 million). This seems to suggest that the overall economic effect of adding these four countries to the VWP would likely be relatively small. According to an estimate by U.S. Travel, the number of arrivals in the United States from these countries would increase by nearly 73,000 visitors at the end of the first three years after joining the VWP.[83] In a separate report, U.S. Travel projected that if Romania were to become a VWP country, annual arrivals from the country would increase by 38,000 and bring $128 million in additional travel spending to the United States.[84] Both reports were prepared before the COVID-19 pandemic interrupted international travel in 2020.

According to figures from the Department of Commerce spending by Israeli visitors in 2018 in the United States on passenger fares and travel-related goods and services was nearly $1.8 billion.[85] U.S. Travel estimated in 2019 that if Israel were admitted to the VWP, an additional 450,200

---

[81] Stephen Bronars, *Passport to Future Economic Growth: How Expanding the Visa Waiver Program Will Strengthen the U.S. Economy and Create American Tourism Jobs*, Partnership for a New American Economy, 2014, p. 2.

[82] U.S. Travel, *Poland is a Logical Next Addition to the Visa Waiver Program*, June 12, 2019, at https://www.ustravel.org/news/poland-logical-next-addition-visa-waiver-program.

[83] U.S. Travel, *Fact Sheet: The Visa Waiver Program Makes America More Secure*, February 12, 2019, at https://www.ustravel.org/research/visa-waiver-program-makes-america-more-secure.

[84] U.S. Travel, *U.S. Travel Encouraged by U.S.-Romania Visa Waiver Program Discussions*, August 20, 2019, at https://www.ustravel.org/news/us-travel-encouraged-us-romania-visa-waiver-program-discussions.

[85] Average visitor spending takes into account travel receipts and passenger fares, but excludes education and other travel-related exports. See U.S. Bureau of Economic Analysis (BEA), *U.S. Trade in Services*, Table 2.2, October 15, 2019.

Israeli travelers would visit the United States over a three-year period, generating $1.2 billion in travel spending.[86]

The U.S. travel and tourism industries support expanding the VWP to other countries, especially populous countries such as Brazil. Brazil was the fifth-largest tourism source market for the United States, with 2.1 million Brazilians visiting in 2018. As shown in Table 1, average spending per Brazilian visitor to the United States was $5,200 in 2018, among the highest of all source countries. The number of visitors from Brazil is projected to reach 2.6 million by 2024 even if Brazil is not admitted to the VWP.[87] In November 2019, the United States announced that Brazil will soon join the Global Entry program, which will reduce waiting time for approved Brazilian visitors arriving at U.S. airport immigration checkpoints.[88]

The VWP and U.S. Travel Promotion Efforts

The VWP is closely related to the promotion of foreign tourism to the United States. The United States no longer has a central agency to promote travel to it; the National Travel and Tourism Office (NTTO), within the International Trade Administration of the U.S. Department of Commerce, mainly provides official tourism statistics.[89]

---

[86] U.S. Travel, *Israel: International Inbound Travel Market Profile*, December 17, 2019, p. 2, at https://www.ustravel.org/research/israel-international-inbound-travel-market-profile-2018.

[87] National Travel and Tourism Office (NTTO), Forecast of International Travelers to the United States by Top Origin Countries, October 2019.

[88] Currently, trusted travelers from Argentina, India, Colombia, Germany, Panama, Singapore, South Korea, Switzerland, Taiwan, the United Kingdom, and Mexico are eligible for the program.

[89] In 1981, Congress passed the National Tourism Policy Act, (P.L. 97-63), which created the United States Travel and Tourism Administration (USTTA) as the nation's government tourism office, but Congress repealed the authorization for USTTA in 1996, placing tourism policy in the hands of individual states and the private sector. U.S. Congress, House Committee on Commerce, Committee of the Whole House, *United States National Tourism Organization Act of 1996*, 104th Cong., 2nd sess., September 26, 1996.

Travel promotion is the responsibility of Brand USA (formally known as the Corporation for Travel Promotion), a nonprofit public-private entity that also is charged with communicating U.S. visa and entry policies to overseas visitors.

Brand USA was established under the Travel Promotion Act of 2009 (P.L. 111-145) and began operations in May 2011.[90] In addition to private funding, since 2010 Brand USA has received $10 of the $14 fee paid by each prospective visitor from a VWP country who requests approval to travel to the United States through ESTA. In 2019, Congress approved raising the ESTA fee from $14 to $21, while reducing the amount available to Brand USA to $7 per traveler. Of the remainder, $4 will continue to go to CBP to cover the costs of administering ESTA, and $10 will be directed to the U.S. Treasury for the general fund.[91] The effective date of the new ESTA fee has not yet been announced.

Brand USA is not without controversy. The Trump Administration's FY2021 budget called for ending the federal grant that matches the private sector contributions to Brand USA and making the revenue available to the U.S. Treasury to reduce the federal deficit.[92] Brand USA remains controversial among other travel and tourism stakeholders too, with some critics asserting that promotion of tourism should be left to the private sector. For example, Airlines for America, an airline industry group representing U.S. carriers, opposed Brand USA's reauthorization, asserting that ESTA funds would be better spent by CBP on border security, vetting travelers and refugees, and modernizing entry and exit processes.

---

[90] The Corporation for Travel Promotion was renamed Brand USA in November 2011; it has an 11-member board of directors and a staff of more than three dozen full-time employees in Washington, DC.

[91] P.L. 116-94, Division I, Title 8.

[92] White House, *A Budget for America's Future: Major Savings and Reforms*, February 10, 2020, p. 181, at https://www.whitehouse.gov/omb/budget/.

In another effort to promote travel and tourism, the United States has indicated that it is considering rejoining the United Nations' World Tourism Organization (UNWTO), which was established in 1975 to promote tourism worldwide. The United States was one of its founding members, but withdrew in 1996 after Congress stopped funding the United States Travel and Tourism Administration. In June 2019, the Trump Administration announced that the United States may rejoin the UNWTO.[93] The announcement met with some criticism,[94] and the Administration has subsequently taken no action. Other countries with large travel and tourism sectors that are not members of the UNWTO include the United Kingdom, Canada, and Australia.

LEGISLATION IN THE 116TH CONGRESS

Proposals introduced in the 116th Congress would give DHS greater flexibility to admit countries into the VWP that do not meet the criteria discussed above. Representative Mike Quigley introduced the Jobs Originated through Launching Travel (JOLT) Act (H.R. 2187), which would reinstate DHS's authority to grant a waiver for the nonimmigrant visitor visa refusal rate. That bill would also change the name of the VWP to Secure Travel Partnership.[95]

---

[93] U.S. Department of State, press release, June 17, 2019, at https://www.state.gov/the-united-states-to-explore- rejoining-the-united-nations-world-tourism-organization/.

[94] For example, see Brett D. Schaefer and James Jay Carafano, *6 Reasons Why the U.S. Should not Rejoin the U.N. World Tourism Organization*, The Heritage Foundation, October 2, 2019, at https://www.heritage.org/terrorism/commentary/6-reasons-why-the-us-should-not-rejoin-the-un-world-tourism-organization.

[95] Unrelated to the VWP, H.R. 2187 would also allow Canadians over age 50 entering on tourist visas who own or have rented property in the United States to be admitted for up to 240 days. Currently, the maximum duration of stay on a tourist visa is 180 days. Additionally, H.R. 2187 includes sections related to visa processing, such as developing a secure remote videoconferencing program for visa interviews.

H.R. 1996, also introduced by Representative Quigley, would solely rename the VWP to Secure Travel Partnership. Representative Dan Lipinski introduced the Allied Nations Travel Modernization Act (H.R. 2946), which would allow countries to be designated into the VWP if, instead of a low nonimmigrant visitor visa refusal rate, they have a low visa overstay rate and agree to spend 2% of their gross domestic product on defense;[96] according to the sponsor, the bill was drafted "to create an alternative pathway into the program for NATO nations like Poland." As noted above, Poland was recently designated into the VWP. In previous Congresses, numerous bills have been introduced to designate Israel and Hong Kong into the VWP.[97]

Senator John Cornyn introduced the Humanitarian Upgrades to Manage and Assist our Nation's Enforcement (HUMANE) Act of 2019 (S. 1303); among other provisions, it seeks to deter VWP overstays by amending the Immigration and Nationality Act's terms and conditions of admission for VWP travelers, the VWP waiver of rights, and the detention and repatriation of visa waiver violators.

The 116th Congress also addressed the spending of ESTA funds. Senator Mike Enzi introduced the Responsibly Enhancing America's Landscapes Act (S. 2783), which would establish the National Park Service Legacy Restoration Fund to help with the backlog of maintenance projects in national parks. This fund would be paid for by increasing the ESTA fee by $16, along with an increase in nonimmigrant visitor visa fees by $25 and a park fee increase of $5. The Further Consolidated Appropriations Act of 2020 (P.L. 116-94), which passed in December 2019, extended the authority for Brand USA to receive fees from the VWP through the end of September 2027 and raised the ESTA fee (as described in "The VWP and U.S. Travel Promotion Efforts" section above). The private sector still must provide at least $100 million per year in in- kind contributions and cash to the Brand USA program in order for it to receive these federal funds.

---

[96] For more information, see North Atlantic Treaty Organization, "Wales Summit Declaration," press release, September 5, 2014, at https://www.nato.int/cps/en/natohq/official_texts_112964.htm?selectedLocale=en.

[97] For example, S. 703, S. 266, S.Amdt. 3933, H.R. 1923, and H.R. 300.

Appendix A. Temporary Visitors to the United States for Business or Pleasure from Selected Aspiring VWP Countries

Table A-1.Temporary visitors from aspiring VWP countries, FY2008 and FY2018

Aspiring VWP Countries	FY2008	FY2018	% Change 2008 to 2018
Israel	388,787	453,620	17%
Brazil	893,186	2,376,392	166%
Cyprus	11,003	10,982	-0.2%
Bulgaria	41,793	32,800	-22%
Croatia	27,772	28,846	4%
Romania	76,799	93,131	21%

Source: Department of Homeland Security, Yearbook of Immigration Statistics, Table 28, "Nonimmigrant Admissions (I-94 Only) by Selected Category of Admission and Region and Country of Citizenship," multiple years.

Appendix B. Selected Immigration Inspections Databases and Systems

Advance Passenger Information System (APIS): CBP database containing information about inbound air passengers and crew members. Air carriers submit passenger information to APIS prior to departing on U.S.- bound flights (or prior to arrival in the United States, in certain cases), and CBP uses the data to identify high-risk and inadmissible passengers.

Arrival and Departure Information System (ADIS): DHS database that collects and maintains biographic arrival and departure information on non-U.S. citizens traveling in and out of the United States. ADIS is maintained by CBP and the DHS Office of Biometric Identity Management (OBIM), and is the main database used by ICE to identify suspected visa overstayers.

Automated Biometric Identification System (IDENT): DHS's primary biometric database. Certain aliens' biometric records are added to IDENT upon admission to the United States, when aliens are apprehended or arrested by a DHS agency, and when aliens apply for certain immigration benefits.

Automated Targeting System (ATS): CBP database of incoming and certain outbound cargo and persons. Advanced screening information is added to the ATS and checked against intelligence data from CBP's National Targeting Center (NTC) and other intelligence and law enforcement databases to produce a risk-based score. Travelers above a certain ATS threshold generally are selected for secondary inspection.

Consular Lookout and Support System (CLASS): DOS database used by passport agencies, posts, and border inspection agencies to perform name checks on visa and passport applicants to identify subjects of terrorist lookouts and watchlists and other individuals who are ineligible for a visa or require other special action.

Electronic System for Travel Authorization (ESTA): Web-based CBP system that screens applicants to enter the United States through the VWP against terrorist, national security, and criminal watchlists.

Interagency Border Inspection System (IBIS): DHS database of shared law enforcement files related to individuals, businesses, vehicles, aircraft, and vessels with suspected criminal violations. IBIS is used by CBP officers at ports of entry (POEs), U.S. Citizens and Immigration Services (USCIS) officers making determinations about immigration benefits, and other U.S. and international law enforcement agencies involved with border enforcement.

National Crime Information Center (NCIC): FBI database for tracking federal, state, local, and tribal crime data. NCIC includes records of stolen vehicles and other articles, foreign fugitives, missing persons, gang members, known or suspected terrorists, and persons with outstanding criminal warrants, among other data.

National Targeting Center-Passenger (NTC-P): CBP, other DHS, and DOS officials at the NTC-P use the ATS to screen passenger manifests and visa records against the FBI's Terrorist Screening Database (TSDB) and other national security records to prevent certain travelers from boarding U.S.-bound flights.

Next Generation Identification (NGI): FBI criminal database of biometric and criminal history information. Biometric records may be checked against NGI to verify that aliens have not been convicted of crimes making them inadmissible to the United States.

Appendix B. (Continued)

TECS (not an acronym): The principal information-sharing system used by CBP officers at POEs to screen arriving travelers for admissibility to the United States. CBP officers use TECS to check travelers against law enforcement and national security watchlists and to record and report on primary and secondary inspection results.
Terrorist Identities Datamart Environment (TIDE): Classified database of known or suspected terrorists maintained by the U.S. intelligence community. Data from TIDE are used to populate the TSDB.
Terrorist Screening Database (TSDB): Also known as the consolidated Terrorist Watchlist, the TSDB is maintained by the FBI's Terrorist Screening Center and includes biometric and biographic records of known and suspected domestic and international terrorists.

Source: Congressional Research Service (CRS) analysis of DHS, DOJ, DOS, and DOD Privacy Impact Assessments and related documents.

In: Visas
Editor: Brian A. Shelton
ISBN: 978-1-53619-966-6

Chapter 10

COVID-19-RELATED SUSPENSION OF NONIMMIGRANT ENTRY*

Jill H. Wilson

On June 22, 2020 President Trump issued a proclamation (amended on June 29) suspending the entry of foreign nationals (aliens) in certain nonimmigrant (temporary) visa categories that allow foreign nationals to work in the United States. Citing the high unemployment rate resulting from public health measures to reduce the spread of COVID-19, Proclamation 10052 suspends the entry of foreign nationals—and their accompanying family members—on H-1B, H-2B, J, and L visas, with some exceptions. On December 31, 2020, President Trump issued a new proclamation extending the June proclamation through March 31, 2021.

Proclamation 10052 follows Proclamation 10014 from April 22 (which it extends through December 31, 2020) suspending the entry of permanent immigrants (see CRS Insight IN11362). In Proclamation 10014, President Trump directed the Secretaries of Labor and Homeland Security to review

* This is an edited, reformatted and augmented version of Congressional Research Service Publication No. IN11435, updated January 6, 2021.

nonimmigrant programs and recommend measures to prioritize the hiring of U.S. workers. According to the June 22 proclamation, the Secretaries found that admitting temporary workers in the aforementioned categories "poses a risk of displacing and disadvantaging United States workers during the current recovery."

The President cited two immigration-related legal authorities. Under Section 212(f) (8 U.S.C. §1182(f)) of the Immigration and Nationality Act (INA), the President may suspend immigration when it would be detrimental to the interests of the United States. Under INA §215(a) (8 U.S.C. §1185(a)) the President may prescribe limitations and exceptions on who may enter or depart the United States.

How Long Will the Suspension Last?

Proclamation 10052 suspending the entry of foreign nationals in certain nonimmigrant visa categories was in effect from June 24, 2020, through December 31, 2020, and was subsequently extended until March 31, 2021. Beginning 30 days after the effective date, and every 60 days thereafter, the Secretary of Homeland Security, in consultation with the Secretary of Labor and Secretary of State, may recommend changes to it.

Who Is Included in the Suspension?

Section 2 suspends the entry of nonimmigrants in these visa categories:

- H-1B (specialty occupation workers);
- H-2B (seasonal nonagricultural workers) unless performing work essential to the food supply chain;
- J-1 (exchange visitors) in the following program categories: intern, trainee, teacher, camp counselor, au pair, and summer work travel;
- L-1 (intracompany transferees);

- accompanying spouses or children of the above (most of whom are not authorized to work in the United States).

WHO IS NOT INCLUDED IN THE SUSPENSION?

Section 3 exempts the following individuals:

- aliens in the United States on June 24, 2020;
- aliens with valid nonimmigrant visas or other official travel documents in the visa categories listed above as of June 24, 2020;
- lawful permanent residents (LPRs or "green card" holders);
- spouses and children of U.S. citizens;
- aliens seeking to enter the United States to provide temporary labor or services essential to the United States food supply chain;
- aliens whose entry would be in the national interest as determined by the Secretaries of State and Homeland Security.

WHAT OTHER MEASURES ARE INCLUDED IN THE PROCLAMATION?

Section 5 directs Secretaries of the following three departments to take certain actions beyond the suspension of nonimmigrant entry. Specifically, it directs

- HHS to provide guidance to DHS and DOS on measures to "reduce the risk that aliens seeking admission or entry to the United States may introduce, transmit, or spread SARS-CoV-2 within the United States."
- DOL to (1) take action to ensure that U.S. workers are not disadvantaged by H-1B temporary workers or workers admitted permanently through the 2nd and 3rd employment-based LPR

categories; and (2) investigate employers of H-1B workers who may not be in compliance with statute.

- DHS to (1) ensure that biographic and biometric information is collected from all aliens applying for immigration benefits or admission to the United States; (2) prevent aliens from obtaining work authorization who are removable or who have been arrested for, charged with, or convicted of a criminal offense in the United States; and (3) "ensure the efficient allocation of [H-1B] visas" including by re-allocating visas from those obtained fraudulently to legitimate applicants and "ensuring that the presence in the United States of H-1B nonimmigrants does not disadvantage United States workers."

IMPLEMENTATION

The proclamation gives DOS consular officers discretion to determine whether aliens qualify for exceptions to this suspension. The proclamation also directs the Secretaries of State, Labor, and Homeland Security to produce standards for determining which aliens fall under the national interest exemption, including those "critical to the defense, law enforcement, diplomacy, or national security of the United States," those involved with COVID-19-related medical care and research, those "necessary to facilitate the immediate and continued economic recovery of the United States," and alien children who would age out of eligibility for a visa as a result of this proclamation or Proclamation 10014.

WHAT ARE SOME IMPLICATIONS OF THIS PROCLAMATION?

The immediate impact is unclear, given that DOS had already suspended overseas visa processing as of March 20, 2020. DOS visa issuance data from 2019 may provide some indication of how many prospective nonimmigrants could be affected were visa issuances in 2020 to remain at 2019 levels. From July 2019 to December 2019 (roughly the same months as this proclamation's effective dates), DOS issued approximately 116,000 H-1B visas, 26,000 H-2B visas, 41,000 L-1 visas, and 133,000 J-1 visas (in all program categories). In addition, DOS issued approximately 135,000 visas for accompanying family members in these categories. Taking into account the fraction of J visa exchange visitors represented by the suspended program categories and the proportion of family members of H-1B, H-2B, and J visitors who would be covered, this proclamation could result in around 360,000 aliens being unable to obtain nonimmigrant visas.

Because this proclamation does not apply to aliens already in the United States or those who have valid nonimmigrant visas, it does not include those applying for a change of status from within the United States. For example, foreign students on F-1 visas pursuing work authorization through the Optional Practical Training (OPT) program, or F-1 students or J-1 physicians wishing to change to H-1B status are not included. In addition, aliens overseas applying for F-1 student visas or J-1 exchange visitor visas in the following categories are not included: physician, government visitor, international visitor, professor, research scholar, short-term scholar, specialist, and student. Temporary agricultural workers on H-2A visas are also not included.

INDEX

A

B

C

D

E

F

G

H

I

J

L

M

N

O

P

R

S

T

U

V

W